CHANGING SCENES

In loving memory of my parents,
John A. and Mary J. Mayne,
who taught me by example and precept
through all the changing scenes of life
to employ my heart and tongue
in the praise of God.

Brian Mayne

Brian Mayne.

30. IX . 03

Changing Scenes

CHANGING MINISTRY IN A CHANGING CHURCH
IN A CHANGING LAND

the columba press

First published in 2003 by
the columba press
55A Spruce Avenue, Stillorgan Industrial Park,
Blackrock, Co Dublin

Cover by Bill Bolger
Origination by The Columba Press
Printed in Ireland by Betaprint, Dublin

ISBN 1 85607 405 6

Contents

Prologue   7

1. Roots   9
2. Ballygally 1941-44   15
3. Malone 1944-52   23
4. Formation 1952-57   40
5. Ballymoney   65
6. Knock   86
7. Knocknagoney 1963-68   102
8. Belvoir   125
9. Involvement with the Ministry of Readers 1969-96   144
10. Belvoir II   150
11. Waterford   164
12. Lecale 1984-2001   182
13. Lecale II   188
14. Liturgical Renewal   205

Epilogue   219

Prologue

'Changing ministry – changing church – changing land.' I began to reflect on these three aspects of life and ministry in the Church of Ireland when challenged to introduce the concepts and ideas that lie behind the modern forms of service that are included in the forthcoming *Book of Common Prayer 2004*. Holy Week in 2002 marked for me a 'jubilee' for it was during it that I yielded to what I came to recognise as the call of God to offer myself for ordination to the priesthood of the Church and found that almost the only person surprised was myself! Looking back I am aware that those fifty years have been years of changes in our understanding of ministry itself, changes in the ways in which we offer our worship to God, and those changes have been set in the context of change within the Church in Ireland not just in the Church of Ireland. Above all they have been years of change, often painful, in Ireland itself, North and South.

Even twenty years ago I could not have foreseen invitations to contribute to two widely-read Roman Catholic publications as well as to the Church of Ireland's serious magazine *Search*: all three essays cover aspects of this changing ministry in a changing church.

This has set me to give fuller consideration to these interwoven themes. I have chosen to do this in an autobiographical way. First, because I experienced the changes in my own life and circumstances and second, because I have found in talking about changes in worship, for example, that I can best explain them as I have related how I came to experience them.

CHAPTER ONE

Roots

No one just happens. Everyone has a father and mother. I am fortunate to have had parents who brought me up in the life of the Church – parents whose own Christian commitment was secure. They were well-rooted in the life of the Christian Church in Ireland. It was only later in life that we were to discover just how deeply-rooted in the life of the Church was the Mayne family. There was a family bible originally belonging to a Simon Mayne dated in the early years of the eighteenth century. Sometime in the late 1950s my father was contacted by a Rupert Mayne, an amateur genealogist on holiday from Kenya keen on tracing the branches of the Mayne family tree in Ireland. As soon as this man walked into my father's office they knew they were related – the shape of head and eyes gave it away. Rupert was quite excited when my father disclosed the existence of the family bible and was able to link Simon (flourishing about 1700) with a Simon on his tree, born in the 1650s at Dinton in Buckinghamshire – a line that ended there. That Simon's father, also Simon Mayne, had been one of those who had signed the death warrant of Charles I – a regicide. Presumably after the Restoration life at Dinton in Bucks. was no longer comfortable and somehow the family went to County Antrim. Does this mean that my roots are strongly Puritan? Perhaps there is a balance – another part of the family in the sixteenth century was also non-conformist but on the other side, producing one of the Roman Catholic Forty Martyrs – canonised as Saint Cuthbert Mayne. There were obviously strong streams of conviction in the Mayne blood.

At the end of the eighteenth century, part of the family from which I directly descend lived at Ballyboley, north of Carrickfergus. Sometime in the nineteenth century my great-grandfather moved to Belfast and opened an iron foundry at McTier Street in the Lower Shankill area. The family wor-

shipped at Holy Trinity Parish Church in Clifton Street which
was destroyed in the Blitz of 1941. I have in my possession a *Book
of Common Prayer* presented as 'a Premium for diligence in the
study of the Holy Scriptures' to my grandfather, Thomas
Mayne, in December 1869 and signed by J. Henry Deacon, the
Rector. It is the BCP 'according to the use of the United Church
of England and Ireland' – the size of the book is 4 inches by 2.5
inches, the typesize is Ruby 32mo – about 4 point. And it was
used! The pages of Morning and Evening Prayer, and Holy
Communion are darkened with the thumbs of the user as are
those of the psalms, the collects, epistles and gospels.
Grandfather also annotated the bits that were added in 1552 and
1559. I wonder was this for use as he taught his Sunday School
classes in the early years of the disestablished Church of Ireland.
Evidence for his so doing was a clock presented to him as
Superintendent of Holy Trinity Sunday School on the occasion
of his marriage to my grandmother in 1878 which used to be
around the house but disappeared on one of our moves.

Thomas Mayne continued to take a deep interest in the affairs of the Church. Like most of the laity of the Church of
Ireland in the early days of disestablishment he would appear to
have been very suspicious of any 'high church' movement. He
had in his possession a prayer book produced by the Protestant
Church of England about 1884. This body had campaigned
against the ritualists in England and had challenged every one
of the innovations. They found no satisfaction in the courts
which had ruled so often in favour of what we should consider
today normal middle of the road Anglican practice as being in
accordance with the *Book of Common Prayer* 1662. Breaking away,
they produced their own liturgy – an exact copy of 1662 but removing every reference to 'priest', 'bishop', 'absolution', 'blessing'. Any possibility of interpreting the baptism office as sanc-
tioning a doctrine of baptismal regeneration was removed, and
its revised catechism taught that Holy Communion was merely
a memorial. Contrary to the Thirty Nine articles, sacraments
were not to be interpreted as efficacious signs. I wonder was
grandfather sympathetic and, if so, what he would make of the
Church of Ireland almost a century after his death in 1911.

Grandfather developed the McTier Street Foundry. When I

went to Knocknagoney in 1963 I visited a family who originally came from the Shankill Road area. Mrs Warnock's father, then in his late eighties, asked me if I had anything to do with Mayne's Foundry. He recalled that he had 'wrought to my grandfather' at the turn of the century and remembered him well and his son, 'Mr William' – my father's eldest brother, whom I never met as he emigrated to Canada in the 1920s when the Depression closed the foundry for ever.

The family prospered at the end of the 19th century and moved 'up the Antrim Road' to a new house in a terrace opposite the gates to Lord Shaftesbury's Belfast Castle, looking up to Cave Hill. This was 'Homelea'. Less than 200 yards down the road on the same side the new St Peter's Church opened in 1900. This would continue to nurture the younger members of the Mayne family. After three girls there were seven sons of whom one died in infancy: my father, John, was the second youngest. Uncle Leslie, who was the youngest, always laid stress on the fact that he was a 'seventh' son but as his father had not been such there was no significance. And I only have one cousin in that line. Two of the girls trained as National Schoolteachers at Kildare Place College in Dublin. Mary and Sarah taught in National Schools (later called Public Elementary Schools) in North Belfast. Mary also sang in St Peter's Church choir almost to the end of her days when she had become very deaf. She couldn't bear not to sing her praise twice every Sunday. Sarah couldn't sing at all, but she loved to worship. After she died in 1966 I discovered her prayer book which used to sit on a table in the lounge beside the lamp. Like that of her father it was well-used, not one page of the psalter remaining attached to spine – those pages had been turned every day for almost forty years.

St Peter's, in the early years of the century, was one of a handful of churches with a robed choir where Morning and Evening Prayer were intoned each Sunday. My father was a choirboy and later an adult member of the choir. He learned to sing the responses, to chant psalms and to sing hymns. It was something he never forgot, something he enjoyed. Right at the end of his life, when his speech had been affected by a stroke, he could still join in the singing with television's *Songs of Praise*, usually with tears streaming down his cheeks. Earlier, in the pew he used to join lustily in the responses and psalms in St John's Malone, ignoring my mother's pleas to sing more quietly.

The rector of St Peter's at that time was Henry R. Brett, a towering figure among Belfast's clergy, obviously one of those who were bringing the Church of Ireland away from its extreme Protestant position, teaching generations the meaning of the catechism and prayer book worship.

My father became a chartered accountant but retained his interest in everything connected with the Church of Ireland. A close friend, a bank official, Charlie Walsh was ordained for the curacy of St Andrew's in 1929, becoming priest-in-change of Ballintoy in 1933. In 1931 Noel Mackey, who was also to be a life-long friend, became curate of St Peter's. This brought my father into contact with numerous other clergy and most of them became clients as he looked after their Income Tax affairs at very small cost or very small profit, depending on how you looked at it.

My mother, Mary Cargill, was born at Glaslough in County Monaghan. Her father didn't live to see his daughter's birth. He was a farmer/miller, one of the Protestant unionist community in that area. Grandmother married again to a Mr Todd and on marriage she moved with her daughter and new husband to Belfast – less than half a mile from the Mayne household, although totally unaware of them. The Todds worshipped at Fortwilliam Presbyterian Church where my mother's two half-sisters were christened. As a child my mother went first to Belfast Royal Academy and later, at the end of the Great War, she was sent to board at a school at Stourbridge in Worcestershire. There she encountered Anglo-Catholic worship for the first time – not understanding it one little bit. However, I think something rubbed off, for as she grew up she became less happy with Presbyterianism. After the Great War her elder brother, Uncle Jack, returned from being a prisoner-of-war. Grandmother was again a widow and the family took the opportunity to return to 'the country', residing at Glaslough and re-opening the corn mill. But partition and civil war were the new experience: the IRA burned down Cargill's Mill and eventually the family went back to Belfast. They lived on the Antrim Road, in Glandore Terrace and chose to worship, not at nearby Fortwilliam Church, but a short tram-ride towards the city centre at Saint

James's Parish Church. My mother's younger sister was confirmed, the others being assured that it was not necessary.
Canon (later Archdeacon) Paul William Nassau Shirley (born on
12 July, hence the middle names!) was the rector and his style of
ministry obviously attracted Miss Cargill and the Todd girls.

It was a comfortable middle-class way of life – obviously my
grandmother could afford to live as a widow – and her daughters enjoyed the quiet society of the Antrim Road in the twenties
and early thirties. Only Eileen entered the world of work, training
in London as a professional teacher of music and finding employment at the Buchan School on the Isle of Man. Mother's mother
died in 1931 just before my mother was to be married. I never
knew any of my grandparents as my father's parents had also
died before he married.

The marriage took place quietly in August 1931. The ceremony
was held in St James's Church at 8 o'clock in the morning and
there was no reception. Archdeacon Shirley was on holiday and
a former curate, Ernest Dixon, officiated. Ernest Dixon was still
rector of Agherton, Portstewart when I was ordained in 1957, in
indifferent health, frequently needing one of the nearby curates
to deputise. He was quite surprised when I told him at lunch
after my first such visit that he had some responsibility for my
being there, in that he had joined my parents in Holy
Matrimony, twenty six years before. When my parents returned
from honeymoon, a decision had to be made where they would
worship – St Peter's or St James's. In the end it was the parish
boundary which decided the matter. It ran along Hughenden
Avenue – the odd numbers were in St Peter's, the evens were in
St James's. Today the parishes are united. My parents' new home
was number 10, and they became parishioners of St James's.
Almost three years later I was born at 10 Hughenden Avenue
and baptized on Sunday 16 September, Saint Ninian's Day.

I was taken to church at an early age. St James's had an 'extra'
morning service at 10.15. I remember little of those services. At
the back of my mind I am aware of hassocks and I am told I was
quite restless. I remember the stained glass windows (and this
must be a genuine memory as they were blown to pieces by the
air-raid of 15 April 1941). I also remember that there were
Sundays when we didn't 'go to Church'. Father and mother

went: it was something special and mysterious called Choral Communion.

The earliest service that I can clearly remember was the baptism of my sister early in 1938. Like my own baptism, it took place at a Sunday afternoon Children's Service with the Sunday School present.

Church services definitely made an impact on this impressionable child and I am told that on Sunday afternoons I would dress up and conduct 'church' in the living room! But the involvement of my parents in the life of the parish made a bigger impact: clergy were frequent callers.

An enormous change overtook 'pastoral visiting' after the Second World War. Archdeacon Shirley and his wife used to go on formal pastoral visits in the afternoon, taking afternoon tea with the ladies of the parish in the avenues off the Antrim and Cliftonville Roads. Indeed, Mrs Jane Shirley visited in her own right. Visiting cards were left with the maids if the lady of the house was not at home. What happened in the smaller streets down towards Carlisle Circus and the New Lodge was probably rather different: I suspect that the curates were left to shoulder that kind of burden. After the archdeacon died in 1954 Mrs Shirley presented me with his private communion set – a real miniature version, of which the wine-flask has remained with me throughout my ministry.

My Antrim Road connection would be broken by the air-raid of 15 April 1941: our house was rendered uninhabitable and we had to seek refuge in the country. St James's Church itself was hit by an incendiary bomb, leaving only the spire to remind those who had worshipped there, or who had been baptized there, of their timeless relationship with God.

CHAPTER TWO

Ballygally 1941-44

The night of Easter Tuesday 1941 changed the face of the city of
Belfast and the lives of many of its citizens for ever. A large
number of churches were destroyed or badly damaged. Holy
Trinity, Clifton Street, where my grandfather was brought up,
was completely destroyed and was not rebuilt after the war.
Incendiary bombs left St James's a shell. Only the tower and
spire remained when the bomb damage crews completed their
work. Until 1951 the congregation would worship Sunday by
Sunday in the church hall. Our own home was rendered uninhabitable and my parents had to seek somewhere for the family
to lay our heads. We spent several days at a farm outside
Lisburn. Then we were able to rent a furnished bungalow in the
village of Ballygally on the Antrim coast north of Larne.
Number One Grace Avenue would be our home for over three-
and-a-half years. In the 1930s our family had spent holidays in
Ballygally, so we were not exactly going among strangers.

Ballygally is a small seaside village, which had developed between the wars. A 16th century bawn – a fortified farmhouse –
had been converted into a hotel. There had been a row of coast-
guard cottages for a century or so but most of the buildings
along the coast road were fairly new. At the southern end of the
bay is the volcanic headland known as a Ballygally Head. Inland
the edge of the Antrim plateau is marked with two small peaks,
of one called Knock Dhu and the other Scawt. The famous Glens
of Antrim begin six miles further to the north but they had been
cut off from the rest of East Antrim until the building of the coast
road in the 19th century. This is an area that has close links with
Scotland, whose coast is usually clearly visible some 16 or 17
miles away, and the local accent is distinctly Scottish as are
many of the surnames.

For young children growing up, the Ballygally area was a

wonderful part of the world to live in. There was a sandy beach and rock pools where sea anemones and tiny fish were to be found. We were always welcome at local farms to watch cows being milked (some still by hand) and sample the rich cream milk fresh from the dairy. In spite of rationing there were always fresh eggs. And in the autumn there was the excitement of bringing in the harvest. As a preacher I would find those experiences most useful in later life. Tractors were just coming into use at that time but horses and carts were still the norm. Also there were woods with bluebells and primroses in spring and every kind of nut and wild fruit in autumn. Country roads were almost totally barren of traffic for walks of exploration and later for first cycle rides. It was little wonder that the war years were actually a very happy time for us children.

My father travelled each day to his office in Belfast by bus, train and tram, leaving on the 8:20am bus and returning home just after half past six. He often said he got more work done in those days when he only got to the office at 10 o'clock than he did when we returned to Belfast and he was at his desk at 9.00am. He carried on all through the war as Honorary Treasurer for St James's, staying with his sister-in-law for the nights following meetings of the select vestry.

The war didn't obtrude too much. Yes, we heard the German aircraft flying in for the May 1941 air-raid and from time to time we saw and heard naval action in the North Channel when the skies were lit up with flares and tracers. We got to know the members of the RAF Regiment who maintained the observation post on the top of Ballygally Head. In the spring of 1944 our roads were choked for days with American and British lorries, personnel carriers etc., prior to their embarcation via Larne for the Normandy landings. We kept in touch by radio and listening to it was almost as important an activity in my life as reading. Certainly I believe that radio had a strong influence in the way my spoken English developed, for I didn't acquire the East Antrim accent.

Ballygally was a small enough place during those war years. We probably knew the names of almost all the people who lived along the Coast Road from the Manse to the 'Halfway House', a public house at the northernmost end of the village, as well as most of those who lived up what we called the Back Road as well. There were families like ourselves who had to leave Belfast because of the air raids. There were some families of members of the Forces from across the water who were stationed in Northern Ireland because of the war.

School came with us! Many of the Belfast schools were dispersed after the air raids. Belfast Inst. evacuated part of the school to Dungannon. Ashleigh House went to Learmount, near Limavady, and Belfast Royal Academy went to hotels at Portrush in the north of County Antrim. Part of the school opened at Ballygally as two of the teachers had holiday homes in the village. A few days after our evacuation, classes began again.

After Easter 1942 the Academy decided to close the outlying schools as a threat of air-raids had receded. It would now mean a bus-ride each day to Larne Grammar School – no problem to an eight-year-old.

The new school was quite an experience. I was at once thrown into learning French, even taking part in a concert, singing French songs on stage. I discovered I needed a bible for scripture classes, so a small edition of the Authorised Version was purchased for me. School Assembly each morning was another new thing, singing new hymns and listening to the headmaster recite the Lord's Prayer. But it wasn't the Lord's Prayer as I knew it; he didn't ask God to 'forgive us our trespasses' but to 'forgive us our debts, as we forgive our debtors'. No one joined in with the headmaster either. I was told that this was the way the Presbyterians did it and that Larne Grammar School was a Presbyterian school. Thus was I introduced to denominationalism.

Tom Salmon, who had been curate in St James's, was sent by the bishop to look after the parish of Larne, as its rector Alan Buchanan had joined up as an Army chaplain. I think he found it very difficult and I remember him cycling out to Ballygally to visit us one afternoon. He must have felt the need of some friends with whom to relax. He never forgot that afternoon and was exceptionally kind to me when our paths re-crossed in the Divinity School.

It was during those years at Ballygally that I began to appreciate Christian faith and the Church. We were a church-going family and, with the car out of action because of petrol rationing, we had to walk to church on Sunday mornings. It was over a mile, uphill almost all the way. We would set out about ten to eleven. Over the months we learned that you had to be at a certain corner at twenty past eleven to be sure of being in church by the half-hour. We called that bend 'twenty-past corner'. Just before we reached it we would hear the engine of the rector's car as, with a full carload, he would sweep by. They didn't have to walk the last steepest part of the journey with tiring legs. On the other hand, after church it was all downhill and we were ready for Sunday lunch.

St Patrick's Church at Cairncastle is a small country church, built on a very ancient site. One of the prebendal stalls in the cathedral of the diocese of Connor is the prebend of Cairncastle, indicating that in the early 17th century it had some greater significance. The present church building dates from the 19th century with a considerable amount of work done just at the beginning of the 20th. It has a tower with a spire, a porch, nave and a chancel into which choir stalls had been placed. To me in those days the sanctuary, into which the rector disappeared when the collection was being taken, seemed far far away. When invited to return to Cairncastle to preach in the year after I was ordained it seemed to have a shrunk to a very small place. The church has a bell to call the faithful to worship; but in 1941 all church bells were silent – the ringing of church bells had been designated by government as a sign that the Germans had invaded the country. But on a Sunday in November 1942 Winston Churchill, the Prime Minister, ordered church bells to be rung again to celebrate the victory of the Eighth Army at the Battle of El Alamein. That Sunday we knew that Germany and Japan would be defeated.

The temporary residents boosted the local congregation in the war years. It must have made ministry more interesting and varied for the rectors as well as more demanding. I don't ever remember being bored by Church. I do know that it was by using prayers and canticles Sunday by Sunday that I came to know them by heart. Nobody ever set me down to learn that the Apostles' Creed or the Venite. My sister and I didn't go to Sunday School for that would have meant walking unaccompa-

nied and there were no footpaths. I don't regret that in the slightest. On the first Sunday of the month the service was slightly different; for one thing it was a shorter and there were different bits
of singing but we had to leave before the service finished; father
or mother or a friend took it in turns to take us children out while
the other remained for Holy Communion. On another Sunday
they used to leave us at our breakfast when the rector, or someone else who still had a car on the road, called to take them to
'early' service. We had to be ready when they returned.

The church organ required hand pumping and this was done
by the postman. Miss Perry, the elementary school teacher,
played and there was a good choir. There was a 'Big House' in
the parish – Cairndhu – the country residence of Sir Thomas and
Lady Dixon. Sir Thomas was the son of Sir Daniel Dixon who
had been a prominent industrialist in Belfast and Lord Mayor a
century before. Whenever he was present, Sir Thomas always
lifted the collection and you could see his pound note on the col-
lecting plate as it came round. In other parishes the 'laird' often
read the lessons at Morning Prayer but I do not recall that happening at Cairncastle.

The Donaldson family used to sit two seats in front of us. Mr
Donaldson senior had retired from a Belfast furniture business,
by then managed by his sons. Holidays had brought our two
families together some years earlier. After the war one of the
boys, Jack, gave up the business, trained for ordination and
served most of his ministry in the west of England. He would
say that he discovered his vocation worshipping in St Patrick's
Cairncastle. I suppose that I must have first heard of the idea of
someone being ordained when I heard that Jack Donaldson was
going to be a clergyman.

Three and a half years and three rectors – that was what happened to the parish of Kilwaughter and Cairncastle while we attended. In 1941 the rector was Robert A. Mollan, but in the
spring of 1942 he moved to Clogher Cathedral and finally became Dean of Clogher.

My father and mother were delighted when their old friend
Charles Walsh was appointed rector in 1942. I found Mr Walsh a
bit over-powering at first but I now reckon it was his preaching
and teaching that drew me closer to the things of God.

So the Holy Spirit was working in my life. It was a huge disap-
pointment early in 1944 when diocesan pressures drew Charles
Walsh nearer to Belfast and he left Ballygally for the County
Down parish of Groomsport. He undertook many important
roles for the diocese of Down and Dromore, separated from
Connor in 1945, and as organising secretary of the future Irish
Council of Churches. Perhaps he never fulfilled his potential, but
it was with a real sense of personal loss that I attended his funeral
in Groomsport Church in February 1968 after his sudden death. I
know that the people of Groomsport had been aware that for
twenty-four years they were pastored by a holy man of God.

We kept regular connections with Ballygally until 1950.
When I was ordained in 1957 one of the first to write and wish
me well in the ministry was Henry Todd Brown, who had succeeded Charles Walsh, and with my boss's permission, he invited
me to preach during the first Lent of my ministry – in both St
Patrick's and in the Millbrook Schoolhouse which served the
Kilwaughter end of the parish.

Idyllic as life by the seaside was, day trips to Belfast to see
members of the family were important events. Transport was genuinely integrated. The bus left Ballygally at 8.20am, connected
with the train at Larne Town station to York Road station in
Belfast, where the tram took you into the very centre of the city.
Other trams took us to family in the Antrim Road area. An es-
sential stop for me was the bookshop, William Mullan and Son
in Donegall Place, in which I would persuade my father to buy
me a book. On another occasion visiting my Aunt Eileen I found
in the book rack of her local shop three hardbound annuals of
the Stirling Tract Company's monthly bible magazine for children. These introduced me in far more detail than before to bible
reading and made the stories of David, Moses and Paul meaningful. There were also stories of those who had struggled to
translate the scriptures into English and of missionaries in the
19th century. This was all part of my faith in Christ becoming
not just something for Church but a personal commitment.

In those years relationships and friendships were never influenced by denominational considerations. Among our friends
and neighbours were Presbyterians, Anglicans and Roman
Catholics. Close friends were the family who kept the local

store, where we were registered for our food rations. There were children and young people in the family with whom we played as children. They were Roman Catholics and they kept a light burning before a picture of the Sacred Heart which you saw when you 'went through' to the family part of the house at the back of the shop. That Ian got the bus going to Garron Tower to Saint MacNissi's School and we got the bus to Larne was the only difference between us. We kept in touch over the next few years, in particular visiting one of the family who had a lot of hospitalisation in the Belfast area. I often said that he understood better than many of my Protestant friends the significance of my going forward for ordination.

Roman Catholics in the Cairncastle and Ballygally areas had to go to Larne for church; one year a mass was held in the disused café and we were able to help out with curtains from our stored furniture – a gesture which was very much appreciated. One of the few buildings erected during the war years was a new church for Roman Catholics on the Cairncastle Road.

Presbyterians and Non-subscribing Presbyterians worshipped in Cairncastle village. Their services didn't begin until noon and sometimes we could hear singing as we walked home from our service. On a sunny Sunday morning we would look at the sundial on the Presbyterian 'Meeting House' as it was entitled – with Double British Summer Time – this would read some minutes after 10 o'clock when by our watches it was after 12.30pm – the effect of daylight saving and the half hour our longitude is West of Greenwich.

By the summer of 1944 it was clear that the war was going to end. With the family growing up, my parents felt they couldn't face another winter in Ballygally. With bomb damage compensation settled, the search for a new home in Belfast was on. By the early autumn 14 Malone Hill Park had been purchased and come Hallowe'en we would be moving. I had few regrets leaving Larne Grammar School: school life was being radically changed under a new principal. John Darbyshire, headmaster when I went there in 1942, had moved to Belfast Royal Academy (and more importantly his son, John, who had been in my class, was gone as well). John and I would meet up again at Queen's in the department of history, a decade later.

Harvest Thanksgiving in 1944 was our last Sunday as parish-ioners of Cairncastle. I thank God for the love shown to us by that congregation, and for the sense communicated there that I was growing up as the Church Catechism, which I had never learnt, says 'a member of Christ, the child of God and an inheri-tor of the kingdom of heaven'.

CHAPTER THREE

Malone 1944-52

It was a return to Belfast but to a completely different part of the city. Malone was a suburb in South Belfast. My sister and I stayed with an aunt for a night during which the removal took place and, on a dark November evening, she took us to our new home. It was beyond the end of the tramlines and so we had to travel by bus – number 16 from the City Hall via Stranmillis Road. The journey seemed to go on for ever. Next morning I looked out – a large back garden and then over the hedge cows were grazing in fields. Life in the city wouldn't be too bad.

Getting settled to school was the next thing. It would be too far to travel to Academy and any way Royal Belfast Academical Institution had been my father's school and that of most of his brothers. He was on the Board of Governors and so it was a formality that my transfer from Larne was accepted. The first week I was on trial in Form One which had one teacher, the formidable Mrs Morris, for all subjects, but the following Monday I was transferred to Form Two (against her advice, she told me!). In that form we had a whole range of different teachers as we had had at Larne. I settled in and never looked back. One of the considerations that had led to my week in the lower form was that Form Two were two months on with French and Latin. The former was no problem, thanks to LGS, but the latter was. Head of Classics, H. B. ('Hector') Hanna took me into his Sixth Form scholarship class to sit at the back and receive about five minutes per period: it didn't work. Next year I started Latin again with Alex R. Foster, who had come out of retirement to meet the teacher shortage caused by teachers being away at the war, and I romped away to an easy facility in the language. Among the seniors in H. B. Hanna's class that first year were Victor Hamilton, later to be my solicitor, and Maurice Stewart. Both would go on to Trinity, the latter being ordained, becoming Vice-principal of the Theological College and later Dean of Saint Patrick's.

Inst. still bore the signs of the war. The front lawn, where junior cricket matches had been played, was still occupied by an air-defence barrage balloon and the 'back field' was covered with air-raid shelters. For months in the year after the war we were taught to the accompaniment of pneumatic drills removing these to give us room to move around at break. Today that field lies below Common Hall, swimming pool and other buildings. Inst. in 1944 was totally secular – there were no prayers at assembly and religious instruction was non-existent. Derided by some as a 'godless' institution, it nevertheless gave several moderators to the Presbyterian Church, two bishops to the Church of Ireland and there were at least three pupils in 1944-45 destined to hold the office of cathedral dean – Maurice Stewart, Hammie Leckey and myself.

My sister was enrolled at the preparatory department of Ashleigh House School which was literally at the top of our avenue. She went on from there to Ashleigh when she was old enough.

The next question was, 'Where would we go to church?' There were 'suspicions' regarding the parish church, St John's Malone. It was reputed to be very 'high' church. My father felt a pull to our remaining with St James's where he was on the select vestry. The first Sunday we attempted the double bus journey across town but the bus service wasn't very frequent on a Sunday. Clearly it just was not possible – certainly there was no way we could have got to Sunday School. Eric Barber, who was now the rector of St James's, came over to see us but recognised the situation. On another Sunday we went to St Thomas's on the Lisburn Road but that involved walking to the tram and then the length of Eglantine Avenue. The matter was settled when Miss Norah Seaver, the Sunday School superintendent from St John's, called to see about our going to Sunday School. This gracious invitation was accepted and at 10 o'clock the following Sunday Elizabeth and I had our first experience of Sunday School. My father took me with him to the 11 o'clock choral matins. It was a little different to Cairncastle but nothing startling and Dad was delighted to find that the sung responses used were those he had learned all those years before as a choirboy. So began our family connection with St John's Malone. At Easter 1945 my father was released from his commitment as Honorary Treasurer of St James's.

The senior classes of Sunday School in St John's were taught by a Mr and Mrs Cautley, with the curate taking those who had already been confirmed. These were two devout and lovely people but they really hadn't a clue how to teach: it was boring, deadly boring – either the text-book was read with head down or there was a long list of questions, a kind of extended catechism week after week. Yet, we stuck it. Highlight was the Christmas party – my first was 1945. I remember the sandwiches and buns in the lean-to corrugated iron building and the fact that most games for the seniors seemed to be designed to scrag the curate, Jack Givern. But the atmosphere at both Sunday school and party was good and we enjoyed belonging.

Confirmation
From early 1946, the year I became twelve, I kept asking to be confirmed. The normal age was fourteen at that time and bishops were fairly rigid about it. I knew in myself that I was ready to make a public commitment but that year I had to content myself. It wasn't any feeling of exclusion from Holy Communion, such as many young people experience fifty years later, as Holy Communion was still a mystery, attendance at which I had yet to experience. It was a sense that I wanted to be fully part of the Church. The rector, Frederick H. P. L'Estrange, agreed to ask the bishop to accept me as a candidate in 1947. By this time Jack Givern had moved on and we had a new curate, Norman Kelly. One sure thing was that he wasn't prepared to be involved in boisterous games at the Sunday School party! But he was to prepare the boys for confirmation and the date was announced for the end of January. I suppose I accomplished my first acts of evangelism when I persuaded my cousin, David, who lived near us and is almost two years older, and two of our friends, John Tyrell and George Kennedy, with whom we travelled to school each day, to come to the classes as well. It wasn't until many years later when Norman Kelly and I had become good friends that I learned that we were in fact his first confirmation class.

Two things stand out. Practical teaching about prayer, all of us receiving a very simple daily prayer guide: this had a special significance for me as the authors or compliers were Archdeacon Shirley, who had baptized me, and Jack Butler who had been curate in St James's. The second was Norman Kelly introducing me to the notes of the Bible Reading Fellowship. While I probably forgot all the teaching, to be encouraged to systematic daily prayer and bible reading was vital in my nurture in the faith and in preparing me to recognise a vocation to holy orders.

Confirmation day was 18 May 1947, a fantastic sunny spring day. At Sunday School in the morning we heard that the Bishop of Connor, Charles King Irwin, was ill and wouldn't be able to officiate. In his place we were to have Bishop John Hind, the former missionary Bishop of Fukien in China. I was terrified that the bishop would ask me to stand and recite the Ten Commandments – I know them but I have always found reciting in public without notes very daunting. Of course, the bishop didn't make any such demands. He was gentle and spoke briefly on the parable of the talents. We had to wait for several more weeks before coming for our first communion: that was the Sunday before my thirteenth birthday at 8.00am, a congregation of fifty-three communicants. Since those days we have realised that new communicants should we welcomed into the main eucharistic assembly and that where possible confirmation should take place within the eucharist. Such an idea would have seemed strange indeed in 1947.

At St John's in 1947 it would have been difficult to define when the main eucharistic assembly actually met. Each Sunday there was a said service at 8.00am usually with around twenty people. Each Sunday there was Holy Communion at noon – fully choral on the first Sunday and with men singers only on the third. At none of these was there a sermon. The 11.00am service of Choral Matins and sermon was the largest assembly of the congregation but many of those who attended week by week never partook of the Lord's Supper. Looking back, it was a curious set-up. In 1947 there would have been very few churches in Belfast that had as many regular celebrations of Holy Communion. Most would have had a similar set-up to Cairncastle, one Sunday in the month Holy Communion would have been joined on to Morning Prayer, with readings from Morning Prayer and after the collects, Holy Communion would have begun with epistle, gospel, Nicene Creed and sermon. After the Prayer for the Church Militant the organ would play, the choir would leave and so would most of the congregation.

Frederick L'Estrange sought to keep the integrity of each rite. I am certain that he personally would have wished to have a full celebration of the eucharist as the main service on a Sunday but he had enough problems trying to live with St John's so-called 'high church' reputation to venture such a move. There were frequent visits from representatives of the Irish Church Union for the Defence of Reformation Principles (ICU) endeavouring to find evidence for the rector breaching the restrictive ceremonial canons of 1871. The 'I See You' people made a nuisance of themselves in a few churches and sought to influence elections to synods. On one occasion a representative complained to Bishop King Irwin that Frederick L'Estrange encouraged his churchwardens to 'bow to the Holy Table' when they acknowledged his dismissal following the presentation of the collection plate; the bishop passed on the complaint indicating that he found no substance in it. How the church has changed! Not only were the restrictive canons removed in 1976 but the bans on there being a cross on the Holy Table and lighted candles have gone as well. Today many churches have all these things. The only time when St John's resembles the church of my confirmation day is Good Friday.

Sunday School – as Teacher
After confirmation I stayed on at Sunday School. The only time I have felt annoyed with Norman Kelly was in September 1947 for he kept me with my age grouping and didn't allow me into the bible class. I was the only confirmed person still in Sunday School but I survived. Next year I was asked if I would act as the distributor of the Bible Reading Fellowship notes each quarter. This built up a number of relationships. Some of the older parishioners were quite surprised when a teenage youth called with BRF notes.

In the spring of 1949 I found myself drafted as a Sunday

School teacher, given a kindergarten class, under the super-intendence of Margaret Seale. We met in the old kitchen and I learned a lot more than I ever succeeded in teaching. Two years later I transferred to the Junior Sunday School where the basic textbooks were *Church Teaching for the Junior Child,* prepared for the English National Society by Canon H. W. Dobson. I got a great deal out of 'Dobson' and I don't believe that there have been any teaching materials produced in the church since to match it. Of course, it would be totally dated if used today. The teaching methods of that period have been long superseded. But for inexperienced and relatively untrained teachers it was just what was required in the 1950s and 1960s. I would successfully introduce 'Dobson' as curate in Ballymoney and use it in Knock and Knocknagoney. It has been a discovery in the last year or so when my Malone connection has been re-built that there are so many of the worshipping community in 2002 who were in Sunday School classes I taught fifty and more years ago.

Involvement in the parish
It wasn't long before my father's gifts and experience in church finance were called into use in Malone. The post-war need for re-building bombed churches and building new ones in new housing areas led to a diocese-wide Bishop's Appeal and my fa-ther became treasurer for the appeal in the parish. A few years later he became parish treasurer. He and I became 'twicers', going to Evensong as well as Matins. Evening congregations were comparatively small – just under a hundred most Sundays. Whereas churches in 'working-class' parishes like St Mary Magdalene's or St Aidan's would expect their largest congrega-tions in the evening, this wasn't the case in an area like Malone where most of the congregation was drawn from professional people. Over fifty years later, evening congregations in almost all Church of Ireland parishes have declined and in many places Evensong is no longer held. In Malone in 2002 a choral service takes place once a month with literally a handful of worshippers apart from the choir – on other Sundays one or two people read the service together. Those Sunday evenings in the late 1940s are memorable for the sermons. The preaching style of rector and curate were completely different. Frederick L'Estrange was ef-

fervescent and enthusiastic. In contrast to Norman Kelly's carefully prepared and quietly delivered teaching, L'Estrange used
to 'turn himself on' as he put it – proclaiming the gospel of personal commitment and the absolute need to allow God to grow
us into the people he wanted us to become. Frequently he referred to Ephesians 4:12, 13, 'the building up of the body of
Christ, until all of us come to the unity of the faith and the
knowledge of the Son of God, to maturity, the measure of the
full stature of Christ'. Often he quoted from the hymn 'Rock of
Ages', especially the verse:

Nothing in my hands I bring
Simply to thy cross I cling.

In my student days, when I used to go and visit Frederick
L'Estrange in his retirement in Dublin, we discussed preaching,
something he never devalued. 'You must have a message,' he
said. 'If you have a message, you can preach.' He used to describe
himself as either an evangelical catholic or a catholic evangelical.
Those are descriptions that I would happily claim for myself.

The other thing I learned those Sunday evenings was the
vital part in the practical life of the church played by lay officials,
churchwardens, secretaries and treasurers. After the evening
service the two treasurers would go to the vestry and the day's
collection and envelopes would be taken home for counting and
bank lodgement next day. The freewill offering envelopes were
recorded by their treasurer: my father brought the loose collection money home, counted it and bagged it for the bank first
thing on Monday morning. The four of us would walk home
from church, one year accompanied by a churchwarden, 'Tiny'
Playle, who would have gone round all the doors and windows
before leaving. Church security was important even then.

The rector used to ask students from the congregation, or
pupils home from boarding school, to read the lessons at Matins.
One Sunday evening he asked me if I would like to read one of
the lessons next week. I agreed but was extremely nervous. I
still remember the passage, from Joshua chapter 24, the one
where Joshua challenges the people of Israel to choose between
the Lord and the gods of the nations. It has a number of words,
wrong pronunciation of which could be very embarrassing.
When it came to the time I was able to read without difficulty ex-

cept the nerves in one of my kneecaps kept twitching. In the following six or seven years I would often read lessons from that lectern. At that time, St John's was without any form of amplification, and I learned to project my voice so as to be heard in the back row or the gallery. As members of our family sat towards the back of the church, I was soon told if I couldn't be heard. In today's church, so often people think that because of microphone systems they do not have to project their voices or enunciate clearly.

Religion in school
At school the 1948 Education Act brought changes to the way religion was approached. A daily assembly with an act of worship became compulsory in 1949. The Principal, John Grummitt, used to read a few verses of scripture, recite a prayer and we all joined in the Lord's Prayer, standard form unlike Larne! On Tuesdays and Fridays we sang hymns, using our own church hymn-books. In a few hymns the words in the three books didn't agree. One of these was 'Onward Christian Soldiers'. The Presbyterian and Methodist books had the words the author had written, 'With the cross of Jesus going on before', but the third edition of our *Church Hymnal* had, in deference to Irish Protestant sensitivities in the last century, bowdlerised this to 'Looking unto Jesus who has gone before.' When we got to those words I am sorry to say that each denomination tried to sing down the other! A 'religious' assembly meant that some pupils, including Jews, Roman Catholics and some who belonged to minority Christian groups which didn't recognise the mainstream churches as Christian, were excluded from the assembly and they went off to a classroom while the rest of us worshipped. One classroom held all of them – about five per cent.

In our last year before Senior Certificate, 'Divinity' became a curriculum subject. Typically, RBAI revived the early 19th century word for in those days RBAI had had professors of divinity before the establishment of the Assembly's College and controversies about the kind of theology taught by those professors. A full-time teacher of divinity was appointed, Will Dunn, from England. He found St John's Malone, the only parish church in Belfast where he felt moderately at home as a member of the

Church of England, standing in the anglo-catholic tradition. As sixth formers, quite frankly we resented two precious periods being given over to divinity: the more so as our section didn't have a 'Holy Joe' to take us. We got 'The Boss', the Principal. He was a brilliant classics teacher, we knew that. You jolly well worked hard in his classes. And he did his best to make the new subject 'work' for somewhat resentful students. John Grummitt had worked in the 1930s for the Student Christian Movement in schools.

In my last year at Inst., I was nominated by my housemaster to be house representative on a group of five prefects who used to take it in turn on one morning each week to read the lesson. The 'Boss' called this group the 'Services Committee'. In the spring of 1951 he called us to a meeting to consult us about a complaint he had received about aggressive evangelistic activity on the part of the School Christian Union. It was a school society from which I had stayed clear. Most of its members were Plymouth Brethren or from similar denominations. It awakened me to the fact that I really knew very little about large parts of the Ulster religious spectrum. Two of the members of the services committee had some experience of the Christian Union – both of them were members of the Church of Ireland. They were able from inside to convince the Principal that it were best to leave well alone and to recommend to the teachers responsible for the Christian Union to invite speakers from a wider spectrum of the church. Reading School News over fifty years on, it wouldn't appear that the Christian Union has changed very much: it still invites as speakers well-known evangelical preachers and workers and appears to use exactly the same kind of language about its activities as it did in the 1950s.

I owe an immense debt to RBAI because of its approach to education. You were never spoon-fed or crammed. You were encouraged to discover and develop your particular interests and bents. In the last year at school, staff prepared you for university by treating you in an adult fashion – Alastair MacDonald, Gwyn Blunt, Joe Cowan, Archie Douglas and John Jamieson were particularly encouraging. The School Debating Society encouraged many who would have before them a life of public speaking. Strange to think that it was in a school debate on education that I first found myself giving a testimony to my Christian profession, following a well-known Quaker member of staff in criticising those who would confine Christian nurture to the confines of a church building.

During the summer of 1950 I would have spent most day-light hours at the school playing fields at Osborne Park. These were open to members of the school for formal and informal games. There were grass tennis courts. Try as I would I could never beat my cousin David except in doubles where I relied on a strong partner. But informal games of cricket could be played on the rugby pitches – proper stumps, gloves and pads were available and old used balls. These were hard: shins, heads and other more painful parts could occasionally be struck. On the way down to Osborne, I took to dropping in to St John's where the clergy read Matins each day at 10am. I found something special in that daily office, as we recited psalms and canticles, listened to the scripture lessons, and I discovered intercessory prayer. Those daily prayers for the world and individuals were so important to the rector. They took me into a new plane of Christian experience. During the next summer they used to allow me to read the lessons. It was sight-reading and I remem-ber the pit-falls the Authorised Version lays before the reader in its way of describing members of the male sex!

Interchurch relations
During those years there was very little contact between St John's and the other churches in the area. There was never a joint or united service with either of the Presbyterian churches in the parish, nor with the Methodists. It was a solidly Protestant area, politically predictably solidly Unionist. The nearest Roman Catholic church was a small one, St Brigid's at Derryvolgie Avenue, attended mostly by those in domestic service and members of the university community.

Families used to go along to Lisburn Road on 12 July each year to see the banners and the bands as the members of the Orange Order walked to Finaghy. None of my family ever had any connections with the Order but to go and see the procession was something we did. There was a St John's Malone Lodge, and probably still is. It had no relationship to the parish but a painting of the Church was depicted on its banner. We would look out for and recognise the well-known figure of Cyril Elliott, Dean of Belfast, a prominent Orangeman. In the 1940s no tensions were felt over clergy membership of the loyal orders.

Youth Conference 1951

I left Inst. in June 1951 and entered the Queen's University of Belfast in October. Many of my school friends came as well but we were soon sorted into different faculties. I continued to live at home and to worship at Malone.

In the autumn of 1951 the Church of Ireland held a large week-long Youth Conference in the Wellington Hall. This was chaired by John Barry, rector of Hillsborough, and the organising secretary was the rector of Armoy and Loughguile in North Antrim, Gilbert Wilson. They put an immense amount of work into the event. Each parish had to appoint two young people to be contact persons and to ginger up young people from the parish to attend. For St John's the task was given to me and to Patricia Morton, also a student at Queen's. Patricia and I hardly knew each other. She was very much involved with her school Christian Union so we didn't have a great deal in common. However, we tried to interest our contemporaries, with very little success. For one thing St John's didn't have a youth group. But I found the meetings very stimulating, and the discussion groups I found fascinating. During the time when people were gathering in the hall on one evening, Norman Kelly introduced me to one who would have a continuing influence on my future, the new Church of Ireland chaplain to Queen's, Edgar Turner.

I suppose the most important words spoken at the Conference were spoken by Jack Barry each evening. It wasn't an 'altar call' but a challenge to each one of us to consider if God might not be calling us to some form of Christian service – could it be to ordination, to missionary service overseas as doctors, nurses, agriculturists? And little shivers went down my spine. Could God be calling me to ordination?

The follow-up to the Conference included a series of monthly talks and discussions on prayer given by Eric Elliott, the Church Education Officer, in the Church of Ireland Young Men's Society rooms in Donegall Square East – a most depressing place, best

known to Inst. schoolboys of a certain disposition for the bil-
liards room! Eric Elliott stimulated my thinking about prayer
just when it was needed. In the next six months we became very
good friends. Rural Deanery youth groups were set up and I
went along to St Polycarp's Finaghy to represent St John's.
Patricia Morton had dropped out by this stage because of pressure of medical studies. Patricia became eventually a consultant
cardiologist and head of the department at Belfast City Hospital.
Welcoming us to St Polycarp's was the Rural Dean, Jack Butler,
the curate who had known me as an infant thirteen or fourteen
years earlier. We arranged a number of Rural Deanery gatherings for the rest of the winter. Will Harris, curate of St Thomas's,
was elected chairman and I was, with a Norman Wilkinson from
St Nicholas's, the committee. I only recall one of the evening
events when we persuaded Norman Barr, then on the staff of
Belfast Cathedral, to give us a talk on the Prayer Book.

For me part of the follow-up was a new interest in the bible. I
had been given an authorised version of the bible by my father
to mark my confirmation in 1947. At that time it was the only
version read in public worship. I began a search for a readable
version in modern English and at Christmas 1951 I purchased a
copy of James Moffatt's New Translation – new, in the sense that
it was the only bible in twentieth-century English, though it
dated from 1926. I devoured it but found it raising questions.
Could there not be a version which would speak clearly to the
post-war world? What would being able to read the scriptures
in the original Hebrew and Greek be like? A few weeks later I
found in a bookshop another translation in modern English –
the New Testament in the *Revised Standard Version* published in
America in 1946. This I found much more satisfactory than
Moffatt because the rhythms of the authorised version were
there. On 30 September 1952, on the day of its publication, I acquired my copy of the RSV, Old Testament and New Testament.
Within a few years this version was what we were using for
reading lessons at daily services. In 1952, I was already experiencing what others were feeling – restlessness with out-dated
language, a growing desire to communicate the eternal truths of
the gospel in language accessible by people, and ultimately to
pray and praise our God using the words we use for human

communication. By the end of the century there would be an immense range of versions of the scriptures, many of which would be recognised in the Church of Ireland as suitable for use in public worship.

Already I was discovering that my focus was moving to life at university, as God continued to press me to yield to his call to offer for ordination.

Queen's in 1951

Queen's University in 1951 was a comparatively small place. The student population was between 1500 and 2000. This meant that you could know people in different faculties, for most people were studying in a comparatively small campus. The facilities for pre-meds, the chemists, the physicists as well as the historians, the philosophers and English students were all grouped around one central quadrangle. And the Students' Union coffee shop was accessible to all. Medical students still came back from the hospital: Jack Kyle, Ireland's Rugby out-half still played for Queen's Rugby Team. Philip Larkin, soon to be a world-renowned poet, worked in the Library. Prof Bates, with his red ties, ran the applied engineering school and was already contributing to space research projects. Over all presided Dr Eric Ashby, the vice-chancellor. Ordinary students could get to know him – you didn't have to offend against university standards of discipline! In 1951 there were still a number of ex-service students, older and more mature than the rest of us and there was also a handful of students from overseas, including the Sudan, Cyprus and the West Indies.

My plan was to read honours history, but in the first year you had to take History 1 of the General Arts course. This was a huge class in which people from all three years were together. History 1 was a course in modern European history from the French Revolution to the beginning of the First World War. Most of us had studied this for Senior Certificate which meant it wasn't exactly exciting. However, we were brought face-to-face with it at a new depth. All the lecturers in the department lectured on parts of the course which gave variety. Essays were discussed in small tutorials and at the beginning of the Hilary and Easter terms there were class exams. Those who hoped to do honours were told at the beginning of the year that the decision would be made on the basis of the June degree exam. Subsidiaries in the first year included a language – I chose French, and thoroughly enjoyed that subject at university level. There was a free choice of a third subject – I chose Geography 1, which turned out to be a course in geology, as geography was my second string in case I didn't make the History School. This was also a course which counted for the BSc degree and in the practicals we mixed with people who had done or were doing chemistry and zoology. Geology 1 was taught by Professor J. K. Charlesworth and was really a course in geomorphology. Charlesworth promised that those who took the course would never be able to look at a land-scape in the same way again. And he spoke truly. In each of these three courses there were others from Inst. and we made friends with people who had studied at other schools.

When you start university, then as now, the 'freshers' are be-sieged by every conceivable university society and club, seeking to inveigle them into become members. I was very conservative and only signed up for the History Society. This was run by members of the Honours School. In my first year there were sev-eral Old Instonians with Tony Stewart is its president. A. T. Q. Stewart was to graduate in 1952 with first-class honours. He later became one of Ireland's best-known historians and pub-lished many books seeking to explain and interpret the compli-cated history of our island from the time of the Tudors. Another Old Instonian, Robert Huddleson, was a Classics student and a member of the Queen's branch of the Student Christian Movement (SCM). SCM specialised in study groups and after the Youth Conference, Bobby persuaded me to come along. Initially suspicious, after my experiences of Christian Union at school, I soon found that SCM gave me opportunities of study-ing my faith with the same integrity as I was studying my other university subjects. The study group which met at a time conve-nient for me was studying St Paul's letter to the Galatians. Led by a Presbyterian theological student, Brian Murphy, the group consisted of Anglicans, Presbyterians and Methodists. Again, it was cross-faculty with medicals, scientists as well as arts stu-dents. One of the members was an agricultural post-graduate student with an honours degree in Botany, John Greer, later to

be ordained and serve the Church especially in the field of education. For the first time my faith was being challenged with fellow students with different traditions of worship. Every Friday
we had a lunchtime service in the chapel of the Assembly's
College across the road and that service was led in different
ways according to the denomination of the leader.

Hearing God's Call to Holy Orders

By the time I was into my second term, the challenge of what to
do after university was becoming sharper. I had gone on to university with the vague purpose of teaching in school. To that
end I was seeking an honours degree in history. However, I
could not get over the persistent niggle that God might be calling me to something else – ordination. There had been those
calls at the Youth Conference. Again and again, the rector
seemed to be preaching on the subject of ordination, and those
sermons made me uncomfortable. Then the bishops issued a
pastoral letter to be read in every parish in Ireland calling on
young men to consider whether God might be calling them to
holy orders. I was finding that every time I prayed the General
Thanksgiving, with its phrase 'giving up ourselves to thy service, not only with our lips but with our lives', I wasn't able to
do it with sincerity. Coming into SCM I was asked if I, like Bob
Huddleson, was planning to be ordained. I could only answer,
'No'.

St Patrick's Day came round. By custom our parish had an
early choral celebration of Holy Communion. That year the service was for me an unforgettable experience. I have often said
that I walked in the courts of heaven that morning. A well
known priest of the Church of Ireland, St John Pike, was at that
time a missionary in the diocese of Gambia. Home on leave, St
John was present at that service, and at the parish breakfast
which followed he told me I was coming out for the day with
him. I hadn't had any intention of doing any such thing but St
John Pike was not someone who easily took an excuse! So off we
went, first to call on former parishioners of his in one of the tiny
streets of the St Martin's area of East Belfast, then to call on his
successor as Head of the Mission, Horace Uprichard. After I was
introduced, Horace asked me if I were an ordinand. My answer

was, 'No'. I heard St John's comment, 'Not yet'. I was conscious
for the rest of the day that inwardly I was churning. Was God
calling me to ordination? I think I had already got to the stage
that if I was sure he was, then I was ready. But how could I
know?

I decided to use the opportunity that the Geology Field Week
offered at the end of March 1952 of getting away from home. I
would give God 'the chance', as it were, to make his call clear to
me. A friend from school, Alan McCutcheon and I shared a
room. On the Thursday night Alan was going to be out with
some of the other students who had organised a fundraising
dance in the local hall, fundraising for themselves that is. I used
the evening as a time of intense prayer, inviting God if he wanted
me to be ordained to 'speak' to me. I don't know what I was
expecting. Perhaps a Samuel-like experience or a voice in the
night such as St Patrick had heard. Nothing happened. I went to
bed content. Teaching, here I come! The next morning was one
of those fabulous north Antrim mornings, a clear blue sky and a
sea of an even deeper blue. The group set out to meet the
Professor on the road to Kinbane Head and White Park Bay. As
we walked along, Rathlin Island was clear across the Sound of
Moyle. You could see the Church in Church Bay. I happened to
say to Alan, 'There's even a clergyman living over there all the
year round.' Alan turned to me, and said, 'Brian, you should be
a clergyman.' And at that moment I knew that I had the answer
to the prayer of the previous evening. Now I had to begin to
come to terms with what I believed I had heard.

The next week was Holy Week. The services of Holy Week
helped me to concentrate my thoughts – the addresses were by
the bishop who had confirmed me, John Hind. By Good Friday
I was ready to make my formal response to God. And at Holy
Communion on Easter Sunday I offered him my life to be used
by him as he and his Church would see fit. I said nothing to anyone for another week because I had an important class exam.
After the exam, the Professor of History announced that he
would be interviewing those who had applied for the honours
course at the end of the next week. This meant I had to come
clean. I didn't want anyone saying that I was going for ordination because I had failed to get a place on the honours course.

So when I came home, at the evening meal, I told my parents and sister that, come what may, I had decided to offer myself for ordination. They were very supportive.

At the weekend I went for a long walk with Norman Kelly. Such walks had been a feature of holiday weekends for some time. I told Norman what had been going on in my mind. I don't know how surprised he was, but he immediately offered to help me learn New Testament Greek. I planned to see the rector the following Saturday after Matins but the Professor fixed an interview for that morning so I went on Friday before lunch. With some diffidence I told him that I wanted to offer myself as a candidate for ordination. He looked at me. 'I knew there was someone in the congregation whom God was calling. That was why I was preaching so much on the topic. But I didn't know who it was.' He seemed very happy and we had a time of prayer together – the first time I had had anyone pray with me in a personal way. I presume he passed my name on to the bishop because I began to get invitations to talks and quiet days. However, nobody ever interviewed me or questioned me about my vocation. How unlike the twenty-first century with selection conferences and psychological profiles. When I went to see Professor Sayles the next morning, it was a very short session. 'Mr Mayne,' he said, 'I am happy to offer you a place on the honours course whatever marks you get in the end of term exams. I suggest you concentrate on ensuring you pass in your subsidiary subjects!'

Thus in a few months in the spring of 1952 the future shape of my life was decided.

CHAPTER FOUR

Formation 1952-57

Queen's College, Belfast, had been formed as a constituent college of the Royal University of Ireland in 1849, achieving full university status in 1908 as The Queen's University of Belfast. By its charter it was required to be religiously 'neutral' although it had a faculty of theology for which teaching was given through the Presbyterian Assembly's College and the Methodist Epworth College. In these, students for the Presbyterian and Methodist ministries were also trained. Denominations were allowed to appoint chaplains, called deans of residences in the 1950s. The denominations are totally responsible for their financing. Students could voluntarily declare their religious allegiance by filling up a card which the university passed on to the deans. The Church of Ireland had until 1945 assigned this responsibility to local rectors. Then an arrangement had been made with SCM whereby its Irish Travelling Secretary was also the Church of Ireland Dean of Residence. Brian Harvey filled the post from 1945 to 1948 before going to India with the Dublin University Mission to Chota-Nagpur. Jack Roundhill succeeded him between 1948 and 1951. SCM then indicated that it couldn't undertake continuing to appoint an Anglican as its Secretary. This led to the appointment of the first full-time dean, Edgar Turner, who had been ordained in the diocese of Birmingham and had served six years there.

The Presbyterian Church had a high-profile student centre at 7 College East, worship facilities in the Chapel of Assembly's, and a very fine Dean of Residence in the person of Ray Davey had been in the post since he came home from war service in 1945. Jack Roundhill had negotiated for the Church of Ireland to have the use for worship on three Sundays each month of the building belonging to the Catholic Apostolic Church in Cromwell Road. The Catholic Apostolic denomination had arisen as a

result of the ministry of a small charismatic revival in the 19th
century. It was also known as the Irvingites after its founder
Edward Irving, originally a minister of the Church of Scotland.
The Catholic Apostolics sought to revive in the life of their
church all the offices and charisma mentioned in the New
Testament, as well as developing a very rich liturgical life. But
because Irving taught that the Second Coming of Christ was imminent they made no provision for the continuation of ministry.
In the 1950s the last of their presbyters was a very elderly man
who would fly over from Birmingham occasionally so that they
could have a eucharist, otherwise a sub-deacon would conduct a
kind of ante-communion or service of the word once a month.
On other Sundays they worshipped in Church of Ireland parishes
– a couple were regulars at St John's at the midday eucharist. By
the end of the decade the denomination decided that their
founder must have been mistaken about the parousia and dis-
banded, recommending its members to join the Anglican churches
wherever they were.

So in 1951, Edgar Turner had a place for worship three
Sundays a month, inheriting the remnant of Jack Roundhill's
group but no other resources. Numbers were small as most students like myself lived at home and many were fully committed
in the life of their parishes. Edgar managed to obtain a flat near
the university. In the autumn of 1952 he organised after-church
gatherings on Sunday evening to which those of us who worshipped at home were invited. Staff and students together discussed Christian faith and living. To these he invited the leading
churchmen from the dioceses of Connor and Down. We had
many stimulating evenings. It was quite clear that the new generation had little patience with the restrictive canons of 1878 – in
particular the ban on there being a cross on the most prominent
place in church, the altar. On All Saints' Day and Ascension Day
there was a corporate communion for all Church of Ireland students and staff at the Cromwell Road Church, followed by
breakfast in the Students' Union. Slowly but surely the Church
of Ireland in the Queen's University of Belfast was becoming a
community – not the social centre that Number 7 was to the
Presbyterians nor what residential Aquinas Hall was to the
Roman Catholics. There was a wonderful partnership in the

community between students and members of university staff like J. C. Beckett, F. H. Newark, E. M. Smallwood, C. M. Crowder and M. Aiken.

By autumn 1953 the Representative Body of the Church of Ireland had been able to purchase 22 Elmwood Avenue, a large double house. Here the Dean of Residence would live with a small group of resident students and facilities would be provided to develop the social life. I was one of those involved as we gradually got the house into order in 1953-54 as a member of the Student Committee. Some of the work was physical and dirty. And I was present on the day in 1955 when the Primate, Archbishop John Gregg and the other northern bishops came to dedicate the Centre. The Primate, who was a man in his eighties, read the prayers that had been drawn up and was quite sure that there must have been a misprint; so he prayed for all who would come to this centre *to work and to pray*. The printed prayer had said *to work and to play* – the centre wasn't to be wholly serious. The groundwork was laid for something that would develop and grow, with its own church erected in what was the back garden of number 22. When the jubilee of the Church of Ireland Centre is celebrated in 2005 the extent of its contribution to the life and witness of the Church of Ireland will be judged as not insignificant.

One of the ways in which Edgar Turner moulded us into a community was through an elaborate nativity play which we performed in the church in December 1952. I found myself playing one of the magi. Although I love drama, I am afraid I am no actor and distinguished myself by fluffing the very few lines I had to speak.

I hope I made myself much more useful as one of the regular team who prepared the church in Cromwell Road for Sunday worship. We had to replace all the furniture used by the Catholic Apostolic congregation on the Friday before their service and take it out to the store-room for the following week. As well as that, Edgar Turner taught Bobby Huddleson and myself how to prepare the communion vessels for Sunday morning and to care for them – lessons that I am afraid we would only get at a very rudimentary level in the Divinity School.

An eye to the liturgy

In the autumn of 1952 the SCM, led by its Presbyterian Irish Secretary Brian Graeme-Cook, known to all as 'BGC', added a series of seminars to its study-group programme. On of these on worship was led by Edgar Turner. It met in his flat on Thursday afternoons. For me, this was literally an eye-opener, as we learned how liturgy had developed, what was happening, especially in England and on the continent, as through the Liturgical Movement worship was being renewed. I devoured books that Edgar was able to lend – Dom Gregory Dix's *The Shape of the Liturgy* , A. G. Hebert's *Liturgy and Society* and the small books by Henry de Candole, *The Church's Offering* and *The Church's Prayers*. I perceived that there was so much more in worship than I had experienced. I learned how Roman Catholics in postwar Europe were seeking to reach out to the un-churched, getting round regulations that required Mass to be celebrated in Latin. In England the Parish and People movement was bringing a Parish Communion to the centre of each Sunday's worship in many parishes like the one where Edgar Turner had been serving. Somehow I knew that liturgy and worship was going to be at the centre of my future ministry.

At about the same time I had discovered, on a back shelf in the Church of Ireland APCK bookshop on Donegall Square West, a small book that had been produced as a Lent Book when the 400th anniversary of the *Book of Common Prayer* was celebrated in 1949. It advocated the regular recitation of Morning and Evening Prayer – the daily office – by lay people as well as by clergy. I had often taken part in daily Morning Prayer and Evening Prayer in St John's but this book encouraged me to put reciting and praying the daily office at the heart of my devotional life. The decision to do this was one of the greatest sources of blessing in my life. It gave and gives me a rhythm to my prayer as well as leading me to read many parts of the bible which I might otherwise miss. It is one of the hopes of the Liturgical Advisory Committee that the provisions for daily prayer being included in the 2004 edition of the *Book of Common Prayer* will encourage more people to pray daily 'with the church'.

Malone 1953-55 – A New Rector

In 1953 a number of things happened in the life of the parish of Malone which involved me. First, the rector asked my father to be his churchwarden in addition to being parochial treasurer. We knew that the rector's health had been precarious for some time as he had been off-duty for three months at the end of 1952. Soon after my father took office he was ill again and it fell to the household of the rector's churchwarden to entertain the preacher for the Dedication Anniversary Service at the end of April. Thus I met Edward William Louis Garrett, then rector of a parish in Fermanagh, and we got on very well indeed. One evening during June, Canon L'Estrange, as he had become a few months before, arrived to see my father and to tell him that for health reasons he was going to retire. This was a great shock for we had all grown very fond of Frederick L'Estrange who had been rector of Malone for almost twenty-four years.

The processes of selecting a new rector swept into action, the bishop being determined not to allow a long interregnum. Edward Garrett was nominated early in August and the Institution, the service used when a new priest is formally entrusted with a parish, was fixed for 18 September. There was just one problem – the curate, Norman Kelly, was getting married at the beginning of September. The bishop insisted that he didn't change any of his plans. With the help of a retired priest who had been helping on and off during the previous twelve months, and Will Harris, Sunday worship and weekday holy communion were covered and I undertook responsibility for the daily services of Morning Prayer and Evening Prayer. I also found myself a kind of 'welcoming officer' as the new Sunday School year began.

Nowadays the Rural Dean makes all the arrangements for an institution service. In 1953 nobody came near the parish to brief the churchwardens, so I asked Edgar Turner to come and indicate what had to be done. Thus the institution went smoothly and for the first time I found myself robed, singing with the choir. The organist seemed quite happy and, until the Sunday before my ordination, I counted myself a member – I could never be a soloist but I believe I pulled my weight and learned a great deal.

Thankfully, the new rector and I formed a happy relationship and as well as continuing to come to the daily services from time to time, mostly on Saturday mornings, there were hilarious long coffee sessions in the rectory. Ned Garrett appreciated having an ordinand in the parish and I learned quite a lot from him. The time for Norman Kelly to move on was coming and he passed on more and more responsibility for Sunday School work. His wife, Noreen, had grown up in the parish, and after they were married I was ordered to stop calling him 'Mr Kelly' – he became Norman to me and I was a frequent visitor at their flat. When in 1955 he was appointed to the parish of Billy in my beloved north Antrim, Billy rectory became a 'retreat' for me.

SCM Irish Conference 1953
An event of great significance for me was SCM's Irish Conference held at Dundrum, County Down, in July 1953. Here I met students from Trinity and Magee College, Londonderry. It was run on the pattern of the UK Conferences held each summer at Swanwick in Derbyshire: a balance of worship, teaching and fun. The Methodist Church had maintained a war-time army camp, giving dormitories, feeding facilities and a lecture room. For worship we went down the hill to the Methodist Church. It is significant that at that time there was no joint communion service. The Presbyterians and Methodists had their communion and Anglicans borrowed St Donard's Church for our celebration. The chaplain for the week was a Welsh Anglican who couldn't get over the ultra-simple church and the lack of all the colourful adjuncts to worship he took for granted. The main speaker was a Methodist minister, originally from Dublin, called Alan Booth. He was superb and opened my eyes certainly to the excitement of the Christian's calling in the post-war world. I bought a book at Dundrum by an Anglican bishop, Stephen Neill, on the church's ministry. It was to become my constant devotional companion for many years. It was re-read every anniversary of ordination. Then I lost it, almost certainly having taken it on holiday. To this day I haven't been able to re-place it.

At Dundrum I made friends with those at Trinity preparing for ordination, in particular Jim Moore and Stanley Baird, as well as Presbyterian ordinands, Donald McIlhagga, an English

Presbyterian who would later join the Iona Community, and Tom Craig, reading history at Magee. Tom Craig would eventually become the Presbyterian minister at Ardglass and share chaplaincy responsibilities at RAF Bishopscourt before his early death. It was a rich experience, one for which I often give thanks.

Over New Year 1954, SCM also brought Dr George Simms, the bishop of Cork, to lead a Prayer School – a kind of follow-up to the conference. Thankfully it was live-in at the Assembly's College and as the weather was very cold one was glad of the efficient heating system and comforts provided for Presbyterian ordinands.

Looking ahead
During the autumn of 1953 I was made to think about my training for ordination. It was suggested that as I would be graduating from Queen's it might be worth considering training at a theological college in England. Three possibilities were suggested: Lincoln, where George Simms had been on the staff and where Edgar Turner has spent a year after completing his course in Dublin, Bishop's College, Cheshunt and Westcott House, Cambridge. The chief advocate of the latter was Eric Elliott: there he had received his theological training and it had access to the whole Divinity resources of the university. I decided that I needed to see what Dublin had to offer. The opportunity arose of a weekend there, linked to a meeting of the Irish University History Students Association Committee. Jim Moore arranged for me to stay from Thursday to Sunday evening at the Divinity Hostel where about half of those training for ministry were housed. I was lodged in the 'Prophet's Chamber', a single room on the top floor of a Georgian house in Mountjoy Square. It was at the time a fairly run-down part of the city about a mile from the centre. There was a chapel and well-ordered worship. Maybe the food was a bit spartan but there was a very welcoming camaraderie. I enjoyed Sunday's worship in the Chapel of Trinity College, and at the recommendation of Michael Ferrar, the Warden of the Hostel, I had secured a matinee ticket for Shaw's *St Joan* at the Gate Theatre – a very famous performance by the great Irish actress Siobhan McKenna, supported by Micheal MacLiammoir. If this kind of thing was on offer in

Dublin, I couldn't think what advantage there would be in crossing the water! Perhaps Michael Ferrar was responsible for keeping me in Ireland. Had I gone to Westcott I would have been contemporary with Robert Runcie and half the English bishops! But my chief consideration was that I intended to minister in the Church of Ireland. By going to Trinity I would be training alongside those with whom I would be working for my lifetime. I never regretted the decision.

History at Queen's and beyond
By the summer of 1954 I had completed the course for History Honours with the exception of the special subject. At that time each part of the course was taught in alternate years so that our second year we had lectures with those in third year and in our turn we had lectures with the new intake. The number in our year was average size with that of previous years – there were seven of us. It meant that there were enough books to go round and the History Library was a comfortable place in which to work. In came as a great shock that the number of those accepted for honours in 1953 was more than double. This meant books needed for preparing essays were in great demand and the more significant had to be read in the main library. Also we had a change of professor. G. O. Sayles, a medieval historian, accepted a chair in his native Scotland but it was not until the beginning of our last academic year that Michael Roberts succeeded him. The larger history school meant greater choice of special subject. I opted for a course in medieval English history, Church and State in the Reign of Edward I, largely because I had found Jack W. Gray, the lecturer who taught it, the member of staff who stimulated my thinking the most. Two of us from the final year and two girls from third year found ourselves wrestling with power politics surrounding medieval archbishops, the papacy and King Edward I's permanent need of money to finance his wars. Definitely good preparation for the ministry of the Church.

Because there were more of us, there was actually more camaraderie between those who would graduate in 1955 and 1956 than in the smaller group. One of the newcomers was my former classmate from Larne Grammar a decade earlier, John

Darbyshire. Coincidentally there were four who would be or-
dained in three denominations – two Presbyterians, Robert
Brown, who would head the religious studies department at
Stranmillis College, and Godfrey Brown from Newcastle, who
would later be elected Moderator of his church; Ambrose
Macauley, who would return to Queen's as Roman Catholic
chaplain, become parish priest at St Brigid's and a monsignor,
and myself. It was a great pleasure in 1997 to invite Monsignor
Ambrose to share with me in an inter-church wedding at Saul.
Little did we think in those days that ecumenical relationships
would move. Among the girls was a former head girl of Victoria
College, Romayne Ferris, who went on to add a law degree to
her history one, enter the civil service, marry another lawyer
who had been head boy at Inst. – my school friend Bob Carswell.
He became Lord Chief Justice of Northern Ireland and, as Lady
Carswell, Romayne became the first woman to be appointed
Her Majesty's Lieutenant for Belfast.

Of the twenty or so, there was an above average early mortal-
ity rate: I know that three or four died before their mid-thirties.
Among them were Margaret Martin, daughter of Very Rev
Alfred Martin, a fearless and passionate preacher of reconciliation. Margaret and I had a special relationship for over three
years and she dared to visit me in Dublin and brave meeting
members of the divinity school. She became a teacher and married an army officer. Another was Anne Smyth. She was the first
ex-pupil of Cross and Passion College, Ballycastle to gain entrance to the honours school. She had an extraverted personality
and was the first girl member of the Roman Catholic faith that I
came to know anyway well. She was rather a non-conformist,
being the child of a 'mixed' marriage, and rather intolerant of
many of the traditions of her Church. As the fourth member of
the Church and State group, she was a very healthy and cheerful
person to have around. Just to show what a 'village' Belfast really
is, when I became incumbent of Knocknagoney, the rector's
churchwarden was Lewis Warren, who joined the history staff
in 1955; he had married Anne.

The teaching of Irish history had been recognised as difficult
because different interpretations were often nothing short of
propaganda and perpetuated divisions.The Professor of

Modern Irish History at University College, Dublin, R. Dudley Edwards, had the inspiration to see the potential benefits of the undergraduate students of history in the Irish universities meeting together and discussing historical subjects. The first 'Congress' was held in 1951, another in February 1952. Queen's was to send three delegates to Cork for the 1953 Congress: one of us had to write a paper and two to speak to papers presented by students from other colleges. I was cajoled into writing the Queen's paper, expanding one of my term essays on 'The Impact of Islam in the fifth and sixth centuries' – sufficiently abstruse to be non-controversial at that point in history!

This was my first visit to the South apart from an afternoon drive to my mother's birthplace in County Monaghan. In 1953 the Irish railways had launched an experimental through express from Belfast to Cork, calling only at Amiens Street Station in Dublin. The train left Belfast at 10.30am and arrived in Cork at 5.30pm. We were joined in Dublin by a number of Dublin delegates including Professor Edwards. One of these turned out to be a final year divinity student, James Hartin, who was to be a guest in Cork of Bishop George Simms. We had a tremendous time. For the first time I became acquainted with the world of the Southern Irish student – the importance so many of them put on the consumption of beer and the smoke-filled rooms! I was fascinated by many things I saw in the South, not least the Honan Chapel at UCC to which Jim Hartin insisted that I accompany him for a pilgrimage. Up to then I don't think I had ever said a prayer in a Roman Catholic church.

My contribution was well received and I found myself the QUB delegate to the committee meeting that would be held in Dublin in the autumn. That centred round an inter debate held at UCD, then based in Earlsfort Terrace above St Stephen's Green. That gave the opportunity for the weekend in Dublin with fare and accommodation paid. At the debate, which was on the subject of German re-armament, I realised that Irish nationalism was very sensitive when a Northerner ventured to speak of his 'Britishness'.

The 1954 congress was held at University College, Galway, and as we were to host the 1955 congress I was again sent as one of the delegates, but all I had to do was speak to one of the papers.

The Belfast Congress was a huge success, Magee College, Derry becoming a participant for the first time. I had great difficulty in persuading any of my year to prepare and present a paper. John McKee, who was then a third years student, came to our rescue and presented a paper on Hitler and Nazism which turned our attention away from purely Irish concerns. John McKee would add law to his history degree and became a county court judge.

The congress was held in February at a time when our thoughts were very much on final examinations. Soon after it was over, at the beginning of the Easter vacation, before finals, I went down with measles. I couldn't bear light and was forbidden to read for three weeks. Bang went my revision programme. I reconciled myself to a poor result – I would discipline myself for the final four weeks. I would do what I could within a strict nine-hour day, broken for the sake of my eyes into ninety minute sessions. On returning after Easter I had to sit a class exam with a minimum of preparation. To my surprise I got the highest mark of my entire four years. A month later the ordeal of finals began: nine three-hour papers between Monday 9.30am and Friday 5.30pm, with only Wednesday afternoon off. And it was a heat-wave.

After finishing the written exams, I went to stay for recuperation with Norman and Noreen Kelly at Billy rectory near Bushmills. The heat-wave continued and north Antrim was at its best. Then it was back for the 'vivas', when the examiners and the external examiner grilled us further on what we had put on paper. We were called in alphabetical order – I was last but one. And I had the longest session. Dr D. B. Quinn, the external examiner, queried my choice of a medieval special subject as my bias seemed to be towards the 17th and 19th centuries. I had no answer other than that I felt at home with the ecclesiastical special subject. Afterwards we sat in the sun waiting for the results to be posted on the library door. No firsts: two of us were more than delighted with our second class honours division one awards – the other two present congratulated us and seemed pleased with their two twos. Then it was home for my twenty-first birthday party.

Preparing for the Divinity School

I had an appointment at Trinity College, Dublin, on the follow-
ing Thursday morning with the Archbishop King's Professor of
Divinity, Dr Richard Randall Hartford, to discover what would
be required from me for the beginning of the Junior Year in the
Divinity School at the beginning of October. I had contacted Rev
Tom Salmon who invited me to stay the night before with him at
his rectory in Carrickmines. That Thursday was St John the
Baptist's Day and it was a special experience to share in Holy
Communion at Tullow Church before breakfast. Tom Salmon
radiated a gentle holiness and led worship in a very special way
as the congregations of St Ann's, Dawson Street, and Christ
Church Cathedral can testify.

I was left into Dublin for my interview with the redoubtable
Dickie Hartford. All he wanted was for me to fill in the application form. To my question about what would be required from
me in the autumn, his reply was 'the complete examination for
exemption from the preliminary year and the pre-term Greek
exam'. To say that I was shattered was an understatement. It
was quite a programme. I was assured that all the subjects
would be taken as 'vivas'. Dr Hartford was at pains to explain
that, at the same time as my divinity course, I would be able to
add a Trinity history honours degree. As a graduate of Queen's I
would be entitled to credit for the first two years. It was necessary in those days to have a Trinity, Oxford or Cambridge Arts
degree to proceed to the Bachelor of Divinity or higher degrees.
The new honours graduate of Queen's didn't like what appeared to be a slight on his recent achievement. I knew I had acquired a good degree in history and I knew enough of the work
required to query how one could possibly read different courses
in history and have time to give to my main purpose which was
an adequate training in theology to equip me for the office and
work of a priest in the Church of God. The subject would come
up again in the autumn as there were three graduates of QUB
joining the Divinity School. The offer of working for a Trinity
Arts degree was put to the three of us and we turned it down,
discovering in the process that the fees due were £30 per term
less! When I told Dr Hartford my decision he said that I would
regret it but that he would never hold it against me. He was true

to his word and six years later certified my results in Divinity Testimonium to the University of London, qualifying me to sit for its BD with honours. Today it would be all but incomprehensible to think that as well as the course for ordination training there would be time for studying for a non-theological degree.

The Divinity School
My experience of the next two years would reveal a huge need for change both in course content and methods of instruction. Bishop Roy Warke, in his *Ripples in a Pond*, has given a very faithful description of the Divinity School a few years earlier. I was coming in at what would indeed be the end of an era.

I worked really hard throughout the summer learning Greek, preparing Matthew and Acts in Greek for the entrance exam. Also we were to be examined on the Church Catechism and an introduction to the philosophy of religion and a book of sermons by an 18th century Bishop Butler. I found both philosophy and Butler almost incomprehensible but I struggled with them. They had little or no relevance that I could see to the post-war world.

So at the end of September, Bobby Huddleson and I set off for 25 Mountjoy Square where we were joined by another graduate of QUB, Harold Magowan, whom neither of us had encountered in our time at Queen's. All three of us received bursaries from the Sir Thomas and Lady Edith Dixon Fund, set up to encourage graduates of Queen's to proceed to ordination. What a link with my childhood: I was the only one of the three who knew the founders of the fund.

Friday morning we gathered in the Junior Year lecture room for the exams. To my amazement these took place in one to one encounters with members of the staff in different corners. After all my hard work and readiness for unseen translation it was a surprise to be presented with a copy of the Greek New Testament, complete with chapters and verses, and to be asked to translate a paragraph: easily recognisable, even if we were required to give the rendering of the Revised Version. Then I was asked to parse a few words – the most obvious irregular verbs. 'That will be 10!' The main hurdle was over. Philosophy just required a short chat with the examiner about one particular chapter. Catechism was an equal doddle. And I managed 7 or 8 on

Butler's sermons. To call the examination a formality was to give it a dignity it did not deserve. However, my diligent work at Greek had proved worthwhile and the system that, on Tom Salmon's advice, I had constructed would see me through all the future term Greek exams and to the prize awarded for highest marks in Greek at the final examination. Before we started the course I came to recognise that the standards required for a university honours examination and those for Divinity Testimonium were worlds apart, but I determined to work for the latter with the same intensity as I had for my degree.

It wasn't long before I discovered another difference. In Queen's we had been treated as responsible adults and were always addressed as Mr X or Miss Y. In Trinity rolls were called at every lecture and we were addressed by surname only. I had developed my own system of shorthand note-taking at lectures but now I was expected to take down every word of the lecturer.

I found the system very frustrating. There were never lists of books for reading. There were few essays. Term exams from the lecturer on the bible were on his teaching. You were required to answer all the questions. Not even in school had I encountered this. There were set books: and you were tested on what the author had written. Systematic theology was studied through E. J. Bicknell's commentary on the Thirty-Nine Articles. That is a very good presentation of what one might call a central approach to Anglican understanding of theology. Conservative evangelicals supplemented it by reading Dr W. H. Griffith Thomas's *The Catholic Faith* and a few from the 'other' wing would look up Dr C. B. Moss's *The Christian Faith*. The latter had the advantage of being very readable and one of the few places where I was ever able to comprehend the subtleties of the classical heresies of the Early Church!

As well as the three main lectures from Dr Hartford, the junior year was divided into two sub-groups, one of which was taken by Tom Salmon and the other by a noted Dublin conservative evangelical, Cecil Proctor. I was pleased to be in Salmon's group but have to confess that my notes of his lectures were virtually non-existent – I simply could not keep awake! He had a very soft voice and the lectures were at 1 o'clock, after lunch. In Senior Year I was in Ernest Daunt's sub-group which he conducted

more like a tutorial with discussion and argument. When one of
the more conservative of our group would make a 'party' point,
Ernest Daunt used to swing round and say, 'Mayne, what do
you think?' There was, however, never any rancour and I am
glad to say that over forty years later I am still on very good
terms with those with whom I debated in that class.

There were wide gaps in the course – little or nothing on
ethics or applied theology for example. Once a year a visitor came
and give half a dozen lectures on psychological problems – the
nature of psychological illness. These were better than nothing,
but only just. Students welcomed this course as the only time the
realities of sex were discussed.

Nor was preparation for practical ministry much better. I
was amazed that, at the inaugural meeting of Junior Year, we
were given a text on which to prepare a sermon that we would
write under exam conditions on the next but one Saturday
morning at 10.30am in the Regent House. Not one suggestion of
how to approach homiletics was offered. I was able to consult
Canon Fred L'Estrange, now living in Dublin, and he gave me
some pointers. This fortnightly sermon writing continued until
the end of Senior Year. Sermons were marked, and each term a
small cash prize was awarded for the highest total. Bobby
Huddleson and I won prizes in each year. On the intervening
Saturday the year divided so that we might practice delivery
and receive criticism from a member of staff. One such criticism
simply consisted in the critic saying, 'Well, that was seven minutes.' Some students were licensed as student readers in Dublin
parishes and inflicted the Saturday sermon on local congregations – and I do mean inflicted – as some of these sermon-essays
were dreadful.

Training in the conduct of worship was equally haphazard.
Apart from the preparation by the Warden for taking services in
the chapel of the Divinity Hostel, which was thorough and careful – but less than half the students resided there – we had weekly
sessions taken by the Wallace Lecturer on Reading the Liturgy
in the College Chapel. John Armstrong was meticulous. He sought
to help those who had difficulties in reading aloud in a large building but he was not an elocutionist nor a speech therapist. Those
whom he reckoned reached an acceptable standard were soon

excused attendance; for me that was at the end of my first term. Even today, those responsible for ordination training, both for full-time and non-stipendiary ministry, do not provide proper training in voice production. Most of those who come through have difficulties and tend to speak too quickly in church, dropping one's voice at the end of sentences is rife, and the ubiquitous microphone is not the answer. Our contemporaries in the Presbyterian Church did take the matter seriously, perhaps over seriously with the consequence that most Presbyterian ministers of our generation tend to speak in exactly the same manner. The lectures in Pastoral Theology were prepared and given with the best of intentions but were woefully inadequate. The 'professors' were Dublin clergy and their experience was of ministry in Dublin or the rural South and had hardly any relevance to those who would minister in post-war Belfast city parishes. Even the instruction on 'how to' conduct services was horrendous: practical training in caring for communion vessels and linen, that Bobby Huddleson and I had received from Edgar Turner over many weeks, was skated over in a quarter of an hour. Only a devotional weekend away near the end of Senior Year, conducted by John Barry, rector of Hillsborough, 'Cromlyn' of the *Church of Ireland Gazette*, began to touch on the realities of the ministry on which we were to embark in a few weeks.

Interaction with fellow-students

Yet I would not have changed my decision of 1953 to train in Dublin. There were priests of deep spirituality. So much of what it was to be a priest in the church was communicated outside lectures – in the worship of College Chapel, in the life of the Divinity Hostel, in the camaraderie of a group of up to forty men who accepted each other as we were. I could and did form friendships with strong evangelicals like Cecil Kerr and Terry Callan, which have not disappeared over the years. Another of these was Oliver Pierce. After I had been living at the Hostel for the best part of the term, Oliver and I walked back one evening up O'Connell Street and he said to me, 'You know, Brian, we were warned about you.' I replied, 'How?' 'That you were the greatest "spike" (meaning extreme Anglo-Catholic) that we would ever have seen, coming from St John's, Malone. But,' he

went on, 'You're normal!' As to who had 'warned' the evangelicals I had no illusions. For before I left Queen's a prominent
member of the Christian Union, who happened also to worship
in St John's, left a note for me with my books in the library asking me to meet him for there was something important he wanted
to discuss with me. We met and he looked at me very earnestly.
'You are going to train to be a minister. I would be happier if I
thought you were right with God.' I fought back my anger at
this kind of impertinence but realised that he meant well and
gave him the kind of answer I have always given to people who
say that kind of thing. 'I am very happy with my relationship
with Christ. I see no reason to doubt its reality as I see no reason
to doubt your relationship with Christ although it may be different. I respect yours and I expect you to respect mine.' He wanted
to give me some literature. Indeed, to this day, there are conservative evangelicals in the Church of Ireland who still don't think
I am a Christian, and enclose tracts and leaflets, often written by
a 19th century bishop of Liverpool, J. C. Ryle, seeking to persuade me that their experience is the only genuine way to God.
One of the advantages of the Divinity School at the end of the
1950s was that we learned to respect one another.

There were a few of the more 'catholic' persuasion who
thought that they had got a new recruit. One persuaded me to
cycle with him to the Sunday eucharist at St John's,
Sandymount, the most Anglo-Catholic church in Dublin. He
was disappointed when I said I didn't find it anyway relevant to
life: it seemed to be imitating the least attractive fashions of
Roman Catholic worship. I was searching for a renewed liturgy
that would be congregational and relevant to life. In the College
Theological Society I soon got a reputation for standing for the
full Anglican position, critical of fundamentalism on the one
hand and of advocacy of Romanist practices on the other. I had
also successfully invaded one of the evangelical strongholds by
entering for the Carson Biblical Prize – a competition in which
one was tested in four ninety-minute quizzes on one's knowledge of the text of the English Bible – including such esoteric information as which Old Testament king had an iron bedstead
(Og, the king of Bashan). My reading of the daily office for five
years had given me a good background and I emerged the winner,

the first winner for years who was not a recognised evangelical. In 1956 twenty pounds was a small fortune – worth two terms' fees for a graduate.

The sudden death, after a meeting of the College Theological Society, of Dr J. E. L. Oulton, the Regius Professor, who had taught all those who had guided me so far like Norman Kelly, Edgar Turner and even Tom Salmon, was an indication that an era in the life of the Church of Ireland was coming to an end. I had great respect, even affection, for him. You could see just by the way he presided at Holy Communion in Chapel that this very shy man had a deep spirituality. It also came out in his singing in the College Choir – *Messiah* and the *Bach Passions*. Richard Hartford, who had been the junior professor, succeeded him: thus the Divinity Testimonia of 1957 are doubly signed Richard Randall Hartford. His best lectures were those he had newly to compose for our final term. I believe he was open to changes in the system and some were introduced by the new Archbishop King's Professor, Frederic Ercolo Vokes, appointed on my very last day in Dublin.

There still survived into my time, giants of the past in the great Dr A. A. Luce, a formidable philosopher, of whom I suspect Dr Hartford may have been a little afraid, and R. M. Gwynn, still living in rooms in College in his eighties. The latter was almost stone-deaf, and many were the legends of his use of an ear-trumpet for viva exams. 'RM' had established many years before a devotional guild, the Dublin University Churchmen's Guild, which met once or twice a term in his rooms to say the Guild Office of preparation for communion, to have tea and buttered barm-brack. Here again was part of the almost hidden spirituality of the Church of Ireland.

Chapel Worship
The worship of the Chapel of Trinity College in 1955-57 would hardly be recognisable by a student of the 21st century. The Provost, if a member of the Church of Ireland, was responsible for regulating the worship of the Chapel; but as the holder of the office at the time was not, the Regius Professor of Divinity was in charge. The College Chaplain, the Dean of Residence, was a kind of 'curate' who had a pastoral care of Anglican students and

arranged weekday services. I renewed a relationship with
Kenneth Maguire that had been formed at that SCM conference
in 1953. He was a much undervalued person whose abilities were
not recognised in Dublin. Subsequently he returned to Canada
where he had been a curate and within two years was elected
Bishop of Montreal.

There was a said service of Holy Communion at 8.00am and
then the principal service at 10.00am. Staff and male students
wore surplices over their suits. Some still wore 'undergraduate
surplices' which were rather like reversed barber shop overalls,
secured by a button at the neck. Fellows of TCD had stalls in
chapel and wore their academic hoods – they took turns to read
the scripture lessons. Female students, including the girls from
the Church of Ireland College of Education in Kildare Street,
wore gowns and mortar boards. Attendance for undergraduates
who lived in College and members of the Divinity School was
compulsory and we had to fill in attendance cards and place
these in mortar boards held by students who were paid a small
fee each term for so doing. Just how far this was followed up in
1955 for the non-divinity student I never discovered.

A section of the choir of St Patrick's Cathedral led the praise
which always included an anthem: they left chapel before the
sermon and a student organist played for the final hymn. Except
for one Sunday in the month the service was Morning Prayer
and Sermon – during lecture term often preached by a distinguished preacher. Each term one of these gave the University
Sermon. It was preceded by the Bidding Prayer, little changed
from the 18th century when the Chapel had been built. On the
Sunday when the service was Holy Communion, the vast majority of the congregation, including those of us who had been at
the early service, left after the Prayer for the Church. It was Irish
Prayer Book worship of high quality, conducted with dignity in
a classical building which I found conducive to worship.

Matins and Evensong were said daily at 8.45am before the
beginning of lectures and at 6.45pm before the formal evening
meal, 'Commons'. From my second term, these were my staple
daily worship, the congregation consisting mainly of the divinity
students who had 'rooms' in College. On Wednesday mornings
and on Saints' Days there was a said service of Holy

Communion. After this there was often breakfast laid on in the
rooms of the Dean of Residence. There was one very special service, the College Carol Service at the end of the lecture term at
the beginning of December. Everyone turned out in full dress
and the Roman Catholic Provost read the Christmas gospel, the
nearest to an ecumenical occasion that College Chapel provided.
Nowadays the Chapel is fully used by all traditions. However,
its use by Church of Ireland students is minimal, the divinity
students worshipping at the Theological College or in place-
ment parishes on Sundays.

The 'Theo.' and social life
There were always a number of divinity students who had
'rooms' in College. Two or three students occupied 'suites' – single
bedrooms, a common room for study and a 'skippery' for
preparing breakfast and snacks. This meant that those of us who
lived at the Divinity Hostel or, like me after the first term, in
lodgings off campus, could have a 'base' with friends between
lectures or when we didn't want to study in the library.

Mention has already been made of the College Theological
Society, third in the hierarchy of College debating societies, which
was headed by the Historical Society (the 'Hist.') and the
Philosophical Society (the 'Phil.'). We met on Monday evenings in
the Graduate's Memorial Building's debating chamber. The officers,
Auditor, Honorary Secretary, Treasurer and Librarian, wore dinner
jackets and the Regius Professor presided. Papers were read and debated. Then the staff withdrew. Members awarded marks for the
contributions to the debate and at the end of the year a prize for
Oratory was awarded. Sometimes private business could also be
frivolous and afterwards all adjourned to somebody's rooms
where a member of committee provided supper and the evening
usually concluded well past midnight with a sing song. I was
'blooded' in the Theo. very early, as Stanley Baird invited me to
be the chief speaker to a paper on the Ministry of Healing. As I
shall relate later, this particular part of pastoral ministry was
going to be important to me. I had the immense resource of being
able to contact Canon Fred L'Estrange, one of those who had revived the practice of healing ministry in the North. His insights,
willingly communicated, enabled me to make a worthwhile con-

tribution. Subsequently I relished the opportunity to speak on my feet – never to win a prize for oratory but to gain a skill that every member of the clergy needs. The years 1955 and 1956 were the four hundredth anniversaries of the martyrdoms of the reign of Queen Mary I. These included Archbishop Thomas Cranmer, who had introduced the First *Book of Common Prayer*. The Theo.'s President's Prize subject was 'Our Debt to Cranmer' and, my entry being successful, I was able to present a paper based on my historical and liturgical studies. In a sense I was setting down markers for future work for the Church of Ireland. For our final year, Donald McLindon was elected Auditor, Bobby Huddleson, Honorary Secretary and I became Honorary Librarian – for the first time two graduates of Queen's were officers of a premier Trinity debating society.

I had expected the SCM to be influential in the Christian life of the College, but perhaps because of the prominence of the Divinity School and the Christian Union, compared to Queen's it was much more low key. I attempted to run a study group like those in Queen's but that petered out after a few weeks.

There was a strong social life in Trinity and the Queen's graduates were warmly welcomed into it. I remained a bit of a loner. I lived in digs outside College, for at the conclusion of the first term in the Divinity Hostel, I contracted a very virulent form of sinusitis and it was recommended that I found somewhere less spartan to live. There was no requirement at that time for all students to live in the hostel. Michael Ferrar, the warden, was very understanding and when he discovered my commitment to daily worship in Trinity, treated me thereafter as if I were one of those under his care. On Saturday afternoons one could watch rugby in College or at Lansdowne Road or take advantage of the many cinemas of central Dublin. I was able to see all the new releases months before they made their way to Belfast for only 2s 6d (twelve and a half pence), about three pounds at today's values. And occasionally one could get a single seat at the Abbey or the Gate Theatres.

On Sunday evenings, I was usually on my own as I had no commitment as a student reader and I visited a number of parish churches for evening worship. These services were often depressing: small congregations and dull preachers. In so many cases school or hospital chaplains seemed to be given the task of preaching in the evening. I only found one church where there was life, and went with a colleague who was student reader there. Both the rector, Alex Camier, and the curate, Dennis McKee, were concerned to make the service in St Mary's, Donnybrook alive. One of those coincidences: this was the church where my future wife was confirmed when she had been at boarding school in Dublin. Once or twice a term I was invited for the evening to the home of a cousin of my father, Marjorie Harrison and her family at Terenure. Reg and Marjorie were members of All Saints' Grangegorman, a parish with a similar tradition to St John's Malone. Their son, Alan, was at this time a member of the choir of Saint Patrick's Cathedral. So it was there that I would meet them for Evensong and then out to relax and be very well fed in their home. Marjorie used to do voluntary work with one of the two communities of Anglican nuns in Dublin and before my ordination presented me with a set of linens for home communions which I have used throughout my pastoral ministry with fond remembrances of that kindness.

Towards parish ministry
So the New Year of 1957 arrived. Dr Oulton's method of matching ordinands to vacant parishes had been in operation for a few months. He had invited me to meet a rector from a large mid-Belfast parish. Interviews like these usually took place in Fuller's Café on Grafton Street and one dull November afternoon I met with a possible future rector. Within two minutes I knew that it wasn't to be. I just could not warm to this man; it was clear that feelings were mutual. And that was it. No more suggestions came my way. I wrote to the bishop of Down and Dromore, for I felt that someone with roots in the Connor part of Belfast might be better off in a different diocese. Bishop Mitchell responded that he had no vacancies and suggested that I apply to the bishop of Liverpool. Such dire shortage in 1952 – was it now to be 'Go to England'? Week by week my colleagues went to meet rectors, visited parishes and were 'fixed up'.

At the end of the Christmas vacation the new bishop of Connor, Cyril Elliott, attended a meeting of Malone Select Vestry. Edward Garrett had obtained permission from the bishop for me to act as a student reader – interesting that the permission specifically authorised me to read the epistle and assist at Holy Communion – not at all normal at that time. The bishop inquired from the rector if I had a curacy yet. My father was at the meeting and he was commissioned to tell me to come to Bishop's House at 2.30pm the following day. The bishop welcomed me into his study and told me that the previous Sunday he had been in Ballymoney. He said that Canon Armstrong must have a curate and that he would like me to be that curate. I had heard that one of the other students had been in communication with that parish. The bishop said that nothing had been settled and that it was his wish for me to go there. He wrote that evening and I found a letter awaiting me in Dublin from Canon John T. Armstrong, asking for details of myself and asking for references. I replied and gave him the names of two clergy in his rural deanery who knew me well: George Guy, rector of Bushmills and Norman Kelly. After further exchanges of letters a meeting was set up at the Midland Hotel in Belfast on a Saturday morning in February. He came off the train and we went and had coffee together. The canon talked about Saint Columba and his own visit to Iona; he asked no questions about my ideas of vocation or anything like that. I instantly formed a rapport and knew that I wanted to work alongside this man. His return train was due. He looked at me and said, 'Well, how shall we leave it?' I replied that if he was prepared to offer me the title to ordination I should be very happy to accept. 'I shall write to the bishop tonight,' was his reply. So I was 'fixed up' with a country town curacy, which at the back of my mind was what I had always been hoping for – far enough away from my 'own country' to be able to learn ministry, confident that my future rector was someone with whom I could work.

There remained the small matter of completing the exams for Divinity Testimonium. It was possible to take these in two parts – before the Easter vacation and at the end of the summer term. An attack of influenza the week before the first set almost set me back but I discovered that the enforced break from revision had been beneficial and all went very well. This meant that the final term was freed from pressure and I was able to benefit from a lovely Dublin spring – a city in festal mood with An Tóstal.

The following week came the final parts of 'Test'. For a generation there had been one incredibly difficult paper for which,
as in all the others, all questions had to be attempted. This had
been set by Dr Oulton himself and was on all the parts of the
bible which had not been covered in other parts of the course, in
reality the more obscure parts of the Old Testament. It was said
that no one had ever scored more than fifty per cent. This time
the paper was set by Tom Salmon and was exceptionally fair, requiring knowledge but not of an especially esoteric kind. It was
such a surprise. I knew I had done well and when the marks
came out 95 per cent was unbelievable. Having had time to work
on the small part of the Hebrew Old Testament set for the
Hebrew section, I was also able to pass in that and so obtained a
first class ranking.

Ready for orders

By this time I was home, had been to Ballymoney to arrange for
somewhere to live, and was as ready as I ever would be for ordination. No devotional preparation was arranged for the seven to
be ordained deacon – pre-ordination retreats were as yet unknown. We reported to the diocesan office for our deacon's
exam, an anomaly which has since disappeared, when the
archdeacon and other examining chaplains appointed by the
bishop put us through our paces, as it were checking that the
divinity school knew its business.

Two days before the ordination Dad was taken to hospital to
have an urgent kidney operation and that meant he was missing
on that day in Saint Anne's Cathedral, Sunday 7 July 1957. Like
all such occasions they flow over you. It was strange to dress
that morning with clerical waist-coat and clerical collar. Another
indication that times were changing was that that day I wore a
starched linen collar. Next day I substituted a plastic version
that only needed a daily wipe or a scrub with vim and water
once a week or so. I never again wore a linen collar. The seven of
us met in the old vestry and robed – cassock and surplice and
also academic hoods which were *de rigeur* at that time. We carried over our arms the stoles that would be placed over our left
shoulders after ordination. In 1957 these were black: clerical out-
fitters at that time provided special black stoles for Church of

Ireland clergy. The ordination in 1957 took place at what is now
the entrance to the chancel in St Anne's, and behind the altar
boarding closed off the choir, for the development of that part of
the cathedral was at last under way. The ordination of deacons
took place after the epistle. One of the newly-ordained was appointed to read the gospel; the choice was determined by the
mark awarded for Greek at the deacon's exam. As I had
achieved the highest mark I was the gospeller. In 1957 it was
made clear in the order of service that only the newly-ordained,
members of their families and friends, were expected to receive
communion. Consequently, at the offertory hymn, members of
the regular congregation departed from the cathedral.
Afterwards there were photographs – one for one of the Belfast
papers because we were the first group ordained by Bishop
Cyril Elliott after becoming bishop.

We had a subdued family lunch because of Dad being in hospital and in the evening I went to Saint John's and shared in
Evensong, now wearing my tippet or preaching scarf. I
wouldn't actually wear it again until my priesting in 1958, as in
Ballymoney the deacon wore a stole at all services. My new boss,
aware of my father's illness, allowed me to wait to the following
Thursday to travel to Ballymoney and I was able to use the family
car to transport my belongings, my sister driving it back. So,
Thursday, 11 July 1957, the new curate moved into lodgings at
49 High Street.

CHAPTER FIVE

Ballymoney

Ministry with L-plates
Becoming a curate-assistant is only a move from one kind of training to another. This latter is of far more significance, for it is ministry learned among and shared with a particular congregation of God's people. They are never 'your' people: you relate to them as one called to particular roles.

As I described above, I arrived on 11 July and began to get to know my landlady and her husband. They were Presbyterians: Andy Nevin was an elder at St James's Presbyterian Church and the Honorary Treasurer. His wife, Sadie, had been brought up as a member of one of the minority Presbyterian denominations – the Reformed Presbyterian or Covenanter Church. I discovered in her a very kind person and her husband a quiet man with all the best qualities of the County Antrim Presbyterian, a man of total integrity who had suffered in his business life because of his refusal to cut corners in the interests of his bosses. They were strict sabbatarians – television and radio were only used on Sundays for the news and religious services. There was no attempt to impose any restrictions on what I did in my study. There were two sons: Sam, a civil servant, living and working in Ballymoney, and Tom, who was principal of Seagoe Church of Ireland Primary School in Portadown, someone who had immense respect for the Church of Ireland for being prepared to appoint him as principal. He knew that school appointments in country areas were at that time very much influenced by denominational allegiances – the likelihood of a member of the Church of Ireland being appointed principal of a school which had a majority of Presbyterians on the management committee being remote. The rector of Seagoe at that time, with whom lay the sole right of appointment of a principal, had chosen the person he believed was the best qualified person for the job. In that

65

way he was setting an example which would be applied everywhere by the 1980s.

I went to bed early on my first night to be awakened by what
I thought was an explosion some time before midnight. It was
the sound of Lambeg drums being beaten with vigour to mark
the Twelfth of July, the day of parades by members of the
Orange Order. The building next to my lodgings was the
Protestant Hall, where members of the loyal orders held their
meetings and where various bands practised. My awakening
was to hear the brethren setting out to march around the town
claiming their territory.

I spent the 'Twelfth' preparing my sermon for Sunday as I
had to report on Saturday morning to the rectory to read it to
Canon Armstrong. That was an interesting exercise as he made
suggestions about how to personalise my sermon and use it to
introduce myself to the congregation. Here was a rector not
afraid of the use of personal experience to light up preaching:
nothing like that had been suggested in College. So I had some
revision to do. Then he took me to the church and asked me to
read the lessons set for Sunday. I thought that I was quite good
at doing that and was appalled to be told, 'Read lessons like that
and you'll bore every congregation to whom you minister.' With
humility I reached for my L-plates and determined to learn. He
was a master craftsman in reading lessons, prayers and as a
preacher. By no means demonstrative or emotional, John
Thomas Armstrong let the words of the liturgy speak for themselves; if scripture described an encounter he took you into the
encounter and his sermons applied the scriptures to living, with
his forefinger raised to emphasise a point.

Every Sunday there was Holy Communion at 8.30am with
fifteen to twenty present: always one of the churchwardens. In
that first year they were John McCook, a bachelor farmer, and
Robert Charters, representative for a wholesale confectionery
firm, married to Margaret who taught geography at Dalriada
School, the town grammar school. You could also guarantee that
Frank Beattie would be at early service. Frank was a breadserver,
an occupation that has virtually disappeared. All the bakeries
had vans on the road who called to homes in town and country
every second day selling loaves, biscuits etc. The development

of supermarkets, combined with a vast increase in the number of homes where the wives were at work, led to the disappearance of breadservers who were vital parts of communication especially in rural areas. Frank with his wife 'ran' the Youth Guild and were demons of the badminton court.

Sunday School was at 10:15am in the old schoolhouse. All ages met for a hymn and prayers and then classes where the old Sunday School Society programme was used. For each Sunday a part of the Catechism or part of the liturgy was set for rote-learning and a passage of scripture for study. Very little assistance was given to those charged with teaching. It was dull and boring. A senior teenager went round the classes calling the roll, one mark for being at Sunday School, two marks for attendance at morning service in church the previous week.

The rector was delighted to hand over the senior or bible class to the curate but that didn't happen immediately since Sunday School was on holiday in July and August.

The 11:30 service was either Morning Prayer or, twice a month, Morning Prayer and Holy Communion. On my first Sunday it was the latter, as the previous week, so that the rector could attend my ordination, a lay reader had conducted Morning Prayer. In St Patrick's Church, Ballymoney, the choir sits in a West Gallery where the organ is also installed. In 1957 the choir was not a robed choir and it did not process, so rector and curate emerged as soon as the opening hymn began. I looked round the congregation – over two hundred and fifty strangers. Then I spotted people I knew from holidays in north Antrim, Dr William Belford and his wife Winifred, their son Shaun and his wife Anne (later to be my neighbours and parishioners in Knocknagoney), their daughter Clare and her fiancé who to my surprise turned out to be someone who had been in my year at Inst., Earle Annesley. It is a small world indeed.

I took as my text words from the Prayer Book Gospel for the Fourth Sunday after Trinity, 'Be ye merciful, as I am merciful', and after preliminary remarks attempted to expound the biblical concept of mercy – God's steadfast love – utterly reliable, utterly dependable. As I look back forty-five years after preaching that sermon, I am so glad that the Holy Spirit guided me to set that concept at the beginning of my preaching and teaching ministry, for I believe that it is that unchanging truth that holds us together when worship, ministry, organisation and the contemporary situations in which we minister change.

Visiting

With a great deal of apprehension I commenced my first round of pastoral visitation. In the parish the rector was spoken of as 'The Chancellor' because he had been appointed as the senior dignitary on the chapter of the cathedral of Connor in 1956, having been a prebendary from 1945. He was a very shy person yet had built up excellent relationships with his parishioners over the years. He maintained a regular pattern of visiting and I was set to follow that pattern, receiving some common sense advice about how to keep conversations going, having obviously recognised in me one who shared his shyness. My first afternoon was to be Charlotte Street: I can still trace the calls to Mrs Slater, to Mr Gordon's rooms (he was of course at school so I left my newly printed visiting card), to the Gillespie family, where I met a housebound former church treasurer and retired country schoolteacher, to Mrs McGrath, whose husband combined the offices of Honorary Secretary to the Select Vestry and Honorary Treasurer, and to the Barkely family. I was pressed to afternoon tea three times! Everything I had heard was true! But because of the involvement of all those households in parish activities, I would never again visit them on the one afternoon. And over the next fortnight I wasn't to be offered refreshment – the Chancellor had them well-trained to expect a short visit as a mutual confidence-building exercise.

There were two main concerns which came up again and again in conversation – unemployment, with mechanisation on farms and the continuing failure to stay of tenants in government advance factories. I was soon aware of the social make-up of Ballymoney parish – common to the Church of Ireland in north Antrim and north Derry. Our parishioners were overwhelmingly artisans, farm and factory labourers, most of whom rented their homes from the local council or, in the case of the village of Balnamore, from the mill. There were two 'big houses' – O'Harrabrooke where Colonel Cramsie and family lived and Leslie Hill, the home of the Leslie family. At that time the head of the family was abroad. We had two farmers in fifty square miles of parish, one doctor and a handful of teachers, civil servants and bank officials. There were only two or three shops owned by parishioners. It was a very Presbyterian town.

Roman Catholics made up about a quarter of the population and were socially very much the same as the Church of Ireland. Relationships were good, and there was quite a bit of inter-marrying. Until very recently it had been the unwritten rule that if a Protestant girl married a Roman Catholic man she 'went with' him and vice-versa.

It is scarcely believable but in almost three years I never met the Roman Catholic parish priest or any of his curates. I was to discover in the mid-1990s that the new parish priest at Strangford had been my 'oppo' in Ballymoney at the time but we never came across each other. I did meet the ministers of the three Presbyterian churches in the town every Wednesday morning, for we all exercised our rights under the Education Act to teach the members of our congregations at the County Primary School for first period.

All three Presbyterian ministers at that time were from what I recognised as 'mainstream' Presbyterianism. The conservative evangelical transformation in the Presbyterian church had not yet begun to take hold. There were four other Presbyterian congregations within the parish area. As well, there were numerous smaller denominations, including Methodist, Reformed Presbyterians and the newly-arrived Church of God, an aggressive American pentecostal group with a unitarian theology. Also present in the area was of one of the most active of the Rev Ian Paisley's lieutenants, Mr Wylie. The latter used to 'preach' at the top of Main Street on Saturday evenings: and I have the distinction of being 'miscalled' – to use the Ballymoney vernacular for being denounced – one Saturday evening, walking back after preparing things in church for the next morning. I was apparently an agent of Satan leading the young people and others of the Church of Ireland to Satan's domain. Paisley had tried to use a dispute in one of the outlying Presbyterian congregations to set up a rival congregation. He wasn't succeeding but was concentrating a great deal of effort on the area, as the *Protestant Telegraph* of the time reveals. It included a massive demonstration of street politics when the local council barred him from using the town hall for an anti-Catholic meeting. Little did we realise it then, but he was honing his tactics for the sixties when challenging authority with marches and provocative demonstrations would open the way for thirty years of violence. I am proud that the lead in recognising that meetings for sectarian abuse were inappropriate in a community hall, and having such meetings banned, was taken by the Church of Ireland chairman of the Urban Council. On my visits following that I was asked frequently why the Chancellor had signed the parish priest's letter to exclude Dr Paisley. The fact that no such letter existed outside the imagination of the Paisley party was just not believed. Here again was a straw in the wind and one of the reasons why, forty years on, Ballymoney is as bitterly divided as any area in Northern Ireland. People will believe utter nonsense if it is what they want to believe.

Once I had completed my first round of visits within the town, it was time to visit parishioners who lived in the surrounding countryside. Their addresses were simply those of the townland – not until the 1970s were roads named and houses numbered, which made rural visiting no problem when I came to Lecale Group in 1984. The Chancellor did not drive a car – and he visited parishioners either on foot or by taxi. Consequently the owner of a local taxi firm, Robbie Hamilton, knew where they all lived and the custom had been for the taxi to be employed for three weeks each year for the curate to visit. It meant I found my way up lanes to labourer's cottages I wouldn't have found easily. We arrived in the yards of Presbyterian farmers to visit maidservants who were Church of Ireland but could rarely get to worship except on monthly weekends when they went home. Again, this was a dying feature of country life – within a decade live-in domestic servants would no longer exist. Those autumn afternoons being driven around the north Antrim countryside at the end of harvesting remain as vivid memories. Having bought a Lambretta scooter just before ordination, I would not need Robbie Hamilton for a second round and I became a familiar figure on the minor roads of the parish – it also meant that I could visit villages like Balnamore in the evening and meet the working men with whom I built up an excellent relationship.

The rector trusted me to get on with the business of visiting and after I completed the first round never once inquired where I was visiting. I kept him informed so that the likelihood of our arriving at the same house on the same day was slight. Two fellow-curates in another parish had different experience of the rector's oversight of their work. On my day off I visited them and after lunch we were enjoying coffee when the phone rang. Neither took the slightest notice. When I asked why they weren't answering the phone I was told that at 2.05pm they didn't answer for it was the rector checking up that they were out visiting in the parish. Another colleague could be found rushing round on a Monday afternoon so that he would have the required forty visits to report at staff meeting on Tuesday morning. By the end of the century a curate would be lucky indeed on 'cold' visiting to find anyone at home in the afternoon. The myth that a house-going parson means a church-going people, if ever true, has certainly ceased to have validity.

One aspect of visiting the Chancellor reserved to himself and that was visiting in the two hospitals. He took the view that he was the chaplain and that while Church of Ireland patients were there they were in his care. I found exclusion from the hospital ministry a minor area of complaint and hoped for a change when I was ordained priest in 1958, but then it was only while the boss was on holiday.

Schools
Every Wednesday morning I took the Church of Ireland children at the County Primary School for denominational religious instruction – a wonderful opportunity to impart the Anglican understanding and supplement the work of Sunday School. The 'Model', as it was still known, was in 1957-60 not yet a re-organised school and all non grammar school children attended it until school leaving age – at that time 15. This meant a large age range from eight to fifteen. I aimed my material at 10 year-olds and hoped it wouldn't be too incomprehensible for the younger children and not too simple for the teenagers. I don't think it was, judging by one memorable question I was asked about St Patrick. 'When St Patrick was in Ballymoney, why did he build his church at the top of the town and his church hall in Castle Street?'

On two other mornings nine o'clock also saw me in a primary school. One of these was in the outlying village of Balnamore where the Primary School was the successor to one established years before for the children of millworkers. The Principal, Wesley Parker, was a Methodist. When I saw him about arranging to come in, he gave me the choice of taking the Church of Ireland children in the warmth of the main classroom or in the dining hall where I wouldn't have had the use of a blackboard. The previous curate had opted for the latter but I chose the former, knowing that Mr Parker would be working away at his desk. There was an immediate plus: discipline was a doddle. Another plus which I could not have expected was helpful advice from an expert on the way of presenting my material. I cannot express my appreciation of this too highly. We were given absolute minimal guidance in college about teaching. Wesley Parker helped me to become a much more effective communicator. He became very interested in the Church of Ireland and before I left Ballymoney had joined his local Church of Ireland parish and was confirmed. The third primary school was a two-teacher, one classroom school: here I taught the Church of Ireland children at one end while one of the staff taught the rest at the other. They were used to it but I did not find this experience very satisfactory, although it was the only one where I was expected to say prayers after a hymn was sung by all the children. This school closed a few years later when the new intermediate school opened.

Ted Gordon, the headmaster of the local grammar school – Dalriada School – arranged for me to have the opportunity to teach non-denominational religious education for a period a week. Several local Presbyterian ministers were also employed as part-time members of staff. I had the top group for a two year cycle – first year, Acts of the Apostles and second year, Old Testament prophets. This was straight imparting of information, with the disadvantage that it wasn't a subject for state examination. I knew from my own experience in my last year at school that a good many would regard it as a waste of time and I wasn't surprised that there were discipline problems – mostly pupils trying to do their homework instead of listening to me! These young people were quite close to me in age, six years or so being the age difference. The majority were not Church of Ireland, only two or three in a class of twenty. But, by and large, we got on well. One of the boys came from an English background, very keen on dramatics for which the school had a high reputation: later in life he would become a television personality, the newsreader Martin Lewis. I must have had some impact, for forty years on a new teacher came to Downpatrick Primary School who had been educated at Dalriada. I told her that I had worked in Ballymoney and a couple of weeks later she asked me if I had ever taught Religious Education in Dalriada. On my confessing, she said that her mother had been in the class and remembered me!

Much earlier in my time as a part-time member of staff, I was invited to address the school Christian Union. I was given a passage from the Old Testament on which to speak – it was either 2 Samuel or 1 Kings. It was wonderful piece where modern biblical scholarship saw two Hebrew traditions intermingled, each of which has a continuing message for the Christian Church. I had a great time disentangling the story and suggesting its application. Although members of staff who didn't normally attend CU meetings afterwards expressed their appreciation, I am afraid my address went down like a lump of lead and I was not invited again in either of the following years.

Youth work

Once the autumn came I discovered youth work. Apart from Sunday School, which I have described above and which from 1958 I was given *carte blanche* to reform by introducing the Dobson series of teachers' handbooks, this meant the Youth Guild, Scouts and Cubs. The Youth Guild seemed to be an umbrella that served 15 to 35 and had two meetings a week – one for badminton and table tennis in the kitchen of the Hall and one with some kind of 'activity' such as a quiz or talk (once a month this was 'devotional' and either the rector or the curate gave a short homily – least well attended session of the month!).

I persuaded the 'experts' to teach me the rudiments of badminton and found to my delight and surprise that here was a game that, with my height, I could perform reasonably effectively. So much so that I found myself playing in matches for the 'B'

team and travelled all over the area for matches that ended in
the wee small hours. In some of the halls the floor space was less
than regulation and the base line was sometimes painted on the
wall behind you. I still have the Fred Perry badminton shirt –
even if it is rather too tight forty years on!

Having learned a little and with the help of some of the
senior members, we introduced a 'junior' group on Saturday
afternoons and there was immense satisfaction there, and later
in both Knock and Knocknagoney, in seeing boys and girls
learning skills and also participating in teams which introduced
them to other churches. In Knocknagoney the aim in which ultimately most of them succeeded was to be able to beat their
teacher comprehensively.

In September 1957, on Friday evening I went along to the
meetings of the scout troop and again tried to help out where I
could, mostly in teaching map-reading. Jim Slater, a skilled
mechanic at Balnamore Mill, was the scoutmaster. Jim is a wonderful churchman and he and I became firm friends rather than
just a curate-parishioner relationship. Many evening were spent
at his home with his wife Eileen and their two small children.
We talked of scouting, church and everything. One evening I
was taken to Coleraine to a district meeting and was introduced
as the new Group Scout Master. This *ex officio* appointment I had
not expected but on consulting the rector it was clearly his wish
that if I was willing I should undertake. I realised that there was
a great deal to learn as I had no scouting experience, if plenty of
goodwill towards the movement. So I began to equip myself for
the role (which also related to the Cubs). Uniform in 1957 was
still as Baden Powell had designed it – khaki shorts and shirt
and a felt hat with a wide brim. The boys could never keep the
brims flat and I soon understood that even with the superior
quality of the leader's hat, how difficult that was. When I moved
to Belfast, how I welcomed the beret that in most groups had replaced the hat.

I underwent the official training programme for the Wood
Badge but there was a problem – practical training involved a
series of weekend courses and a curate could not have weekends off. After my first camp at Downhill in County Derry in
July 1958, the rector decided that to enable me to complete the

Wood Badge training he would pay for me to go to the Scout Movement's international training headquarters at Gilwell Park in Essex the following spring. That was a wonderful experience at which I met people from all over the world and had a range of training in scouting that I could never have got elsewhere. It was totally exhausting and I slept for twenty-four hours in a London hotel afterwards.

A feature of Youth Guild life at that period was what were called and advertised as 'parties': the games were country dances like the Walls of Trory, Strip the Willow, Gay Gordons and wild Canadian Barn Dances. The music was provided by a couple of young men with piano accordions and the eats were provided by the committee, lemonade being purchased whole-sale from a parishioner whose travelling van supplied shops with minerals. To comply with entertainment regulations admission was by invitation – but you had to pay two shillings (10 pence) for your invitation. When it was discovered that the un-married curate was quite good at dancing, he never had a moment's peace. And he enjoyed these evenings! Usually, as well as the 'paying guests', youth guilds from other parishes from Ballycastle to Aghadowey would be invited and reciprocal invitations could be anticipated. This was just before the revolution in the kind of music that was acceptable to young people changed to rock and roll and the like – a change that I would encounter in a few years when I went to Knocknagoney Parish.

In service training 1957-58
The bishops of Down and Dromore and Connor introduced a joint programme of post-ordination training with the Dean of Belfast, Cuthbert Peacocke, in charge. It was known from its initials as COPOT – Committee on post-ordination training. Not for a few years, when such programmes became universal in every diocese, did this gain the nick-name 'potty-training'! Once a month those ordained in July met at Belfast Cathedral, with the Dean in the chair. We had speakers tell us about different aspects of ministry and we discussed our experiences, good or horrendous 'in the field'. One or two were left on their own the Sunday after ordination – provision was made for priests to come and 'do' communion as required but they were baptising

and solemnising marriages as deacons. It simply horrified me. My rector had allowed me to perform one baptism, so that he could be sure that if an emergency cropped up I could do it properly. Even when he was on holiday he arranged that a neighbour should conduct the one wedding scheduled – I was present but he didn't believe that solemnising marriages belonged to ministry of a deacon – and he had guided six men through their diaconate before me. It struck me that what was needed wasn't training for deacons but training for rectors – and that conviction still remains. One memory of those Friday mornings remain – advice given by Dean Peacocke – on which I had no intention of acting – that it was good for a clergyman to join the Orange Order for it enabled him to get alongside so many of the men in the parish. At that time he sincerely believed this to be true. Later experiences which are in the public record showed him another side of Orangeism and as bishop of Derry he resigned from the order.

I regard the tradition of clerical societies in the Church of Ireland as a form of in-service training. Usually on a monthly basis, the clergy of an area, like Lurgan or Downpatrick, meet to study the scriptures together and to listen to a speaker invited because of his or her expertise in a subject. I was introduced to the Coleraine Clerical in the autumn of 1957. Gilbert Wilson, rector of Armoy, arranged to collect me at my lodgings and take me along to the hotel in Coleraine where meetings were held. He was considerably senior to me but insisted in the car that I should call him Gilbert. I obeyed and continued so to address him personally when later he became bishop of Kilmore. These monthly meetings involved clergy from parishes as far apart as Castlerock and Ballycastle. In 1958 I made my first contribution as we studied the report of 1958 Lambeth Conference of Anglican bishops on the use of the bible in church. After leaving north Antrim, I have on three occasions been back to the Coleraine Clerical – in 1962 to give a paper on the Church in Ulster in the late 17th century, when our present traditions were formed, in 1987 on liturgical renewal before the publication of *Alternative Occasional Services*, and in 1997 on how the church might use the Internet. That kind of range of study has kept clergy in touch with what is happening in the world church. Most areas have clergy with knowledge about a wide range of subjects or who are in touch with people of particular expertise. I find that in the new century there is much less willingness to commit oneself voluntarily to such study groups. In some places these have been replaced by rural deanery chapter meetings: these can be excellent or they can be dominated by 'business'. In areas of sparse population the lack of opportunity to study and have fellowship together has been an impoverishment of ministry.

A curate in north Antrim had one other opportunity: to be a 'day-boy' at the annual Clergy Refresher Course which met in Portrush in the week after Low Sunday each year. These courses, organised by the clergy for the clergy, had been going on since 1936. They had unofficial approval from the bishops but were totally independent. Some of the most significant scholars from the Church of England were speakers. W. R. Matthews, dean of St Paul's, was the speaker in 1958.

For me the course of 1959 was to be a watershed. The main visiting speaker was someone who had published some scholarly work on the Church, John A. T. Robinson, dean of Clare College, Cambridge. His lectures were entitled *Liturgy coming Alive* and described with full theological rationale the way in which insights from the liturgical renewal movement had been implemented in the Chapel of Clare College. This followed on from my studies with Edgar Turner at Queen's and everything I had been able to discover about the parish communion movement since. The bishop of Connor gave permission for these 'daring innovations' and the Clare College rite to be used at Holy Communion on the final morning. I was on my scooter to Portrush at 7.00am to be present – a loaf of ordinary bread and a bottle on wine were brought up in an Offertory Procession, the prayer for the church militant was broken up with silences between the paragraphs, we said the prayer of humble access together. It was a vision of what was already possible. It reinforced me in my desire to help people see the eucharist come alive for them.

Priesting 1958 and after

Because the meeting of the bishops of the Anglican Communion was to begin early in July, ordinations would be brought forward

– those of deacons were to be on Sunday 29 June. I was concerned lest the bishop would bring the ordination of priests back to Trinity Sunday or St Barnabas's Day (11 June) in which case I would not reach the canonical age of twenty-four. The bishop chose St John the Baptist's Day, a Tuesday, at 11.00am in Lisburn Cathedral. This made just about impossible the presence of any parishioner or friends with a day's work to go to. Only the Chancellor, his wife and one lady travelled with me in Mrs Armstrong's car. At least this time my whole family were there including my father, fully fit. It was about as dreary a service as the Church of Ireland could put on, from the sermon to the music. I remember very little about it except that the curate of the cathedral, having moved the bishop's chair after the ordination, placed it in front of my nose as I knelt at the altar rails for the communion. Yet it is that occasion, my priesting, that I remember with thanksgiving each year and make a point of somehow getting to Holy Communion to do so. And so far I have succeeded each year. When the laying on of hands took place I knew I was now what the Lord had called me to be, a priest in the church of God.

There was an innovation that year. For the first time the new priests, their rectors and friends were entertained to a buffet lunch. Then it was back to the car, arriving in Ballymoney at 4.30pm, just in time for closing prayers with the cubs, where I would give the blessing for the first time.

With great joy I celebrated Holy Communion on Sunday, St Peter's Day, for the first time, and then it was off in Mrs Armstrong's car, kindly lent, to lead morning worship in Portrush and afternoon worship in Ballywillan Hall, as Portush's rector was in Belfast for the ordination of their new curate.

Then holidays beckoned. My sister, Elizabeth, and I had planned a week in London. It was our first foray across the Irish Sea and we travelled overnight Belfast-Liverpool on one of the old-style Belfast Steamship Company ships, the *Duke of Leinster*. This was first class travel with a steward to bring morning tea and toast; stewardesses wore black frocks and white aprons.

By mid-morning the train had arrived in Euston and we took a taxi to our hotel in Bloomsbury. We had a great week of sightseeing. We went to a theatre and to a West End cinema to see

Around the World in Eighty Days in the wonder of Todd-AO. A
Canadian graduate student who had also had a room in the
same flat as I had in Dublin met us on Saturday morning,
arranged a tour of the Houses of Parliament and took us to the
city and the church of St Bartholmew the Great. Of course we
went to Westminster Abbey and St Paul's. While at the latter we
discovered that the opening Holy Communion of the Lambeth
Conference was to be there on Sunday morning. We decided to
be there. Arriving at 9.30am we were met by a steward in morning dress: 'Your tickets, sir and madam?' We had no tickets and
our spirits fell. 'Just the back three rows, I'm afraid.' It was
enough. We sat there and watched the cathedral fill with people,
many in colourful African and Indian dress.

It was a very good point from which to watch the procession
as the bishops of each province came in. The African bishops in
1958 were nearly all white missionary bishops and we spotted
Bishop St John Pike who had the previous year returned to
Africa as bishop of Gambia and the Rio Pongas. Right at the
back came the churches of the British Isles and our own Church
of Ireland, headed by the archbishop of Dublin, George Simms,
as the archbishop of Armagh, John A. F. Gregg was too frail to
process. The service was the 1662 Holy Communion service
sung to the music of Merbecke. In 1958 that rite and even that
setting would have been recognised in a large part of the
Anglican world. Forty years later, when the 1998 Lambeth
Conference would open in Canterbury the rite would be from
Kenya and the music from Mexico and other parts of the world.
The preacher in 1958 was the Metropolitan of India, Pakistan,
Burma and Ceylon who, in a powerful address, called on the
Anglican Communion to take the task of achieving visible unity
seriously and not to cast away those provinces who were prepared to enter into locally united churches. It would, however,
take twenty years before the Indian, Pakistani and Bangladeshi
bishops of the united churches were welcomed back into the full
fellowship of the Anglican Communion.

After the service people milled about on the cathedral steps
and we had the opportunity to greet Bishop Pike and as we were
talking to him Archbishop Simms with our own bishop of
Connor came over to greet us. After lunch Elizabeth and I went

to Westminster Abbey for Choral Evensong and listened to the
Primus of Scotland preach. The Monday issue of *The Times* carried a photograph of the procession and congregation. As we
were able to pick out ourselves at the back of the picture we
arranged to get a proper copy of the photograph. After that experience, being a member of the Anglican Communion became
very important and I began even then to assemble a collection of
worship books from other parts of the Anglican World, with the
prayer books of the Episcopal Church of the USA and Canada.

Second winter and change of leadership
My second winter was the time when I really got to know the
people of Ballymoney. I oversaw the re-organisation of the
Sunday School, which thankfully was received well by everyone. Confirmation normally took place every second year. A
group had to be prepared for 1959. The rector asked me to take
the class for boys. Being determined that the members would
have some permanent record of their classes I obtained a very
basic postcard duplicator mechanism, messy and primitive. This
meant that very brief summaries had to be prepared on my new
typewriter – unfortunately it couldn't spell very well! I had six
teenagers all but one of whom was also in the scouts. The odd
man out was several years older. He was the son of a family of
which the rector used to say 'didn't work very hard at their
church'. He had come forward for confirmation because of the
influence of his partner in the cab of a milk delivery firm who
was an enthusiastic member of the Church of God. Raymond
was very diligent in attendance at classes and asked many questions – some of which, like ' was confirmation the same as baptism in the spirit?', were quite outside my ability to answer. But
my answer that I believe God does something in response to the
bishop's prayer and that confirmation is a means by which we
receive gifts of the Spirit, seemed to satisfy Raymond and his
mentor. The problem was going to be anchoring him into the
worship life of the parish after he was confirmed, especially
since he had only one work-free Sunday morning in seven. A
couple of years after his confirmation I met Raymond delivering
milk at Norman Kelly's rectory; in reply to my question as to
how he was getting on he confessed somewhat sheepishly that

he had joined what he knew I called a 'sect' and was totally involved in the Church of God. I wished him well and he drove off considerably cheered. I don't know what it was about my confirmation preparation, for one of those I prepared and presented in my Knock days became a pastor in a Pentecostal church in East Belfast!

The Confirmation Service was on a Friday evening and I was delighted to be able to welcome Edgar Turner, presenting as candidates two students from Queen's University.

During my second Christmas in Ballymoney the rector's sons, who lived in England, persuaded him that it was time for him to retire because they didn't want him to be left curate-less when the time would come for me to move on. At the end of January he told me of his plans and asked if I would stay until retirement took effect and a successor had been found. To this I was only too happy to accede as I was having a very fulfilling ministry. Being so far from Belfast could have been a lonely existence. However, Norman Kelly was rector of Billy, the rectory 12 miles from Ballymoney and it became a regular thing for me to go out there most Mondays. We would go for long walks at the Giant's Causeway which was in the parish, or on damp days worked at carpentry and constructed two bookshelves for my study. Frequently we met up with Warren Jones, rector of Ballintoy, and with Alwyn Maconachie, rector of Killowen in Coleraine. The three rectors were producing their own parish magazine.

A stint in charge

Far sooner than one realised, the time came for the rector to retire. The Armstrongs bought a bungalow in Ballycastle and at the end of July 1959 I found myself in charge of the parish during a vacancy. The new Rural Dean was Fred Moore, rector of Dervock, but apart from a kindly call to say that if I needed help I had only to ask, he left me totally on my own.

This meant chairing meetings of the Select Vestry and that meant, at my first meeting, seeking to keep the peace between the gentry and the working class membership over a potential dispute about seating in church.

There were two significant experiences during the weeks of

vacancy. Several people offered to assist me in the conduct of
worship, by reading the lessons. Some of these were good readers and some were not. One Monday I was stopped in the streets
by a railway signalman with a request – a fine churchman who
used to come in his working clothes to the 8.30am communion
service if he had been on the night shift. He told me about one of
his friends who had been coming to church regularly for over a
year, a man who was unable to read or write. The request was
for me please to read the lessons myself for the only way his
friend could get to know the bible was by listening and they just
couldn't hear some of the readers. If the rector's words two
years before had challenged me to make the lessons come alive,
this was an even more important challenge – how vital good
reading can be for there are those for whom the read word is the
only way they encounter the Living Word.

The other experience changed my approach in minstering to
those who are sick. I had, of course, been accustomed to saying a
prayer after paying a sick call or at the hospital bed once I was
allowed to visit in hospitals. One of our select vestry members
was ill. The members of this particular family had become personal friends beyond a curate-parishioner relationship. When I
went to visit, he was in bed. We chatted for a long time and I
rose to go home for my evening meal. He caught my arm.
'Surely, you aren't going without a prayer.' I was rebuked and
never again left a sick room without asking for permission to say
a prayer. This man was diagnosed with tuberculosis and moved
to the chest hospital in Londonderry, forty miles away. His wife
travelled back and forward most evenings. On one occasion she
called at my digs and asked me if I would drive her over, for her
husband would like me to come to see him. When I walked with
her into the side ward I knew that there was something different
that I had to do. So I explained that I would like to pray with the
laying on of hands. The three of us prayed and I laid hands in
prayer for healing for the first time in my ministry. There was
something about that moment – a deep sense of peace. We
didn't stay long. In a few weeks the treatment began to work
and before Christmas the family was re-united in Ballymoney
where we shared Holy Communion, still in the sick-room.
Before I left the parish I learned the reason that his wife had

asked me to drive her: she had been told that her husband's condition was becoming critical. I have no doubt that his recovery, and it was a total recovery, was God's response to the ministry of prayer for healing. This was to lead to a total re-assessment of the place the ministry of healing was to have in my ministry, including the conviction that Canon L'Estrange had shared with me years before that it is part and parcel of pastoral ministry, not something for great 'healing missions' – and that there are no healers but the Lord God who, through the Holy Spirit, bestows 'gifts of healings' (1 Corinthians 12: 9 – the Greek original being plural).

New rector

In October 1959 the new rector was to be instituted: Robert Stewart, rector of Ahoghill. My experience of the institution of Ned Garrett in 1953 proved invaluable and I was able to re-hearse the churchwardens so that they were able to carry out their ceremonial duties on the night with quiet confidence. An unexpected emergency hindered getting the church itself ready the day before as we had planned. There had been a road traffic accident in which three local people, en route to a greyhound racing meeting in Belfast, had been killed. The three funerals were to take place on the day of the institution. The three friends had each belonged to a different denomination. The Roman Catholic was buried after morning Mass and the Church of Ireland funeral was timed for 1.00pm. I stood with the sexton at the church door and, at five to the hour, the doors of the three public houses across the street opened and a steady stream of mourners poured into the church, packing it solid. The atmosphere was more spiritous than spiritual! These were people of all three denominations – and inter-church funerals were unknown in 1959. The funeral of the Presbyterian victim of the crash took place in one of the rural churches at 4.00pm.

The Institution Service went well. I was thanked for my months of care and I settled in to the business of getting to know my new boss. He had his own ideas – I didn't agree with all of them and found myself biting back my 'but...'. We had logistical problems for with the rectory undergoing major modernisation, Bob Stewart, his wife Kay and their two boys were living in a rented farmhouse eight miles out of town.

With the vacancy, the usual conventions that rectors seeking new colleagues didn't approach curates without the consent of their present rector, didn't apply and I had two inquiries. One was a move to Belfast Cathedral where the Dean was anxious that I should become Dean's Vicar. I had difficulty in arguing my way out of this as I could see little scope for work with young people, but the dilemma was resolved as the Dean would have required me on 1 January 1960 and I had promised to stay with Bob Stewart for up to six months. The other was a message to contact W. J. Whittaker of St Columba's Knock. A meeting was set up and we explored the possibility of my joining Jimmy Moore as junior curate. I expressed my interest but declared that if I was wanted before 1 April I had to decline as I had given an undertaking. I well remember WJ slapping his thigh and saying, 'Well, you have a conscience.' It was agreed that I should move to the dicoese of Down in April. The bishop of Connor wasn't all that pleased when I informed him of my impending move. He had, he wrote in reply to my letter, been going to recommend me to the rector of St Peter's on the Antrim Road. Little did he know that my Aunt Mary was in the choir and Uncle Tommy was People's Churchwarden. That wouldn't have worked at all.

I worked out my last few months in Ballymoney. I eagerly supported the new rector in his plan to have a monthly parish communion, not tacked on to Morning Prayer, but with hymns and sermon and general communion. The only frustration was the bishop's insistence that Morning Prayer be a public service earlier in the morning and that children should attend that.

In the next few years this children's Morning Prayer would become very popular and one of the aims of the parish communion movement, to accustom whole families to worship at the Lord's table together, could not be achieved. Suffice it to say that after the Sunday in March 1960 when we held the first parish communion, I was greeted in the town by enthusiastic parishioners who said it was the most wonderful service they had ever been at.

In a country town parish we set out to welcome temporary residents like bank officials and police officers. Among the latter were Constable John Hamill with his wife – I would find them years later when I went to Belvoir. Another was Head Constable

Arthur Irvine who took charge of the police in 1959. There was great speculation and competition among the three Presbyterian ministers as to which congregation he would attend, for previous holders of the post had all been Presbyterians. Arthur never let on where his allegiance lay and on his first Sunday, when he dressed in full uniform and with his wife Olive went out of the station to go to church, he arrived at the parish church and I had the pleasure of welcoming him. Over the next several years he would give great support to Bob Stewart and helped totally to re-organise the finances of the parish. After his retirement, Arthur with Olive settled at Castle Ward near Strangford. It gave him enormous pleasure to welcome me when I became rector of Ballyculter in the Lecale Group in 1985. For ten years he was a stalwart in parish and group and a very dear friend of my daughter, Hilary, to whom, as for so many others over the years, he opened up vistas in the life of the countryside. Although we had been on Christian name terms in the years between 1960 and 1985, on the day before my institution he said that he would call me 'Rector' for I was now his priest as well as his friend. And so it remained, 'Rector' or 'Canon' until his sudden death in church on 7 July, 1996. At his funeral I could not have refrained from drawing from his full life lessons for Christian discipleship.

It was quite a wrench at the end of March 1960 to pack up and move, preparing for new adventures in a different diocese.

CHAPTER SIX

Knock

First impressions

All Fools' Day wasn't perhaps the best day to start in a new parish, but it was on 1 April, 1960 that I reported at 29 King's Road, Knock – the Rectory. Canon William Joseph Whittaker, always known as 'WJ', was a native of Co Tipperary and could pile on the blarney when he wanted. Over the years we would become very good friends but that I couldn't have imagined at that time. I was a little wary of my third 'boss' in twelve months. He eased me in to the job. Jimmy Moore was moving on after Easter so I was to be senior curate after all. In fact another priest who had been offered and accepted the junior post had changed his mind, so I was to be on my own for at least a year.

I didn't have to preach for three Sundays and could use the time to prepare to take over the reins from Jimmy. Of immediate importance were the confirmation classes – forty-eight boys and girls, with confirmation early in June. I would see these in two large classes once a week and they would also be together in church on Sunday afternoons in the rector's bible class. Youth Guild was run by an excellent committee to whom I was to be introduced at a committee meeting in the home of one Valerie Hennesey on Sunday evening. I inquired about the scouts and was told that the rector and Jimmy Moore knew very little about what went on. That evening the new curate dressed up in his scout uniform and arrived at the meeting of the 64th Belfast Troop. Such a thing had not happened before. I was made very welcome and, after a try-on or two to see if I knew my stuff, was warmly welcomed. Of course, it wasn't long before one of the patrol leaders discovered that his brother had known me at school and my school nick-name, 'Jab', became my scouting name in East Belfast.

The parish of Knock is a leafy suburb in East Belfast and in

April all the blossom on the magnolia and cherry trees was in full flower. The parish was largely middle-class but there were terrace house streets in the old 'village' of Ballyhackamore and a new Belfast Corporation housing estate, Clara Park, on the south-eastern edge. In the previous decade St Columba's had 'given birth' to two new area parishes, Gilnahirk and Stormont. This had reduced the number of Church of Ireland households from 1500 to about 750.

Knock parish was financially in a very strong position, having been a pioneer in using a directed 'Planned Giving' programme in 1958. Planned Giving had been introduced to Ireland in the parish of Bray in County Wicklow. St Columba's had been one of the first in the North. These early campaigns were directed by a company with American roots. They charged hefty fees for the 'know how' and employed a professional who spent up to a month in the parish training and directing parishioners as visitors. WJ and others defended the employment of professionals against criticism, likening this to the employment of architects and surveyors in the design of church buildings. Certainly I know of no parish which brought in the Wells Organisation that had any cause to regret their decision. I would personally learn much from the second directed campaign in Knock at the beginning of 1962. A year or so later the Church of Ireland set up centrally a Christian Stewardship Office, imitating many of the methods, but also seeking to teach principles of giving time and talents as part of discipleship, and through it would transform the giving of its members throughout the land. In 2002, after forty years, the Christian Stewardship Office was wound up. It is hoped that the lessons pioneer parishes like Bray and Knock learned have now been truly applied church-wide.

Sunday worship in St Columba's involved three morning services. At 8.30 there was Holy Communion (said). At 10.15 it was Morning Prayer on the first, third and fifth Sundays in a month; Holy Communion on the second and fourth; for this there was a second choir which didn't wear robes and never attempted anything elaborate. For the 11.30 service of Morning Prayer there was a full choir and although the office was not intoned, unlike St John's Malone, at every service one of the canticles was sung to a cathedral setting and there was an anthem.

On the first Sunday Holy Communion was a fully sung service,
usually to the setting Stanford in B flat. By and large the later service was attended by an older age-group and its shape had been
determined by a previous incumbent for whom church music
had been a central feature in his ministry. Evensong was rather
like Morning Prayer except that the congregation was very
much smaller. The verger used to turn the lights out during the
sermon at Evening Prayer – very conducive to suggesting sleep
to the congregation. One summer evening I was delighted to
look down the church and see my father sitting near the back. It
was the first time he had come to a church where I was preaching. After the service, of course, he found someone in the congregation with whom he had been at school. Because of later
illness he would never be able fully to participate in a service
when I was in a church of my own.

The 10.15 service had developed from the requirement that
there should be Morning Prayer on parish communion Sunday
and WJ's desire that the Sunday School should experience worship at least once a month. The only concession on the first
Sunday of the month to the fact that there were between 150 and
200 members of that congregation under 13, was that there was no
setting for the canticles. The preachers' book of the time reveals
that the combined congregation on the first Sunday of the
month was well over four hundred, and totals of five hundred
plus occur from time to time. During his time as curate, the
rector had allowed Jimmy Moore to encourage those who were
recently confirmed or who were in confirmation class to be worshippers at 10.15, setting up a system of rotas in which month by
month junior churchwardens and sidesmen were appointed,
giving the young people full responsibility, the elected churchwardens literally taking a back seat. I noted that especially popular with these young people was the 'straight' Holy
Communion service with hymns on the second and fourth
Sundays. Yet time and again at Youth Guild discussions I would
receive pleas for hymns in a more modern mode – this was 1960.

At that time the bishop required curates to live in or near
the parishes in which they served. I set out to fulfil this requirement but could find nowhere in the neighbourhood which
would offer the same facilities as I had had in Ballymoney. I

eventually found accommodation with a member of the congregation who had been widowed a year or so earlier. It was convenient and I tried to be as little nuisance as possible, but after a week she said that I wasn't sufficient company in the house and that she would prefer a female lodger who would be away at weekends. I reported this to the bishop and said I would buy a car and live with my parents on the other side of town. With reluctance he agreed and I acquired my first car, a second-hand Morris 1000. I was able to do my work efficiently and immediately took on responsibility for most of the hospital visiting, as apart from the Ulster Hospital all the main Belfast hospitals were closer to home than to the parish. I was to be one of the last curates for whom parishes made no housing provision. St Columba's acquired a series of curates' houses for those who would join the staff in later years. Today one of the criteria for a parish being allocated a curate is the provision of an equipped residence. Potential curates examine carefully the accommodation on offer before accepting nomination.

I found the responsibility of preparing so many young people for confirmation the most demanding and yet the most rewarding of my curacy days. I 'inherited' forty eight boys and girls for whom Jimmy Moore had covered half the course, and I had simply to deal with worship and the rite itself. In the next year there would be thirty four candidates and forty in the third year. The reason for these above average numbers was simple: these were children born in 1946 and 1947, the years after the return of their parents from war service. My first task was to visit their homes and, because they came from all corners of the parish, I was quickly getting a 'feel' of the parish. I wanted to provide notes of teaching given but the parish had no facility for reproducing material until after the second Wells programme in 1962. However, Edward Garrett at St John's Malone, made available the parish duplicator and also allowed me to incorporate in my teaching material ideas from his own excellent notes. On his advice and drawing from his experience, I instituted individual pre-confirmation interviews at which I promised always to be available as a priest for the young men and women wherever I might be in the future. I was to be amazed how often in the next twenty years that offer was to be taken up. It is a matter of great regret that under Safeguarding Trust, the Church of Ireland's child protection scheme, such individual interviews cannot be contemplated and classes nowadays have to be held with another adult present or within earshot. The time commitment to confirmation preparation is an investment in the future of the church which I have proved to be well worthwhile. It doesn't mean one hundred per cent success, if we mean all become regular worshipping members of the church Sunday by Sunday. It does mean that those who do are people who understand what worship is about and something of what Christian commitment involves. It gives one a great thrill and joy thirty years later to go to a church as a visiting minister and find as churchwarden one whom you presented for confirmation.

The actual services of confirmation 1960-62 saw all the young ladies dressing in white frocks and wearing veils, which parents would have purchased. I had great difficulties in convincing them that what was required was a plain veil. Shops would try to sell their mothers the kind of thing designed for Roman Catholic First Communions. These were not suitable for a rite in which the bishop lays his hand on the head of the candidate. It was also necessary to tell the boys, suitably dressed in dark suits or school blazers, to refrain from putting oil or haircream on their hair. With a huge congregation gathered (520 in 1960) it was all very splendid. Disastrous features were Bishop Mitchell's two addresses. These were far too long and seemed designed to cover everything that twelve confirmation classes had attempted to communicate. From the curate's seat I could see glazed expressions coming on the faces of those young people who had come excited and expectant. There were also a number of weeks before the newly-confirmed came for their first communion. At least this took place within the Sunday 10.15 Holy Communion with which they were already familiar, and at which our hope was to integrate them as part of the fellowship. We had moved that far since 1947.

Scouting in Knock
In the summer of 1960 the Knock group of scouts celebrated its 21st birthday with a fortnight's camping in Guernsey. I was able to be one of the party, warranted as an Assistant Scoutmaster.

Michael Reid, 'Mikko,' a young engineer, was leader-in-charge. It had been a tremendous logistal programme by the committee, involving two overnight sea-crossings on the way out and a night in London on the return trip. We made it successfully, arriving on the channel island on a morning after an 'Irish' downpour. The local authority suggested accommodating us in a barn but that was not the way of the 64th! I was very impressed by the sheer professionalism of all the leaders, including the experienced patrol leaders, as by lunchtime we had everything set up. Thereupon, the sun came out and we never saw any more rain or cloud for twelve days. During that time we did all the touristy things with special coaches laid on; we walked to the beach, for swimming and games. To the amusement of English scouts sharing the site we even put on a Gaelic Football match. One of the ASMs, a small man, prematurely bald and a dead ringer for the then president of the Irish Republic, Seán T. O'Kelly, was solemnly introduced to the teams, as the Irish National Anthem was played on a harmonium! On both Sundays we paraded to Vale Church and on the second Sunday the rector, now knowing that I was a priest, asked me to assist with the chalice. The St Columba's magazine duly recorded the fact that they received the chalice from a person wearing uniform with hairy knees at eye-level! In the two following years when I also accompanied the scouts to camp in the Mournes, we set up outdoor celebrations of Holy Communion on tables made out of tree branches. These were most memorable and I know of one young man for whom faith came alive at Holy Communion in Mourne Park – a life-changing encounter with Christ. Those years under canvas were useful for building relationships which gave opportunity for ministry both then and in the future when the trust established allowed young men to seek out a priest they really knew.

Rector sidelined!
In the third week of my holiday I received a call back to the parish as WJ had developed a throat problem that required hospitalisation. In addition to the Sunday services etc. suddenly I had to take over for him a wedding preparation interview, rehearsal and the wedding itself. I had already sat in on one of his pre-marriage preparation interviews and had officiated at my

first wedding early in July. For the next eighteen months I officiated at all the marriages in St Columba's. The pattern of marriage preparation that I learned from WJ, and which my own future wife would insist he went through for us, was one that I have not wanted to change in forty years.

But it was also the baptisms: and in Knock because of the Clara Park estate there were three or four a month. The sacrament was administered at 4.00pm on Sunday afternoons. The clergy visited the parents (and godparents, if possible) on some evening in the week previous to go through the service carefully. As it was *Book of Common Prayer* only in those days, this required a large amount of what was virtually translation of the six-teenth-century language. I felt at times that it must seem like some mysterious rite – hard to relate to discipleship in 1960. These evening meetings did mean that I met the dads and that was important. I continued this practice when I had parishes of my own – in my first twelve months in Belvoir in 1968-9 I would have thirty five baptisms. Was I thrilled when the experimental new form of the baptism service was issued in 1969! Here we had an order of service which said clearly what it was about – not perfect but such an improvement.

WJ had a strict rule that before the baptism the parents would come to the altar rails for the Prayer Book service of Thanksgiving after Childbirth, commonly called the Churching of Women. We hadn't used this short rite in Ballymoney. I disliked it at sight for it carried the implication that something about giving birth required purification as in the Old Testament. Calling the service Thanksgiving may have been all right but the bold title in the Prayer Book was the Churching of Women. As one under authority I dutifully used the service as long as I was the curate but I have never used it since. One of my successors, Stanley Baird, persuaded WJ to allow him to compose an alternative thanksgiving rite and the bishop allowed it to be used instead. In the services in *Alternative Occasional Services* (1993) a new Thanksgiving service was provided and this will find its way into the new edition of the *Book of Common Prayer*.

The autumn of 1960 dragged on into the winter and WJ wasn't making any headway. The parish was ripe with rumours about his health but it was simply a matter of years of wrongly using of his vocal chords. It required a simple operation and then months of total silence after which a speech therapist taught him to speak again. Amazingly, when the silence was broken the rich Tipperary brogue was stronger than ever. Some more assistance with Sunday worship was required than the occasional visiting preacher. A retired canon, St Clare Stewart, was available and as he lived convenient to my home I transported him each Sunday to Knock. Canon Stewart was the father of Bob, rector of Ballymoney, and he used to get great amusement from the 'fact' that I had been his son's curate and he was now mine! The Canon and WJ got on extremely well, the latter writing jokes on his erasable pad and the former taking the pad and writing replies on it! After Christmas the bishop decided that it was too much to ask someone in his eighties to travel each week and asked a young lay reader, a research student at Queen's, who intended to go on to ordination, to be my regular partner. That student was Robin Eames. After a couple of weeks I succumbed to flu and this left Robin Eames responsible for all the preaching, a couple of curates were brought in for the Sunday communions and the rectors of Stormont and Gilnahirk looked after those on weekdays. Needless to say everything went smoothly. I was glad when, on St Patrick's Day, a deacon was ordained for the junior curacy and I could share with Alex Smith some of the responsibility. WJ re-appeared in church on Easter Day when he gave the blessing, but preaching and so on were our responsibility until the beginning of July. So I still had to take the weddings – we had two on Easter Monday, with home communions sandwiched between. Snow showers were more apparent than showers of rice.

WJ left the running of the parish to me. I reported to him every week but he never took a single decision during those many months. That included my chairing the Select Vestry. It was suggested that perhaps the Rural Dean might undertake that role but the rector did not want that kind of interference. He trusted me and he trusted his vestry members. It was a trust that was not misplaced. It involved all the details of the planning of the new parochial hall. So many problems arose over the site originally designated, across King's Road from the church, that it had to be abandoned in favour of the unused area below the

rectory garden. It was wonderful training for one's future independent charge.

In a way, although I had a rector behind me, I had almost
twelve months to all intents and purposes in sole charge. I had,
of course, to organise my time as efficiently as possible and to my
surprise found that there were sufficient hours in the day.

Keeping up my studies
At the end of my time at Ballymoney, I begin to think of studying for a higher degree. I knew that I was barred from a Trinity
degree because I hadn't the qualifying Arts degree from that
university and so I inquired from the University of London
about its external BD degree. The exam syllabus showed that
1962 would be the best year to attempt as the special subject
under church history was the Church in England in the seven-
teenth century. To encourage clergy to undertake further study,
a canon theologian had just been appointed to Belfast Cathedral,
Anthony Hanson, one of twin theologian brothers. Anthony had
spent over a decade in South India, as a presbyter in the united
Church of South India. This united church was made up of former Anglicans, Presbyterians, Methodists and Congregation-
alists. Some of the Church of Ireland bishops had never been
happy with this united church, indeed Archbishop Gregg is reputed to have taken the lead at his last Lambeth Conference in
opposing welcoming CSI to full communion. The appointment
of Hanson did not have the full support of the bishops – F. J.
Mitchell, the bishop of Down and Dromore, was noticeably cool
and didn't go out of his way to encourage his clergy to seek his
assistance in pursuit of their studies. I responded to a general invitation to meet the canon theologian at Belfast Cathedal and
found someone who was a complete enthusiast for the London
University course, especially when he found that one of the Old
Testament books on the course was Job, on which he and his
wife had written a commentary. He laid on two hours of lec-
tures/tutorials three mornings a week for me and two others,
one of whom was working for a Trinity BD.

Working with A. T. Hanson gave structure to my BD studies
and, in spite of the work-load at Knock, I was able to complete
preparation, sitting the final examination – nine three-hour papers

– at the College of Technology (!) in May 1962. I awaited the results with great trepidation because to fail one paper was to fail
all. I knew I had done a first-class paper on my special subject
but I knew just how little I had understood the Philosophy of
Religion part of the course. Norman Kelly was in London on the
day the results were posted at the Senate House and very kindly
went to read the results for me. At lunch time he phoned to say
that I had passed with Second Class Honours. St Columba's
Select Vestry was very kind and bought my BD degree hood for
me.

That autumn, still keen to be academically active, I went to
see J. C. Beckett at Queen's about doing research for an MA in
history. I had assembled some material about Richard Chenevix
Trench, the last archbishop of Dublin to be appointed before the
Church of Ireland was disestablished. Beckett made it clear that I
would need some primary material like letters etc. and I planned
to discuss this with the Librarian of the Representative Church
Body. Professor Roberts came in while I was with J. C. Beckett,
inquired about what I'd been doing, congratulated me on my
BD, and made some pleasant remark about supposing I was
going to do research on some bishop. J. C. Beckett in characteristic puckish way said, 'One better, Michael, an archbishop!'
However, before I could take things further I was appointed as a
Curate-in-Charge – no time for research and the following
spring a biography of Tremch was published. On reading it I
discovered that the author had no more information than I had
acquired so there were no primary resources to be tapped.

The autumn of 1962 also saw me take office as president of
the Belfast Junior Clergy Reading Society. This was a junior version of the Belfast Clerical, the curates meeting on their own,
doing much the same kind of thing as I have described earlier in
relation to the Coleraine Clerical. BJCRS was just beginning to
suffer from the decline in absolute numbers of curates, which
meant a proportionate decline in the numbers of those who
could be bothered to attend. Post-ordination training was being
organised in a new way in both Connor and Down and Dromore
with compulsory attendance one morning a month. Within ten
years the society was defunct. I believe that this was disastrous
in that doing one's own thing, pursuing and presenting to one's

contemporaries the fruit of one's study and receiving their criticism was stimulating and rewarding. It was also good for clergy
in Belfast, a city which sits astride two dioceses, to meet and
share experiences. My presidential address was on the
Liturgical Movement which had been growing in influence for
seventy years. I called it 'A Revolution in Worship'. In fact the
revolution was about to break out with power as a result of the
Roman Catholic Church's Second Vatican Council. One of the
great things about the president's lunch was the custom of inviting previous presidents who would offer their comments.
Senior past president in 1962 was Canon J. T. Armstrong who
travelled up from Ballycastle with another past president, J. N.
Goulden, and made characteristically generous comments.

Liturgical experiments
A weekend at Murlough House, Dundrum, Co Down, seaside
home of the Marquess of Downshire, at that time available to the
Church of Ireland as a retreat house/conference centre, was
planned for the Sunday School teachers and members of the
Youth Guild. It took place on the first weekend in March 1961.
We managed to get cover for the services in St Columba's and I
was able to persuade Anthony Hanson to give the talks on
'Worship'. I planned to do the communion very much on the
Clare College lines I had experienced at Portush two years before. The group co-operated wholeheartedly and joined in parts
of the service which they had hitherto only heard the celebrant
recite. One girl, confirmed the previous summer, said that receiving a broken piece of bread with a bit of the crust on it made
her realise for the first time what it meant to be part of the Body
of Christ and how Jesus wanted to share his life with us.
Hanson's knowledge of the liturgy of the Church of South India
helped our group realise that what we were attempting was part
of a worldwide movement. The fact that he had a review copy of
the *New English Bible* New Testament, being published later in
the month, from which he allowed us to read lessons at the services, also made it special. The view through the window behind me of the sun shining on the snow-covered Mourne
Mountains may also have helped. In the afternoon, at our last
session I was challenged: was this enlivening experience just to

be for Murlough? Could we not do something like it in the parish church?

I reported back to WJ and he gave me the go-ahead to bring the insights we had found at Murlough to the 10.15 Holy Communion next Sunday. Using the telephone, I was able to get all who weren't Sunday School teachers to promise to be at the service and I arranged everything except the single loaf to be as at Murlough. My sermon was an explanation and the young people carried everything off perfectly. One of the ultra-conservatives tried to stir things up by asking one of the churchwardens what he thought of 'all that'. I am profoundly grateful to that churchwarden for his reply: 'Just wonderful! Really meaningful worship.' Over the next few months the same pattern – offertory procession, congregation joining in Prayer of Humble Access and the post communion thanksgiving became established at both the 10.15 and 11.30 services. It was one of the things that prepared St Columba's for the experimental services of 1967 and 1972.

Apart from a few occasions when I managed to get parents to bring their children for baptism at one of the main services, that was the height of liturgical renewal during my time in Knock. I had seen what could be done and was eager to have further opportunities to promote renewal in worship. Following the announcement at General Synod 1962 of the approval of the House of Bishops for the use of the *New English Bible*, we introduced its use for the New Testament lessons. At one of our classes in May I had told Anthony Hanson of the House of Bishops announcement. He said he would have preferred approval of the *Revised Standard Version* and said he would write accordingly. In the autumn the bishops added the RSV to the list of approved versions and within a decade it was to be found on many lecterns. There were always people who declared a preference for the 'old bible' and to this day lessons are read from the 1611 *Authorised Version* in a great many churches in Ireland, notwithstanding that in many places it is both inaccurate and unclear. Many rectors have had an uphill task in persuading people that the important thing is to hear what the Holy Spirit is saying through the scriptures, and not relaxing by listening to the sound of sixteenth century English.

Youth Guild

I inherited a very lively Youth Guild from Jimmy Moore which unusually had a number of young marrieds and professional people in their later twenties. These 'senior' members indicated that they would back me for 1960-61 but after that they wanted to hand over to the younger folk. Committee meetings were usually held in the homes of members and featured execellent suppers. My first, on my first Sunday evening, was held in the home of Valerie Hennesey, a bank official, an evening never to be forgotten. Little did I think then that the tall dark-haired girl who welcomed me would be the one who would share my life in future years as my wife.

Youth Guild activities involved planned visits to places like Belfast City Hall and the new state-of-the-art Castlereagh Police Station, and visiting speakers. I was able to set up a strong programme for the coming winter as we brought along people like the Dean of Belfast, the BBC Religious Broadcasting Advisor and even the Bishop himself – all willing to submit themselves to cross-examination.

Knock Youth Guild, under the leadership of Jimmy Moore, had been a strong supporter of the creation in the outbuildings of the Rectory in Strangford of Youth Guild House, where guilds could spend self-catering weekends. St Columba's Parish had helped in the furnishing (no luxury!). I took the Guild there twice and Alex Smith would do so twice more. It was a place with great potential and I know that the early morning communion services were much appreciated. Indeed four young people who came to an awareness of faith in their lives through the Youth Guild and were confirmed as a result, made their first communions at Strangford on Palm Sunday in 1962. But there were problems and these would ultimately see the Youth Guild House project come to an end. The rector and his sister objected to any noise after 9.00pm, and it just wasn't possible to keep young people on a weekend quiet at such an early hour. On my first weekend the group of young people walked the two plus miles to the Parish Church at Ballyculter for Morning Prayer at 11.45 and back again, which meant a very late lunch. On subsequent visits they rebelled on the grounds that there had been Holy Communion before breakfast in the House. They wanted to be out and about. The local rector, who was warden of the centre, complained to WJ. Knock Youth Guild weren't the worst offenders but the bishop intervened. If visitors wouldn't attend the Parish Church and obey the Warden's rules they couldn't use the facility. In 1960 I didn't know of the existence of the lovely Old Court Chapel just up Castle Street in the de Ros estate. If only we had been able to use it for worship. I do know that on one of the weekends a number walked across the road to Star of the Sea Church and attended service there – partly out of curiosity, partly in rebellion against one whom they regarded as their persecutor! On each occasion I had had to leave Strangford to get back to St Columba's for the 10.15 service.

Ecumenical activity
One would have to confess that there was even less ecumenical activity than I had found in Ballymoney. There were two large Presbyterian churches and a Methodist church inside the parish boundaries. Another Presbyterian Church was sited just across the Upper Newtownards Road. Yet we had no relationships with them nor with St Columcille's Roman Catholic Church. We did nothing together that we could do separately, with the exception of Christian Aid Week where St Columba's had responsibility for collectors in a small corner of the area, including Clara Park Housing estate.

There wasn't even any shared relations at primary school level for the only Primary School in the parish was a junior school in Clara Park which only catered for the first three years of a child's school life. I used to visit it regularly but it was nothing like school work in Ballymoney.

But things were changing. My time in Knock coincided with the reign of Good Pope John XXIII who allowed a fresh move of the Holy Spirit to blow through the Roman Catholic Church. We observed with great interest the opening of the Second Vatican Council and when one of the 'experts' who was advising the Council expressed a willingness to share with others what was happening, we eagerly welcomed Dr Cahal Daly, then a lecturer at Queen's, to an informal gathering of clergy and laity. Things were just beginning to move. Then Pope John died and, with the rest of the world church, we awaited the election of his successor with more interest than hitherto. There was a fear that the progress we were seeing towards a new reformation in the Roman Catholic Church would be halted. However, those fears were to prove groundless as the post Vatican II church would *de facto* be quite a new community – one with whom we in the Church of Ireland would be able to forge new relationships, unthought of even in 1957.

Pastures new

During August 1962 I had my first experience of ministering in another province of the Anglican Communion. Norman and Noreen Kelly planned their holiday to meet up with me in Edinburgh and later to travel to Argyll. There we stayed in the village of Ballachulish and, having previously contacted the local rector with an offer to give him a holiday, Norman and I conducted the services in St John's and in the outlying churches of Duror. It was very much Jacobite country in the 18th century and there has been a enclave of episcopalians from that period when the Scottish Episcopal Church suffered persecution. Officiating meant wearing full eucharistic vestments for the first time at the morning services. Afterwards we were thanked by one of the churchwardens, a man from the Hebrides, with a distinctive way of speaking which renders the letter 'v' as an 'f': 'Our serffices were fery much appreciated.'

The weather in the West of Scotland was generally wet except for the day we went on a trip round Mull with the object of getting to Iona. The objective was reached but we had less than two hours – enough for me to determine that I would return and spend time to absorb something of the atmosphere that even that short visit had impressed upon me.

Once the autumn season had commenced, it became clear that with a rector back to full-time duty and Alex Smith, both priested and married, there wasn't actually enough work for three of us. I had passed oversight of the Youth Guild to Alex. Confirmation preparation wouldn't start again until the New Year. I discussed this with WJ and on my behalf he put out feelers to rectors who had semi-autonomous areas in their parishes like he had had before Gilnahirk became a parish on its own right. Nothing came of these and apart from an approach to take

Jimmy Moore's place as the archdeacon's curate in Bangor we agreed to leave any thought of moving on to the following summer.

Then on Thursday 8 November 1962 after the 10.30 Holy Communion, the rector said the bishop would like me to go round to the See House. Wondering what he could be wanting, I drove round. Bishop Mitchell told me that his chaplain, Jim Hartin, with whom he had just been on pilgrimage to the Holy Land, had intimated that he wanted to return to Dublin for full-time academic research and teaching. This would leave the new area parish of Knocknagoney without a priest. His question was, 'Would I be willing to take over?' I was quite staggered: one, by Hartin's impending departure as we had regarded him as one of the 'coming men' in the diocese, and two, with the responsibility for overseeing the building of a new church, the first designed on liturgical movement principles. Perhaps I was precipitate and didn't investigate the proposition fully enough, but I couldn't have turned down the offer, even if I had been aware of problems ahead. I had several times stood in for Jim Hartin on Sunday evenings and had found worship in the temporary church building, a former army hut, meaningful and worthwhile.

So, on 1 January 1963 I was to become Curate-in-Charge of Knocknagoney Parish (Bishop Elliott, congratulating me, emphasised the importance of the hyphens). I would be the youngest incumbent in Ireland. I was aware of a huge responsibility, but this was again that to which I believe God had called me and for which five and a half years as a curate had prepared me.

CHAPTER SEVEN

Knocknagoney 1963-68

Origins
Kocknagoney Parish, the name in Irish meaning 'hill of the rabbits', was one of the new areas created by Bishop Mitchell's church extension programme to meet the needs of new housing estates springing up on the edge of east Belfast and along the north coast of County Down. It was unique in that it was formed out of two parishes – St Mark's Dundela, in which there had been a church hall since 1956 and Holywood. In 1960 it consisted mainly of three distinct estates of public housing (rented) and a handful of fringing owner-occupied avenues. Holywood Road and undeveloped land stretching north to Belfast Lough formed one boundary, and Old Holywood Road, a very dangerous piece of roadway, was a *de facto* southern boundary. The Belfast Corporation bus service (Holywood Road) terminated at the bottom of Knocknagoney Road and some of the Bangor Ulster Transport buses came up and along Old Holywood Road, but this latter road had no footpath. The church site had been purchased in a strategic position on the map, but subsequently planners banned housing development beyond the church towards Holywood or on the hill side of the Old Holywood Road. Thus, by 1962, there was no further development permitted for the foreseeable future. This meant that a church development envisaging a parish of six to seven hundred households was immediately constricted. Around two hundred and fifty families acknowledged some allegiance to the new parish. One of the estates consisted of post-war bungalows constructed of aluminium. Those where the original tenants still lived were beautifully kept. However, these were the exception and many, where tenancies had frequently changed, were in a deplorable condition. The other estate was more recent and the majority of the tenants had come from areas near the Queen's Bridge where housing had

been cleared for the new by-pass. Some of these had had close church connections with St Martin's and were ready to support the new parish. Most disappointing had been the response from the Redburn estate on the edge of Holywood. It could have been looked on to provide leadership for the new parish but for the dangerous road which discouraged children from attending Sunday School or organisations, and the fact that they were mostly Holywood people, who went to school in Holywood, shopped in Holywood and many had been and were active worshippers in St Philip and St James's Church there. Had I but known, I was on a hiding to nothing! Knocknagoney would be a problem parish for the diocese for up to thirty more years.

A large corner site had been purchased and in 1960 an ex-army hut had been dedicated as the temporary Church of The Annunciation. This was one of a number of dedications for which an enthusiast had left a sum of money to the diocese. I had led worship there on several occasions for Jim Hartin. These had conveyed the impression of a small keen dedicated group of people. The truth of that impression would be borne out in the months and years ahead. The problem was that it was so small. One unusual feature was that a cross constructed of stainless steel was suspended on wires above the holy table. By this the letter of the canon prohibiting a cross being placed on or behind the table was circumvented. In the plan for the new church, passed by all the authorities, a similar cross was envisaged. In the event, because a bill was before the 1964 Synod to rescind the canon, the offer of the suspended cross was withdrawn pending the outcome of the bill. It passed. However, the offer was not renewed and to this day there is no cross in the Church of The Annunciation.

Introduction and Sunday worship
My introduction was to be on the evening of 1 January 1963. The event was over-shadowed for me because my father had suffered a stroke on the previous Sunday and was seriously ill in hospital. It meant that my mother and sister, now a qualified doctor, were not able to be at the service. The family was represented by my mother's two sisters, Eileen and Biddy and the latter's husband, Hugh Larmor. Bishop Mitchell had decreed

(and I had agreed) that since there was to be a 'big' day on 2 February when the foundation stones of the Church and Hall were to be laid, there shouldn't be a party after the service. Unfortunately the ladies of the parish took this as a judgement that they weren't capable of putting on a 'do' for visitors and, to all intents and purposes, they boycotted the service. Canon Mervyn Dickson, rector of Down in 2002, was at that time a parishioner of Knocknagoney and recalls that for all kinds of reasons, this latter among them, my ministry in the parish got off to a dreadful start through no fault of mine. The weather was also dreadful: we had had to dig ice off the flagstones on the path leading to the church, and as the service went on the feet of those who were there got colder and colder. It is significant that no numbers for the congregation are recorded in the Preacher's Book, the collection amounting to less than £6!

The following Saturday evening the parishioners put on a social to welcome me as their new rector and I have good memories of a warm friendly evening in the hall in Garnerville Road, where the community had first come together in 1956.

Sunday worship consisted of three services, a 9.30am Parish Communion with sermon, 11.30 Morning Prayer with sermon and 6.30 Evening Prayer with sermon (the latter being Holy Communion once a month – my first experience of evening Holy Communion). Undoubtedly Jim Hartin had intended to build on the 9.30 Parish Communion and at first I continued the practice, having significant events like the Boys' Brigade enrolment at it. But I found that it just was not working and, when the new church came into use, developed a monthly Family Communion at 11.30am which by then was the service attended by the largest congregation of the day. I retained the tradition of a short homily, often *ex tempore*, at 9.30 and over the years 'preached through' the *Book of Common Prayer* Collects, Epistles and Gospels.

New Church and Hall under way
In January 1963, beside the temporary church, the steel skeleton of the new church and hall was rising. It was going to be a revolutionary diamond-shaped building with a copper roof, speaking of a tent or tabernacle for the worship of the people of God.

A crypt chapel was being included. This was to be the Chapel of the Magnificat, a diocesan chapel for the members of the Mothers' Union. Vestry and hall were to be linked to the church on the north side and the rectory was similarly to be linked on the south. In the centre of the complex there was a large cross in pre-stressed concrete. To the east the architect had planned a landscaped garden. It was a grandiose plan. I suspected that it would be expensive but when I was appointed I was told that all the money was in hand. The laying of the foundation stones was scheduled for 2 February but exceptionally bad weather in mid January meant that this had to be postponed for a month. However, the foundation stone of the church, on which the font would be placed, had already been cut from Mourne granite and incised with the original date and details. Some would see something symbolical with there being a falsehood built into the foundation stone of the church!

A week or so after the ceremonies of 2 March, which had gone off very well, the designer of the buildings, Desmond Hodges, phoned me to say that he had the adjusted costs and that they were as he had communicated to the Building Committee six months earlier. When I heard the breakdown I had a terrible shock. For they were about double those that the bishop had indicated to me and for which funds were available. Contracts had been signed and all that could now be done were massive reductions. I felt that I had been totally deceived but, with the help of the bishop and a group from the diocese, we were able to pare back the plan. Out went the linked rectory, the vestry was reduced in size and the link to the hall cancelled, as were a number of embellishments to the basic church building. We were able to negotiate a loan from the bank to cover the comparatively small difference. At that time bank rates were low; by 1968 they had risen and were a constant problem through the seventies. We were going to have a new church, bare of all but basic furnishings.

Lack of leaders

In January 1963 the Parish Honorary Secretary was Joe Cully, a layman who had grown up in north Belfast, whose vocation to Holy Orders had been recognised. Because of family commitments he had been allowed to study for ordination at home and, over a period of years, had completed the requirements of the General Ordination Examination of the Church of England. After Easter, the bishop arranged for him to spend two terms at the Theological Hall of the Scottish Episcopal Church, so he was also immediately removed from my support team. The Rector's Churchwarden was Dr Lewis Warren, lecturer in history at Queen's (married to my former classmate Anne Smith), but almost immediately he resigned on his appointment as Warden of the Queen's University Halls of Residence. One of the leaders of the Sunday School, Mervyn Dickson, had also been accepted for training for ordination and went off to the Theological College in Dublin in the autumn. I seemed to be losing leaders hand over fist! It proved very difficult to find people with education and experience who could negotiate with banks and church commissions: those we did find, like civil servant Bill McIntyre, didn't put down roots for long enough. Without the support of police officers like Bertie Gamble and Billy Nicholl I should have been truly on my own.

Boys' Brigade
One element in the life of the parish was very encouraging. This was the 110th Belfast company of the Boys' Brigade. I had never had any great enthusiasm for the BB, having always been drawn to the Scout Movement. However, I determined to 'grit my teeth' and play whatever part the rector had with the company. The Captain was a Dubliner, Jack McClure, a senior Bank of Ireland official, who had grown up with BB in Dublin and was a one hundred per cent Church of Ireland man, parishioner of St Mark's Dundela. Whatever bias BB might seem to have towards Presbyterianism, given its origins in the Church of Scotland, Jack made sure was corrected. Whenever the 110th went to camp and the chaplain went too, there was a camp celebration of Holy Communion and they loved to have a cross on the table when outside Ireland! The weekly bible class was given equal status with company night and the young men were trained over the years to lead the studies and the prayers. It is no accident that 110th BB gave three ordinands to the Church of Ireland, Canon Mervyn Dickson, Canon Walter Laverty and

Noel Beattie. I have often said that in them the wider church and diocese was well repaid for any monies it invested in Knocknagoney. Jack McClure and his family became great friends and Mrs McClure personally worked, in wool, the long communion kneeler for the new church, which has stood the test of time. I would only accompany the BB to one summer camp – Scotland in 1964 – a new experience for a scouting man. They were very tolerant of my scout shirt and envied my shorts on some very hot days.

A new home
I took over the 'temporary' rectory, a detached three bedroom house in Glenmillan Park. Because of the illness of my father it was again my aunts who were to the fore in helping me to furnish the house and I was able to draw on friends in Malone and Knock with the 'right' connections in supplying furniture and electrical things like fridge, washing machine and vacuum cleaner. I had to supply and purchase these and all carpets and curtains. The small first incumbency grant about paid for one carpet. Nowadays a parish has to provide all these basic furnishings for a rectory. All that Knocknagoney provided was the cooker. It was mid February before I was 'in residence' although I drove over each morning. By this time my father was out of hospital, although he would be handicapped and his speech restricted for the rest of his life. I still went home for mid-day meals and tried to share in some way the caring burden that fell on my mother. My sister was at this time a house surgeon at the Royal Victoria Hospital with the long hours that role demanded of her. I had a parish to serve, a house to keep and a garden to construct. In due time I hired a woman to come in once a week and do the cleaning etc. I also managed to find a gardener who came once a week in the summer and we made a garden out of a very unpromising site.

New relationships
It was a time of building new relationships – a considerable number of baptisms, a new group of confirmation candidates and more than a few weddings. Because it was primarily a new area there were fewer funerals. Services for funerals in 1963 were

either in the home of the deceased and thence to the cemetery, or took place in a funeral parlour. Some of the latter were terribly depressing although I always wore a cassock when officiating. I found the custom in east Belfast of keeping the coffin open until after the service very difficult to come to terms with. I enjoyed the weddings: almost without exception I found young men and women who wanted the very best for their joint futures and were quite happy to marry one another in the temporary church. The confirmation groups were also very responsive: I found those who were members of the BB particularly alert. For the first time I had one girl who at the end of the course declined to be confirmed. She decided she wasn't yet ready. Next year she returned, went through the whole course again, was confirmed and became a regular communicant. After leaving school she went to work in Switzerland where she married in a civil cere- mony as required there. On the first opportunity, a year after the wedding, she and her husband came to N. Ireland and al- though I was by then in Belvoir the family came to the Church of The Transfiguration for a service of blessing of their marriage.

Refresher and Summer School
After Easter I spent a week with the Kellys at Billy and was a 'day-boy' at the Portrush Refresher Course. I was elected to the committee and was responsible for the next ten years for the running of the course bookstall. This was a very positive in- volvement. 1963 however was the last time I could be a 'day- boy' for Norman Kelly had decided to accept an invitation from Jack Roundhill, Vicar of Dorking in Surrey, to work with him in the three church parish there. By the summer his address was Ranmore Parsonage in Dorking. I had booked a summer school place at St Augustine's College at Canterbury, formerly a theo- logical college for training priests for overseas mission areas, at that time the central college of the Anglican Communion. It gave me a further opportunity to discover more about the worldwide communion in a fortnight of fellowship with people from America, Canada, Australia, Japan, Madagascar and Mauritius. Billy Macourt, his wife, Esmé and their son, Malcolm, were other representatives of the Church of Ireland. Each morning we worshipped at the Holy Communion celebrated according to

the rite of the celebrant's province and in their native languages. Thus we had Holy Communion in Malagasy and Japanese. The use of eucharistic vestments was general. Someone complained to the leader, Canon Leonard Schiff, that there was no north-end celebration by the Church of Ireland. He replied that this was usual but that summer they had a priest from Australia which had an equally 'low' tradition and he had given him the opportunity of celebrating in his way. The priest in question came from one of the few Anglo-Catholic parishes in Sydney and so there was no north-end celebration. One service took place in the open air in the ruins of St Augustine's Abbey where I encountered for the first time a celebration of the Holy Communion with the minister presiding, facing the people over the altar. We were also encouraged to receive the sacrament standing and, with one exception, a very conservative catholic from Central Africa, heeded the request. It was all part of the experience which had concentrated on the way the eucharist was the service for the Lord's people 'in a strange land' by which the lecturer from the Church of the Advent in Boston, USA, meant the post-Christian age into which he believed we were moving. Ernest Southcott, from the parish of Halton in Leeds, a pioneer of house church communions linked to the weekly parish communion, was the other main speaker. He was an excellent communicator. There was also the sublime experience of Sunday worship in Canterbury Cathedral. For me it was more evidence of the movement towards liturgical renewal in the Anglican communion in which I wanted the Church of Ireland to have a part.

Saturday socials

Autumn of 1963 saw a project which began as an attempt to meet a need for a social activity for the throng of young people in the area. We created a Saturday night Club with a membership card as well as a weekly subscription of two shillings (ten pence but with a value in today's money at least ten times that!). The club also provided bottles of lemonade at a shilling (five pence) and packets of crisps which sold for fourpence (two pence). We had contacts with a mineral water manufacturer which delivered our order to the hall caretaker and collected the empties each week. I became quite an expert at ordering and paying accounts like that. The activity was dancing to records – what would later become known as a disco but at a very simple level. A licence was obtained from the Phonographic Performance Society and a list of recordings used returned each month. 1963-4 was the year of the outbreak of Beatlemania. I first heard those Beatles records like 'She loves you, yeah, yeah!' dinned into my ears each Saturday evening. The dances were a terrific success and financially fantastically profitable. As a result I was able to buy the linens and soft furnishings for the new church. The frontals and falls, burses and veils were almost all paid for by the young people of the area through the Saturday Club. I had the support of a number of adults and our presence meant that behaviour was good. Now and again someone would bring a visitor who didn't know the situation and there would be a bit of aggravation. As the evenings grew less dark in the Spring of 1964, I decided that a rest from the Saturday Club would be a good thing and announced that the Club would be closed for six weeks 'because it was Lent'. A group of non Church of Ireland young people came as a deputation demanding to know to whom I had lent the hall! Although we attempted resurrecting the Club in the autumn of 1964 we had, after a few weeks, to close it again. Sadly the reason was the emergence of sectarian violence. Boys and girls from both Protestant and Catholic communities on the Lower Newtownards Road discovered the Garnerville Saturday Club as a venue to express their mutual hostilities – the availability of bottles, easily broken and used as weapons made continuing dangerous. For several weeks in a row we had to call the police and the Select Vestry decided it was unfair to the residents as well as dangerous to the young people. Sadly, one must see this as one of the first shoots of what has been and is a sad harvest for Northern Ireland.

Teaching ministry
School ministry was a major part of weekday work. There were two primary schools, Redburn at the Holywood end of the parish, where I went once a week for five and a half years, and Knocknagoney. The latter in 1963 was a two teacher school on the corner of the church site. A new school was being built and it would be there that future developments would take place. I

persuaded Stuart Black, the minister of Garnerville Presbyterian Church, whose new building was also in the course of being erected, to join me in teaching at Knocknagoney. At first he was hesitant and loath to divide children denominationally but he accepted my point that each of us could build a useful relationship of trust with our own children. Subsequently Knocknagoney Primary School established a tradition of holding their annual carol services in the two churches alternately.

Canon Eric Barber, Vicar of Holywood, was anxious that I would become involved in teaching at Holywood Intermediate School and, although only about ten per cent of the Church of Ireland children at the school were from Knocknagoney parish, I very much enjoyed the years teaching 14 and 15 year olds. It was that experience that opened my eyes to a social change. I can illustrate it in this way. In my first year, discussion came round to the commandments and a girl asked me in all seriousness what adultery was. She had been wondering why people passed it over quickly. She thought it was something to do with selling bad quality goods ('adulterated'). When I explained it simply and directly the class was genuinely pleased that someone had answered a question they knew was important but at age 14 still didn't understand. By 1967-8 the questions I was getting were about teenage pregnancy and what girls should allow boys to do when out on dates. Yes! We were into the 'swinging sixties'. This was a very perplexed generation, as well as one much more knowledgeable about sex. Drugs was not yet even a vestigial question.

Another educational institution opened in the autumn of 1963, the Northern Ireland College of Catering and Domestic Science at Garnerville. This was a residential third-level college and I requested the privilege of being its Church of Ireland chaplain. In their first few weeks some of the girls, led by one of my St Columba's 1960 confirmation class, appeared at the 9.30 service. I was invited once or twice a term to meet any Church of Ireland students who would like to come along. These became discussion groups exploring our Church's history and ethos. I enjoyed them and continued in subsequent years although it became rare to see students at church, most preferring to go home at weekends when, under pressure, the college relaxed the rules.

Garnerville College later became part of the New University of
Ulster and transferred to the Jordanstown campus.

The Consecration of the Church
It was a very busy few months as the time drew near for the
completion of the church and the service of consecration. It was
on St Mark's Day and the liturgy used was the service in the *Book
of Common Prayer* as it had been adapted for the consecration of
other new churches in the diocese. I was delighted that the archbishop of Dublin, George Simms, had agreed to be the preacher.
In the evening the bishop returned and preached at a service of
dedication of the furnishings for the Chapel of the Magnificat
which had been presented by the branches of the Mothers'
Union in the diocese. On the morning of the second Sunday after
the consecration, Bishop Mitchell confirmed seventeen young
people, and in the evening Canon J. T. Armstrong came from
Ballycastle, and gave a very characteristic address of the kind I
remembered so well. He chose to stay in a City Centre Hotel to
which I brought him after the service. It was in fact to be the last
sermon he ever preached and the last time I saw him, for during
May he took ill and died on 7 June in his eighty-first year. After
all these special services refreshments were laid on in the new
hall with which the Mothers' Union and other ladies coped most
capably.

There was a mixture of excitement and sadness on the part of
the congregation when we held the last services in the temporary church for that had been important in the spiritual development of so many. We had tried out 'samples' of the pews that
were for the new church and in that way found plain but extremely comfortable seating which also allowed people to kneel
in comfort. In my experience this is rare in new church buildings. Those who complain about the decline in the practice of
kneeling in the Church of Ireland should examine the seating
and kneeling facilities provided (and I do not exclude any of the
cathedrals that I know from this judgement).

There was immense interest in the new church building.
Requests for invitations (!) came from all over Ireland and both
television companies sent camera teams to interview me in the
days beforehand. 'What did we hope for the new building?'

'Why was it so different?' For it was the first building designed primarily for eucharistic worship in the twentieth century Church of Ireland. Clearly the Holy Table was prominent with lots of space setting it off. However, I was never satisfied that sufficient prominence was given for the ministry of the Word. Many who would preach in the church felt exposed as there was no protection for their legs. In my successor's time a pulpit from a redundant church was brought to wrap around the north ambo: aesthetically a disaster.

The day of the consecration came. The contractors were working up to the last moment. Indeed, the electricians were still connecting up the hot-water geyser in the kitchen as the service began. The archbishop arrived an hour or so before the service and sought somewhere quiet to think and we gave him the privacy of the crypt chapel where, characteristically, he put the finishing touches to his sermon. The chancellor of the diocese, the legal official who drafted all the documents, was absolutely delighted with the building as it gave him full scope to proclaim in wig and gown the Deed of Consecration and present it with due flourish to the consecrating bishop.

The first few weeks in the new church were exhausting in more ways than one. It was a very warm May and we discovered that the evening sun beating in on the windows of south and west made the church quite hot. It would have made a good greenhouse for growing tomatoes. The first of many architectural problems were not long in raising their head – copper sheeting on the roof cracked with expansion and contraction – this would produce problems with rain ingress, problems not solved almost forty years later. Another problem arose with some of the wooden window mullions: they would warp and crack the panes of glass. It was exciting new architecture, but it was not without problems, some of which were due to mistakes in the construction, others were design errors. None were as serious as those which affected another new church, St Brendan's Sydenham, consecrated a year earlier in 1963, which had a different architect. During an extremely strong gale on 13 January 1965 it collapsed, becoming a total loss, and had to be rebuilt to a new design in 1967.

A few weeks after the opening of our new church I was an

honoured guest at the dedication of Garnerville Presbyterian
Church, members of whom conveyed to me that they would
never have persuaded their central committees to let them have
a new church had the Church of Ireland not gone ahead. If that
were so it was a significant ecumenical gesture. The possibilities
of co-operation were there and in the years ahead would be
grasped.

Holidays and personal
After eighteen months I needed a holiday. My sister, Elizabeth,
having almost completed two years at the Royal Victoria
Hospital, and was working for her MD degree, suggested that
we should go to Devon and Cornwall where she had done one
of her pre-qualification placements. We flew to Exeter, hired a
car for ten days, and toured. It gave opportunity to visit a married cousin in Topsham and, because we had established a base
at Falmouth for a weekend, could also visit my mother's brother
and his wife, who lived close to their married daughter and her
husband, a consultant physician in Truro. Although driving in
the narrow roads of Devon and Cornwall isn't easy, that last ten
days of June was a real rest cure – good weather, an experience
never to be forgotten, visiting Exeter and Truro Cathedrals and
another liturgical movement parish church, The Ascension in
Plymouth, where carved over the west door are the words:
'Now the real worship begins: in God's world.' That coupled
with wonderful cuisine in the hotel overlooking Falmouth
Roads, and some equally great meals in country inns, definitely
recharged batteries for both of us.

  When I look over my diary for 1963, I note occasional entries
for Sunday evening – 'Henneseys'. I normally went across Belfast
for Sunday lunch with my parents. And after evening service if
there wasn't a parish meeting I had an open invitation to drop in
for supper to the home of Valerie Hennesey and her mother.
Valerie was a bank official and had been on the Youth Guild
Committee as well as being a Sunday School teacher in St
Columba's. We had occasional meals out including a Saturday
in north Antrim in the summer of 1963. I ceased making diary
appointments in 1964 as it became the rule rather than the exception. They were top of my personal invitation list for the consecration celebrations. When I came back from the Devon holiday I

knew that I wanted to ask Valerie to be my wife. Intending to 'pop the question' I invited her to dine out with me on 30 June: totally impossible as bank officials in those days worked late into the night for the half-yearly balance. So it wasn't for another month that the dinner could be re-arranged. Suffice it to say that the following afternoon I had my answer as we went for a picnic on the hills above Ballygally.

Valerie's mother was delighted to give her 'consent' and it was a joy to my family also. On Sunday afternoon we called at St Columba's Rectory. W. J. Whittaker thought we were coming on some church business as Valerie was at this time Secretary of the Youth Committee of Irish Churches. When we asked him to join us in marriage, he was totally taken aback, 'Glory be to God and his holy mother!' he exclaimed (an expression learned in his Tipperary youth). Then, because he liked to think he knew everything that went on in his parish, he asked, 'And where did you two do your courting?' We didn't enlighten him. The wedding was arranged for the first Saturday in December. It couldn't be sooner as Valerie had to give three months notice to the bank directors. In 1964 banks did not continue to employ women officials when they married. Within a few years that would change but we both knew that we would have to rely on one salary from the start.

Wedding preparations took in all the free time there was in the autumn of 1964. Valerie informed the YCIC that she would be giving up and I was warmly welcomed to this ecumenical group at a party held after a meeting at Murlough House. Strangely enough, just as she came off the committee so the authorities of the Church of Ireland appointed me to membership for 1964-5. I am afraid that I found the Youth Committee little more than a talking shop, valuable for making contacts but as an ecumenical instrument rather toothless.

Bobby Huddleson was my choice for best man and he was willing to act. He had returned from a year's scholarship study in Greece with the Orthodox Church and had grown a suitably 'orthodox' beard. At the time he was without an appointment, being reluctant to return to parish ministry after two curacies with 'difficult' rectors. In the end he went to work for Christian Aid, in Geneva and in East Africa.

Valerie insisted that WJ should give us exactly the same marriage preparation as he would for any other couple: with this I
agreed totally. I might have performed fifty marriage ceremonies: in this one I was the bridegroom. We had invited
Norman Kelly to assist in the service and to celebrate Holy
Communion at the marriage. It had also been arranged that after
our honeymoon in London we would go to stay with the Kellys
at Ranmore Parsonage, Dorking, for the second weekend away.
Our wedding day was a typical wet December day but that
didn't matter. All our families, including my father, were present. But, again typical of the era, only the clergy, bride and
groom received communion.

We had a super week in London. It was December and pre-
Christmas. We went to The Temple Church for Sunday Matins
after Holy Communion at Christ Church, Lancaster Gate. We
spent our money on theatres and concerts and ate simply at
Lyons' Corner Houses, which sadly no longer exist. On the
Friday we travelled to Dorking and spent a pleasant weekend,
extended because of a one-day airport strike. During the weekend, discovering that Valerie's mother had grown up in
Rathmines before the First World War, where Norman's mother
had also lived, Norman un-earthed a book which showed that
his mother and Valerie's aunt had been best friends. Truly,
Ireland is a village.

Back home to Christmas and a great welcome from
Knocknagoney parish for the rector's 'new wife'. They were obviously delighted for me, giving us a party and a generous wed-
ding-present. They were also delighted because Valerie was
ready and willing to encourage the small choir, and having
known the organist in her CIYMS Tennis Club years helped. Mrs
Senior, the Mothers' Union Enrolling Member, was delighted
that she could soon step down and return to her home branch in
Holywood.

Progress?
The first enthusiasm for the new church wore off only too quickly
and we were faced with maintenance problems. There were
always enough volunteers to clean the church and make it ready
for Sunday worship. But we couldn't afford a caretaker and

organisations proved notoriously irresponsible when charged with the upkeep of the hall. No one wanted to make sure the toilets were kept clean, and how crazy had been the design of these so close to the main door. How seldom are architects of church halls members of organisations which use them. There was also the unbuilt area surrounding the church – grass-cutting the plot in front of the hall and church was a major operation. The plan for landscaping had been scrapped early in the economy process. Part of the grounds were granted to parishioners for garden allotments, but young people from the estates stole lettuces and other vegetables and those who had planted them lost heart. We took advantage of a government scheme to supply young trees and thorn quicks to go along the Old Holywood Road boundary. This was reasonably successful until December 1965 when the conifers were pinched for Christmas trees. Year on year we tried to cope and were still trying when I was moved to Belvoir. Many years later, when the block on house building to the east of Knocknagoney Road was lifted, the parish was able to sell off the greater part of the surplus ground for housing. The church now nestles among homes. It has given it greater security at the expense of having a commanding position.

Ecumenical
It will have been noted that no mention has yet been made of a Roman Catholic population in Knocknagoney. The reason for this is simple: there was none except in the Redburn district. Our partner church was the Presbyterian. Its minister was Stuart Black who was many years senior to me and had served in the church overseas. For Sunday in the Week of Prayer for Christian Unity in 1965 I invited him to come with his congregation for a joint prayer service at which he would be preacher. His response was to treat the invitation with suspicion. What were my motives? What would be the purpose of the service? Once I had convinced him that I had no sinister designs and simply wanted to respond to our Lord's prayer that all might be one that the world might believe (John 17: 21) he co-operated fully and regular annual visits to one another's churches were inaugurated.

Just next door to the Church of The Annunciation was Knocknagoney Mission Hall, a typical small Belfast evangelical mission. They didn't consider that we were Christians and were always inviting people to go to their hall for a converting experience. I don't think they were any more sucessful in evangelisation in the area than the main-line churches. Close to the area was the Northern Ireland headquarters of the Church of Jesus Christ of Latter-day Saints, the Mormons. We were constantly visited by Mormon missionaries and they attracted a number of our young people to their exciting social events and games occasions. A number succumbed to the 'charms' of the young elders and underwent Mormon baptism. For the vast majority this was a passing whim.

Occasionally clergy receive anonymous letters and treat them with the attention they deserve. Quite early in my time at Knocknagoney one such letter was pushed through my letterbox and I saw a man in a grey waterproof coat pedalling away on a bicycle. It contained a diatribe of abuse both of me and of Canon Eric Barber for our involvement in matters ecumenical. Full of biblical quotations on the one hand and the foulest language on the other. It always amazes me how these fundamentalist enthusiasts can stoop to use language of the gutter.

In 1966 a meeting of the Rural Deanery Chapter, which consisted of all the clergy of the area, was told by a rector who was also a member of the Orange Order that the Order was launching a campaign against the World Council of Churches and everything ecumenical. This represented the growing influence of Ian Paisley's Free Presbyterian Church fomenting suspicion of the greater openness that was following the Roman Catholic Vatican Council. The chief Anglican observer at Vatican II had been Dr J. R. H. Moorman, the bishop of Ripon. He had accepted an invitation to address a meeting in Belfast to give his impression of Vatican II. Because of the number who wanted to hear the bishop the gathering was to be in Belfast Cathedral and people had to apply for tickets through their rector. The Orange Order declared that they would mount a massive picket of the Cathedral. On the Sunday I announced tickets would be available, my churchwarden, who was an Orangeman, told me that he would like to hear the bishop but was afraid that he would have to be outside in obedience to his Order. For the first time I began to realise the sinister power that it represented. In the event the Dean of Belfast, Cuthbert Peacocke, yielded to pressure and withdrew the invitation to use the Cathedral. The bishop came and spoke to a much reduced gathering elsewhere in the city. Ian Paisley and the Orange Order had won a victory. Many observers see this as the beginning of a process that would lead to the 'Troubles' – the revolution which destroyed the life of Northern Ireland and its people.

A second manifestation came when Ian Paisley picketed the annual meeting of the General Assembly of the Presbyterian Church in Ireland leading to street violence, and, I believe, set in train a sequence of events that led to the withdrawal of that church from the World Council of Churches, marginalising many faithful pastors within it.

During Lent 1966, when I was giving one of a series of addresses on the words spoken by Jesus from the Cross, one of our most regular attenders, one who would have regarded himself as primarily a Protestant, walked out after the sermon, saying to the churchwarden, 'I won't be back. I have seen the Romish trend.' The warden, who had in his time been a member of the Irish Church Union for the defence of reformation principles, said to me in the vestry, 'Mr Mayne, I know what to watch out for. I didn't hear you say anything that I could complain about nor did I see you doing anything wrong!' All I could think of was that we had sung a hymn kneeling. But not once while I was in charge did that man attend another service in the church, and he was someone who had put a great deal of work into building it up. I suspect that he knew my views on the bishop of Ripon affair and was reading into my words and actions something to confirm his resentment. This kind of thing has been part of the burden which clergy throughout the North have had to bear for many years.

New Liturgy
In 1967 the Liturgical Advisory Committee of the General Synod, which had been formed five years before, produced its first order of service for trial use in churches and chapels of the Church of Ireland. *Holy Communion 1967* was a slim A5 booklet with a white card cover and contained a service re-ordered in accordance with the guidance of a liturgical group set up imple-

menting a resolution of the 1958 Lambeth Conference at which
the archbishop of Dublin had chaired the section on Prayer Book
Revision. The members of that liturgical group, the influence of
whose work has dramatically changed Anglican worship since
the 1960s, were Archbishop H. H. Clark, Primate of Canada,
Archbishop Leslie Brown, archbishop of Uganda who had been
one of the architects of the liturgy of the Church of South India,
Bishop C. J. Sansbury, bishop of Singapore and Professor
Massey H. Shepherd Jr, of the Standing Liturgical Commission
of the Episcopal Church of the USA. The guidelines were drafted
by Dr Leslie Brown. In this way the insights which the Church of
South India had brought to liturgical worship in the 1950s came
profoundly to influence the change in Anglican worship before
those of the Roman Catholic Vatican Council's *Constitution on
Liturgy*.

Holy Communion 1967 diverged from the document in one
major way. The Liturgical Advisory Committee was not persuaded that the penitential section at Holy Communion should
be part of the Preparation and retained it in its *Book of Common
Prayer* position after the intercession. The new service did provide for three readings with a psalm between the first two – at
one fell swoop the supposed need for Morning Prayer as well as
this order of service on a Sunday was done away with. The
familiar Prayer for the Church, mildly amended, was given in
the full form; the Liturgical Group's recommendation of a litany
was an alternative. What I suppose I must call the Clare College
insights for congregational participation, described earlier, were
all built in. The churchwardens readily agreed that I seek the
bishop's permission to begin experimental use of *Holy
Communion 1967* in Knocknagoney. In the directions for using
the service there was no requirement that the priest must stand
at the north end of the holy table, and I requested the permission
of the bishop in using the service to stand facing the congregation, for which the Church of The Annunciation had been designed. Imagine my horror when he ruled that I must adopt the
standard Church of Ireland position, but I was prepared to obey.
However, on the Saturday before our first use of the service,
having consulted the legal officers of the diocese, he phoned to
say that I could celebrate in the westward position. I must still be

sure not to offer any prayers with my back to the congregation. So the Church of The Annunciation became one of the first parishes in the diocese to use *Holy Communion 1967*. In a sermon on worship that day, I ventured to prophesy that worship in the Church of Ireland would never be the same. We had started on an adventure which would release our offering of worship to the glory of God from what can only be described as a virtual straight-jacket. Knocknagoney parish has throughout its life participated to the full in the worship developments of the church and preserved a lovely sense of being a tabernacle where God is known.

Family growth and upheaval

In June 1967 our first daughter, Barbara, was born – of course, being a clergy first-born, she arrived on a Sunday. I left Valerie to hospital before the 9.30 communion. By lunch-time no baby had arrived nor before I had to leave for an evening confirm-ation at Belvoir where I was presenting a candidate and acting as chaplain to the bishop. It was late evening when the mes-sage came that our daughter had been born. Grandparents were informed and I went to see my wife and daughter. How different today when fathers are routinely present at the arrival of their offspring!

Barbara Elizabeth was baptised on the Feast of The Transfiguration by Canon Whittaker – one of four baptisms in the principal morning service. One of the others was Andrew Forster who would be ordained to the ministry of the church and is now archdeacon of Elphin. I had securely established the rule that the administration of Holy Baptism always took place at a principal service, even though with thirty baptisms in the year it meant almost once a month, morning or evening. Each time I used the rite in the *Book of Common Prayer* I mentally cried out for a rite that would be simpler and better appreciated. During a Mothers' Union branch discussion one member, better educated than some, had said how she hated the service because it said there was something sinful in the way children were con-ceived and born. No one had ever explained what the words 'conceived and born in sin' meant, or that they had nothing to do with the act of procreation. A new baptism rite was being prepared: it couldn't come soon enough.

Before our daughter was a year old something happened that would see us moving across the city. Early in May the phone rang about lunch-time. It was the bishop. He wanted me to take over the new area parish of Belvoir, from which Jimmy Moore had just been appointed to be rector of Groomsport in succession to Canon C. H. Walsh. I was completely taken aback and asked for time to think about the request. He replied that he wanted an answer by five o'clock that afternoon. Valerie was surprised and I decided I needed to know if there was any special reason why Jimmy Moore was moving from what was the most successful of all the extension parishes to the seaside parish of Groomsport. I spent an hour with WJ, seeking his advice, knowing that he would be aware of any reason why I should not move, and he assured me that from his sources there was nothing to prevent my accepting. I then went and spent the rest of the time praying in the Chapel of The Magnificat. I returned to the rectory, entirely at peace as was Valerie. I phoned the bishop and was invited to go and discuss details next morning.

I discovered that Bishop Mitchell wanted me to move on 1 July as he didn't want the momentum of Belvoir parish to slacken with a lengthy interregnum. Only one Sunday would intervene between Jimmy Moore's farewell and my introduction. My family were especially delighted as Belvoir was just across the River Lagan from Malone, a couple of miles or so from my former home. I had been present at all the significant events in the life of the young parish of Belvoir and had been a speaker at their Men's Society. On Sunday afternoon we went to see Jimmy and Mary Moore and the temporary rectory, 3 Brerton Crescent. I took an immediate liking to the bungalow and we began measuring for curtains etc. straightaway. In no time we would be moving. The Belvoir Select Vestry also moved with great speed, redecorating and preparing the house for us to move to by mid-July.

There was very little leeway for us to have the family holiday we were just in the process of planning. In the end we got a week at St Ernan's, Donegal, a week particularly remembered for incessant rain, and Barbara, not yet a year old, discovering how to crawl at speed along the wide corridors of the house. When I informed the churchwardens and parochial nominators of Knocknagoney on 19 May that I was being moved to Belvoir they were very much taken aback but I received nothing but support from the whole parish.

Coventry 1968

I had secured a place on what was called an in-service Ministerial Course at Coventry Cathedral. Thankfully, I was still able to go, making further discoveries about the changing church in a changing world. My wife had been one of the Church of Ireland Youth Delegation during the weeks of festival that had followed the consecration of the new Coventry Cathedral in 1962. She had been keen for me to have some experience of its worship and life but it wasn't until 1968 that I managed to get a place on one of their courses for clergy and the sponsorship to enable me to travel and participate. I travelled by sea and rail via Liverpool. This gave me the opportunity to visit the recently opened Roman Catholic Cathedral, so early in the morning that Mass was being celebrated. This was the first time I had worshipped at a Roman Catholic service. To my surprise, it was in English. The revolution that followed Vatican II was beginning. I also visited the Anglican Cathedral at the other end of Hope Street – so vast and lofty that it seemed to say, 'What is man?'

The course director at Coventry, where I arrived in the afternoon, was the canon residentiary in charge of education projects, Canon Horace Dammers and we also had to opportunity to listen to Provost H. C. N. Williams, whom I regard as one of the unrecognised prophets of the mid-twentieth century. The participants came from several denominations, including Roman Catholic, and we had a full opportunity to share in the cathedral's international ministry, staying in John Kennedy House, the cathedral's youth facility, seeing various aspects of its reconciliation programme which brought together people from what had been former enemy countries in Europe and even reached out into communist East Germany. We also saw something of the work of the industrial chaplains and of the outreach to people of other ethnic groups. Coventry and much of the Midlands was already a multi-racial society. The children and teenagers we

met in 1968 are the parents and probably grandparents of the
21st century – not immigrants but people whose roots are now in
English city life. Until very recently this has not been a major
issue for ministry in the Irish churches, but it is something we
must accept for the future and be prepared for adjustments.

Of course we shared in the Sunday Communion, where the
liturgy had been re-shaped to allow maximum lay involvement.
I took notice of the fact that no one took part in the worship
without being fully rehearsed by the Precentor, Canon Joe
Poole. Even when I was asked to read a lesson at Sunday
Evensong I had to rehearse it on Friday afternoon to satisfy him.
This, he said, was because worship is the church's 'shop window' and therefore anything in it must be of the highest quality.
I found the way daily evening prayer in the Lady Chapel was organised by the chaplain – a women lay minister – immensely
satisfying, with the careful reading of scripture, psalms and canticles, she having first ascertained where the worshippers came
from and whether they had anything special they would like
built into the prayer. I was converted to become an advocate of
the ordination of women through that encounter. By the end of
the ten days I felt part of a significant worshipping community
wrestling with the needs of a modern city and a potentially violent city. I felt that I had been on a very special kind of retreat
which was preparing me for the new adventures in ministry
which would begin when I returned to Ireland.

CHAPTER EIGHT

Belvoir

First years :1968-72

The parish of Belvoir had been formed in 1962 out of the western end of the parish of Knockbreda. To all intents and purposes it consisted of the Housing Trust estate of Belvoir Park, a couple of houses on Newtownbreda Road and Brerton Crescent, a private development of bungalows, one of which was the temporary rectory. One of those who lived on Newtownbreda Road was Hubert McManus, whose family had been living almost opposite the house in Hughenden Avenue when I was born, and had known me as a very small baby. He was a faithful churchgoer and regular communicant, to whom I was able to minister at the end of his long life, officiating at his funeral and the burial of his ashes. Here was just another of those coincidences which have been a feature of the ministry God has given me.

Belvoir Park estate had been the home of the Deramore family which had close ties with the Duke of Wellington. Just like the village and castle in Rutland, the pronunciation was French, and sounded like 'beaver'. Amazingly no one seemed to have any problem, unlike Belvoir Street off Newtownards Road which was always 'bel-voy-er'. The estate had been developed at the end of the fifties by the Northern Ireland Housing Trust at exactly the same time as the Andersonstown estate in West Belfast, with the same variety of housing types. Strong local management in Belvoir, with a manager who lived among the people, ensured that tenants realised their responsibilities for upkeep. There were plenty of green spaces and a daily patrol of litter wardens. The housing was almost all on the eastern side of Belvoir Drive, leaving a clear view towards the Forestry Department's forest which would become part of the Lagan Valley Park. There was a central avenue connecting to the Newtownbreda Road which was ultimately replaced by a dual carriageway, forming part of the Belfast ring road: on this avenue were both the Presbyterian Church and the Church of Ireland Parish Church of The Transfiguration, the latter having the higher ground! Just off this avenue was the shopping centre, library, doctor's surgery etc. The church was just three minutes walk from the rectory. Because the latter was small, the vestry also served as the rector's study, with phone switchable from the rectory, and the Select Vestry had it fully shelved for my coming.

The Church of Ireland and the Presbyterian Church had appointed clergy as the estate developed and Jimmy Moore and his Presbyterian opposite number, Gordon Gray, had worked in tandem from their appointment. Togther they visited the streets of new homes as they were occupied. Jimmy would take one side of the street and Gordon the other, after which they met to exchange information. Together they visited Belvoir Park Primary School and, as well as leading assembly in alternate weeks, each taught the members of his congregation in the senior class. I would be happy to continue this, finding that the Principal, J. B. Stevenson, was a very well-known Old Instonian. The two congregations sought to set up organisations which would be complementary – the Presbyterians offered Boys' Brigade and Girls' Brigade and we offered Scouts and Guides. There was an early attempt mutually to share youth club activities – but by 1968 that had collapsed leaving badminton and table tennis at the Church of Ireland and a Christian Endeavour group at the Presbyterian Church. As with Knocknagoney the Church of Ireland parish building was ahead of the Presbyterians for in 1965 the Church of The Transfiguration – a building incorporating both church and hall – had been consecrated and opened. In 1968 the Presbyterian building was not yet quite complete and I would attend its dedication.

By the time of my introduction, the estate had grown to about 1,800 households of which some two-thirds had some connection with Presbyterian churches. There were about forty Roman Catholic homes (Roman Catholics tended to apply for tenancies in Andersonstown), a relatively small number of Methodists and a scattering of adherents of assorted evangelical groupings, including Free Presbyterians. At either end of the parish were Baptist Churches. These maintained strenuous programmes mostly aimed at children, enticing them with clubs and parties to change churches. In July 1968 over four hundred homes were Church of Ireland, of whom fifty continued their allegiance to down-town parishes. I had churchwardens for St Stephen's, Christ Church, St Philip's and St Mary Magdalene's living in the parish in 1969! How much stronger the new parish could have been with their active involvement. Nevertheless, after a Christian Stewardship programme in 1967-8 the parish was well on the way to being self-sufficient and it had the reputation that one needed to be at church in good time to be seated. It was a good reputation but built on one or two Sundays. However, unlike Knocknagoney, there were few empty seats at the 11.00am service.

The church was, like that in Knocknagoney, diamond shaped, but was in area a hundred square feet smaller. The sanctuary area did have an apse in which sat the Holy Table, constructed out of redundant bank counters by one of the parishioners. Over the first few months I gradually moved the table out to prepare for celebrating facing the congregation with the 1967 service. At either end of the communion rail were identical ambos, one being the lectern, the other the pulpit. Outside the sanctuary were two rows of choir stalls, the clergy desk being behind the choir on the south side, the electronic organ in a similar position on the north. Seating took the form of chairs, well-finished and vinyl hassocks were provided but not universally used. Where there were walls these were finished in rustic brick which imparted a warmth to the building while the north and south apexes were double glazed with obscured glass. At the east end was a window in hammered stained glass, depicting the Transfiguration. The colours of this were especially rich. Parishioners had travelled to France during the planning to meet the artists in their studio. The church was normally seated for 180 plus the choir and there was a small gallery at the west end over the foyer. On either side of the church at the west end were the clergy vestry and a somewhat larger room, which was choir vestry and committee room. Between the church and the foyer was a folding screen with glazed wooden doors: this could be folded back so that the foyer could be used for large congregations. As well, between foyer and church hall was an identical

screen which in theory allowed the hall to be used by large congregations, but in fact sound doesn't travel well through a low
archway. I describe this in some detail because the Church of
The Transfiguration took the full force of an IRA bomb directed
at the Forensic Science Department on Newtownbreda Road in
November 1992 and, though rebuilt on basically the same
foundations the present building is significantly different, the
colours in the Transfiguration window being somewhat less
deep than the original.

It was to a large congregation on the evening of 1 July 1968,
that I was introduced as the second Curate-in-Charge. W. J.
Whittaker preached the sermon, for some inexplicable reason
failing to refer to my five and a half years in Knocknagoney!
However, the people from Knocknagoney were given their opportunity at the reception which followed. My new parishioners
were very welcoming, getting rectory and study ready for the
new man.

Once in residence I was able to publicise the fact that prayers
were said in church, morning and evening every weekday, and
people were very welcome to join me. I cannot say that it was
very often that I had a congregation, but unless I was away the
daily office was said. Sunday worship was 8.30am Holy
Communion, 11.00am Morning Prayer (Parish Communion on
the second Sunday of the month), 7.00pm Evening Prayer (Holy
Communion on the fourth Sunday of the month). Holy Baptism
was scheduled for the first Sunday in the morning, third Sunday
in the evening and in my first twelve months there was usually
an infant for baptism. This meant the pre-baptism visit and I
found a far greater willingness to discuss and think about the
meaning of baptism than in either Clara Park estate in Knock or
Knocknagoney. Was it something to do with the fact that by and
large the social make-up of Belvoir was drawn from a better-ed-
ucated social group? I was also fortunate to have resident in the
parish a Church of Ireland priest, Harold Fennell, teacher of
Religious Education at Annadale Grammar School, and until
1971 a tremendous stand-by and encouragement. Without any
problem I could get away for holidays in June 1969 and 1970. It
was my joy to prepare one of his sons for confirmation. He and
his wife were both very supportive on the weekend when our

second daughter, Hilary, was born, for on that day also my wife's mother died.

1968 was the year of revolution and student demonstrations in many parts of the world. The Civil Rights demonstrations began in Northern Ireland as Roman Catholic citizens began to organise their protests at the discrimination in housing, employment and public representation they undoubtedly suffered. How the Protestant community had been able to stand by for so long without shame is a mystery. Probably because from the setting up of Northern Ireland as a state, there had been a sense that the Protestant community had been under attack from the IRA at various times, and the fact that Roman Catholics and Nationalists had been unwilling to accept the legitimacy of the *de facto* six county state. West of the Bann local government had been manipulated to give the smaller Protestant community control of many local councils, and local councils had used their powers of housing allocation to maintain its majority. Discrimination in housing did not apply to the Housing Trust and so didn't affect Belvoir. But I soon found parishioners who had personal knowledge of that discrimination in Tyrone and Fermanagh. I could see that the Civil Rights protesters had right on their side. The Unionist government under pressure began to recognise that reform was needed and Terence O'Neill, the Northern Ireland Prime Minister, began a programme of reform that indeed would lead to his downfall. That was because the Rev Ian Paisley began militant opposition to the Civil Rights agitators on one hand and against what he saw as appeasement by O'Neill and the Unionist government. Nearly every weekend there was a confrontation on the streets of the country towns of Ulster with the Paisleyites mounting counter demonstrations to those of the Civil Rights movement, which rapidly became riot situations. This impinged quickly on the parish. Not because we had demonstrations in Belvoir but because almost a quarter of our families were headed by policemen. We had almost all ranks, from District Inspector to Constable, living in the estate, partly because police could afford the rents. As the winter went on they suffered tiredness and minor injuries. For all this I never heard any sectarian comments. They hated being 'piggy in the middle'.

Liturgical change

After a few months I persuaded the churchwardens that it was time to use the experimental *Holy Communion 1967* in Belvoir. It was introduced on the second Sunday in December in 1968 with Canon Brian Harvey, Anthony Hanson's successor, giving a brilliant introductory address. The pattern was established: on the Sunday of Parish Communion we used the service in the *Book of Common Prayer* at 8.30am; the one member of the Select Vestry who disliked the new service always came to 8.30 on that Sunday.

In autumn 1969 the second set of trial services was issued, lightly revised orders for Morning Prayer and Evening Prayer, and an order for the Baptism of Children. 'The little red book' was warmly welcomed, being genuinely user-friendly and not so revolutionary as to frighten the horses. The Lord's Prayer was in what came to be called 'modified traditional' and Holy Ghost was replaced by Holy Spirit. The Baptism service was indeed an answer to prayer, making preparation meetings so much easier, making it easier for all participants. Few actually noticed that for the first time in Church of Ireland worship the Almighty was ad-dressed as 'you' and second person plural forms were used throughout. In this way the 1969 Baptism service marked the be-ginning of the real revolution in Irish liturgical forms.

By 1972 when a further revised order for Holy Communion came, now also with 'you' language I had the full confidence of the parish and the 'little blue book' was quickly accepted. I only encountered opposition to one feature – the Lord's Prayer in the 'Our Father in heaven...' form. We decided to stick with the modified traditional Lord's Prayer and, apart from one or two who usually availed of an alternative time of worship, *Holy Communion 1972* was firmly part of Belvoir's liturgical life for the future. We were one of the first congregations to learn a musical setting for the rite – by a then little known composer, John Rutter.

From the start of its life as a worshipping congregation, one of the evening services each month was Holy Communion. Strangely, evening celebrations of the Lord's Supper had been until the late 1950s sure signals of a 'low' church evangelical tradition. Canon Fred L'Estrange would have been horrified and there were no evening communion services in St Columba's, Knock. Because Knocknagoney had started in Garnerville Hall with evening services only, a monthly evening Holy Communion service was part of its tradition from the start and I had no problems with it. I found it an opportunity to worship in a more relaxed and quieter way when we celebrated the eucharist in the evening, and it became the natural service at which to introduce publicly the ministry of laying on of hands with prayer for healing from 1977 onwards. At Christmas in 1970 I introduced a 'midnight' celebration of Holy Communion, not without some anxiety for I had read reports of parishes having problems with over indulgent Christmas revellers producing problems in some places. I need not have worried and the midnight eucharist (usually beginning at 11.30pm) became firmly established. When I went to Waterford that congregation was also responsive, though, unlike Belvoir, organist and choir did not support it.

Holy Week services too easily slip into a pattern of Evening Prayer or Compline and an address. In 1972 we tried an ecumenical approach, using forms suggested by the Joint Liturgical Group of Great Britain: I invited John Lappin and his congregation to share in this and he responded to the extent of preaching on one of the three evenings. A handful of Presbyterians came along with him. More successful in what it led to was my invitation to Cyril Haire, the Methodist minister of Ballynafeigh, who had responsibility for Belvoir's Methodists. For three nights we had tried an ecumenical observance of Holy Week and, to be honest, I think we were happier on Maundy Thursday with Holy Communion on our own. On Easter Eve I used the JLG form of Easter Vigil, using dimmed lights for the readings, switching on full lighting for the Exsultet and using St Patrick's Breastplate as part of the welcome to the Risen Christ. A small congregation shared in this, a rite that I used every Easter Eve for the rest of my full-time ministry, never with large congregations but always valued. I would hope that in years to come an Easter Vigil service will be produced for the Church of Ireland and that it will become as familiar as other rites of Holy Week.

Community problems and pastoral ministry 1969-71

While the liturgical life of the parish was growing and it was moving towards achieving fully established parochial status, the wider community was becoming de-stabilised as we entered what are known as 'the Troubles'. As 1969 progressed, the pattern of street demonstrations leading to mini-riots continued. A general election, in which Terence O'Neill had appealed to the Unionist community for backing for his modest reforms aimed at meeting moderate Nationalist grievances, returned a number of hard-line uncompromising members to the parliament at Stormont led by Reverend Ian Paisley and his Democratic Unionist Party. The latter thundered, 'O'Neill must go', and eventually O'Neill did resign and disappeared into private life, disillusioned with his attempts to build bridges with the republic and to redress genuine faults in Northen Irish life.

In the summer of 1969 it all boiled up, with almost continuous evening rioting in West Belfast – exhausting members of the police, many of whom received minor injuries, and placing immense strains on their wives and families in my pastoral care. Events in Londonderry and in the streets which link Falls Road and Shankill Road, after the Apprentice Boys' Demonstration in Derry, led to the deployment of the army in aid of the civil power – their appearance welcomed by the Roman Catholics who were in genuine fear in the face of Protestant attacks on their property. The exact truth of what happened on the night of 12 August, 1969, will never be known. Those who were there included one of my churchwardens who was with the special constabulary. He came to see me in great distress a few days later, and he had only the vaguest understanding of a night of fear. He gave me a picture of two communities confronting each other, terrified that the one was out to destroy the other, that guns were being fired and that fire bombs were being used. A later judicial inquiry wasn't able to discover what actually happened and the muddled impressions of traumatised people on both sides have become the stock of folk-memory. At the crucial time in August 1969 the Church of Ireland leadership was at an all-time low, as Archbishop James McCann had just resigned and the bishops of Derry, Connor and Down and Dromore were about to retire. George Otto Simms, a man of quiet holiness, was appointed to Armagh. Arthur Hamilton Butler, the bishop of Tuam, was elected bishop of Connor and came north in early 1970. Archdeacon George Quin was elected to the see of Down, and Dean Cuthbert Peacocke to the see of Derry: both these bishops were consecrated in Belfast Cathedral on the feast of The Epiphany in 1970. But there had been a significant leadership vacuum.

The autumn and winter were not used to re-build but became a period of human misery as a process of separation of communities into Nationalist and Unionist blocs began. Instead of normal allocation of homes in Belvoir, emergency re-housing began to take place. We welcomed to the parish wonderful church families from Whiterock parish (where Protestants left the mixed Ballymurphy estate in droves), people who had owned their own homes and lived happily with Roman Catholic neighbours in the Springfield Road and in Suffolk beyond Finaghy. Some of these were to become fully integrated into their new parish. On the other hand, quite a number of the Roman Catholic families in Belvoir were intimidated into leaving. Some of their neighbours, Presbyterian and Church of Ireland, did their best to dissuade their friends from going – sitting with them night after night to give support. In the end, most of those with families moved out to what became known as Roman Catholic areas. The forty or so families of 1968 became what you could count on two hands.

Pastoral ministry continued, building up, welcoming, consolidating what had begun. In spite of difficulties faced at this time in parts of the city, we were able to operate all our organisations as before. The Guide Company developed its senior branch as Ranger Guides were inaugurated, while the Scouts developed a junior group below Cubs with the Beavers.

Soon after I arrived I was approached about the formation of a dramatic society. This found a ready response with me as I had been involved with one in St John's Malone, and even suggested the name, the Belvoir Players. This made use of the excellent staging in the hall. Pressure of space led to conflict with the existing Badminton Club as stage and minor hall had hitherto allowed for table tennis. As long as I was in Belvoir there was a smouldering battle between the two; other organisations tended to side with the Badminton Club when they found 'their' nights claimed by the Players when putting on a production. The rector was 'the man in the middle' as allocation of use of the hall is one of his prerogatives. The Players unearthed some amazing talents among parishioners – Jim Button's stage sets were to win awards at Drama Festivals, a young man discovered that he had a flair for lighting and electrics in spite of the fact that his parents disapproved totally of drama and said so. Richard Mills proved to be an outstanding producer and within a few years the Belvoir Players were among the top half-dozen in amateur drama in Northern Ireland. Later he would receive an MBE for his services to amateur drama. The Players went independent of the parish in the early 1980s and now have impressive premises on the northern side of Belvoir Drive. In the 1970s, in difficult times for down-town theatres, the annual pantomime played to full houses in the church hall.

Richard suggested several times that we should try to put on a Passion Play and we searched around for a suitable text without success. He then challenged me, 'Why don't you write one yourself?' And in the spring of 1974, I did just that. We were blessed by having a group of young people who had been in the Confirmation Class of 1973 and had shown an interest in the dramatic society. So it was a teenage cast that performed *The Valley of the Shadow* in the hall on the Tuesday and Wednesday of Holy Week in place of the Holy Week Service. The geography of the Church ruled out its use in a play that required lighting effects, and off-stage voices. There were, of course, one or two parishioners who denounced this as blasphemous, especially as I had an actor playing the part of Jesus appear in the resurrection scene. One of those who wouldn't have countenanced attending any other play came and afterwards told me with tears in her eyes how moving she had found the passion play to be. I shall always be grateful to Dick Mills for pressing me to write the play, to him for directing it and to that incredible bunch of youngsters who so faithfully interpreted it, revealing a depth of spiritual understanding that I don't think they realised they had. I recall in particular the acting of the girl who played Mary of Magdala and, of course, the fact that the young man who played Jesus, in the resurrection scene, wearing my longest

surplice, which was fine, even if on the first night forgot to re-
move his trainers before going on stage.

I resumed my connections with Scouting and became Group
Scout Leader of the 106th Belfast Group. In the five years that
had elapsed titles had changed: no more scoutmasters, we were
all 'leaders'. Shorts had been replaced by mushroom coloured
long trousers and shirts were dark green not khaki; the floppy
hat had gone, all wore berets. We prepared to mark the tenth anniversary with a camp in Scotland and I went along with Ray
Rennix, the scout leader, and our first Queen's Scout, Terrence
Smythe, to help us run it. Auchengillan is on the north side of
Glasgow with great views of the Highlands. Apart from discovering that Scots have a different language when it comes to
catering (what we call 'sausages' have to be ordered as 'links')
we had a wonderful week. 'Educational' tours to Edinburgh and
of Glasgow city educated the leaders to realise that Ibrox
Stadium, home of Rangers FC, was the most significant place to
be visited in the eyes of the scouts of 1971. By 1972 Ray Rennix
had moved, Terrence was at university and I found myself the
only available person to take the troop to a planned camp at
Cobham in Surrey. The Scout District gave me a young student
as an assistant. It was a good camp but I realised that as rector I
could not hope to have the same relationship with the boys as I
had had twelve years previously a young curate. They almost
made my life a misery but I had one day's escape, to Norman
and Noreen Kelly's vicarage at New Haw, the other side of
Weybridge from Cobham. The high spot was a coach trip to
Windsor Safari Park: that I could cheerfully have left a couple of
the patrol leaders as fodder for the lions indicates how I was
feeling. During the camp the Camp Warden called me in anx-
iously for me to phone home in case any relatives had been
caught up in the day of bombings in Belfast, known as Bloody
Friday. Thankfully no one had anyone involved and although
the bus station at the centre of the attack was the one from which
buses served Belvoir, no parishioner had been injured.

It was virtually the end of my active scouting. I remained in a
supervisory role. Thankfully the scout district was able to provide leadership for the remainder of my time but it was never as
effective without commitment to the parish as well as the move-

ment. The contrast with Cub scouting, managed by Susan
Headden and the Fletcher boys, was only too noticeable.
Capable home-grown leadership took over the Guides which
had been begun by Milda Glenny and Elsie Neill and under
Elizabeth Grenville and Noelle McCoubrey the company went
from strength to strength

Parish 1971-75
Full parochial status was granted in 1971 and the procedures of
nominating the first rector were solemnly conducted. Constitution-
ally it could have been someone other than me, and I would
have been out of a job and homeless! But the forms were observed and I was offered the nomination. My institution was
fixed for 4 December.

I had been to London for a meeting of wardens of readers.
For the four days that I stayed with Norman and Noreen Kelly
at New Haw in Surrey I had been really unwell, suspecting that
the blisters round my eye and on the hair-line might be shingles.
On the day after I returned, my doctor confirmed my diagnosis
and told me to take time off. There was to be a wedding on the
Saturday and I was determined to officiate. My signatures in the
registers and wedding photographs are the only evidence that I
did. I have no memory of being there at all. From then on there
was no question, I was off duty. Valerie was expecting our second child and her mother, terminally ill with cancer, was staying at the rectory. It was a difficult fortnight. And I had left the
bug at New Haw: Norman contracted chicken-pox and was
rather ill for the month of December.

I was well enough to organise the rehearsal for the institution
on the previous evening. I had endeavoured to communicate
that although this focused on Brian Mayne becoming rector, it
was to be treated as a celebration of the parish's 'coming-of-age'.
Bishop Quin had invited John Duggan, bishop of Tuam, to be
the preacher but hadn't given him a proper briefing. His sermon
suggested that I was someone coming anew to the parish as he
talked about the way the parishioners should welcome their
new rector! However, the reception in the hall afterwards went
some way to redressing the balance and Sunday's service with
the first Curate-in-Charge, Jimmy Moore, preaching completed

a weekend celebrating the first nine years of parish life in Belvoir.

Early in 1972 a second daughter, Hilary, was born. On the same day her grandmother, Mrs Mabel Hennesey, died in the same hospital. It was as if she was waiting to be sure that all was well with her daughter and grandchild before she departed this life. It was a very difficult time for Valerie, as her brother and I arranged the funeral at which she couldn't be present. We had tremendous love and support from parishioners. Throughout the infancy of both daughters, members of the Mothers' Union and others were baby-sitters of the very first class.

By this time elder daughter, Barbara, was a pupil at Belvoir Park Primary School. There were over seven hundred pupils on the roll in that year, the high point of enrolment at the school, making it one of the largest primary schools in the Greater Belfast area, with three intake classes. It was an indication of the age of the estate. It also ensured a very dedicated staff. Barbara had a superb grounding and flourished in every department, as did Hilary when she entered in 1976 in time to have her first formative years in the same school. About this time I was elected as a parent representative on the Management Committee and continued to serve on that committee for the rest of my time in Belvoir. It was almost the easiest experience of school management that I have had. I did have to be aware that school teaching appointments were minefields. In those days there was far more freedom for the committee as it made appointments than was the rule when I was again involved in school management after 1984.

By 1972 Derek Baxter, the new pastor at Milltown Baptist Church, had joined the visiting clergy and thus it was now every third Wednesday that one led assembly and I had found that I was able to speak to the children informally and without notes. After the new Presbyterian Church had been opened a pattern of holding the school carol service in it and the Church of The Transfiguration in alternate years began – and Derek Baxter proved willing to come to these and to read a lesson.

The General Synod of the Church of Ireland reviewed the canons which governed worship and a new set came into force in 1975. One of these permitted the clergy to wear stoles in the

liturgical colours. I availed of this provision and to a very few
who passed comment I simply replied, 'Do you still have black
and white television?' To which there was no reply. I never had
any inclination to wear full eucharistic vestments which still remain outlawed.

The community 1972-74
In the summer of 1972 I had received a phonecall from the
Worshipful Master of an Orange Lodge somewhere in the
Milltown area, which was outside my parish boundary. He said
that the members of his lodge would like to attend morning service at my church (sic) on the second Sunday in June. Would
they be welcome? I assured him that they could be made welcome if they simply wanted to come and worship with us, but
that there was a problem since the service on that Sunday was
Family Communion which might not suit members who were
not Church of Ireland. He wanted me to move the Family
Communion to another Sunday but I said that was impossible
due to Sunday School prize-giving. A later phonecall indicated
that the lodge would not be coming after all. On the morning
concerned we heard the sound of a band as the lodge walked to
the Presbyterian Church. I learned that it was being stated that I
had refused to allow the lodge to attend the Church of The
Transfiguration. There was no refusal, just a pointing out of
problems. However, I was never approached again.

The background to ministry in Belvoir continued to be the
security situation in the province. I continued to preach brother-
hood and reconciliation. I am quite sure that if it had been in my
make-up to use the pulpit for anti-Roman Catholic teaching and
to affirm a hardline political position, I would have had larger
congregations and less problems but that was not my understanding of the gospel.

Increased overtime meant that many police were now earn-
ing enough to seek to own their own homes and many moved
out of the estate into new owner-occupied housing in
Newtownbreda. Some did continue to attend but many transferred to Knockbreda Parish.

This did affect the life of the parish to some degree. More
serious was the deteriorating political situation. I was encour-

aged to find a number of our most influential parishioners taking an interest in the new cross-community Alliance Party and there was widespread welcome for the Sunningdale Agreement and the first power-sharing executive. But following the general election of 1974, militant Protestantism, supported by paramilitary elements, brought about the Ulster Workers' Strike. Government proved helpless because the militants had control of the power stations and held the executive to ransom. Although it was never proved, most people believed that Dr Ian Paisley was a moving spirit encouraging what was a virtual rebellion. For him it had been, 'O'Neill must go', 'Chichester-Clark must go' and now 'Faulkner, Fitt and all must go'. The executive resigned and a chance of stability was lost for twenty-four years.

In Belvoir there was unprecedented co-operation, as the churches mobilised to help those most at risk with the loss of electric power and the deliveries of basic necessities. With the assistance of social service agencies for whom the strikers were prepared to provide petrol, we made sure that the elderly and homes where there were babies and young children had hot water and adequate meals. Below the Church of The Transfiguration the Guides built a huge altar-shaped fire on which cauldrons of boiling water were kept going for the several days that were necessary until the crisis passed. It was an example of co-operation when the pressure was on. Baptists and Free Presbyterians worked together with us and nobody asked any question about the religious persuasion of those in need. The following autumn the social service agencies held a meeting to set in place procedures for the 'next time'. I am afraid I became rather angry that anyone should be thinking and talking about any 'next' time. What we should have been looking for was a way forward that would avoid any 'next' time. For that all the churches should have been praying and working. But my words fell on deaf ears. Thankfully there never was a 'next' time.

But there was an endless pattern of devastation due to bombs and a seemingly endless toll of death.

It is a matter for thanksgiving that I never had a police funeral at Church of The Transfiguration although it did happen in my successor's time. I had to bury one victim of IRA murder, an educationally retarded teenager, David Walker, who had been overheard boasting that he knew the leaders of the UDA, had been kidnapped, tortured and murdered in June 1973. His parents were parishioners who had come from an area of tension and, with the exception of a daughter in the confirmation class, the family had only slight church commitment with the result that they hardly knew me nor me them. There was an immense crowd outside the funeral parlour in Dunmurry where I conducted a service and also at the interment at Ballylesson Churchyard. These events all occurred outside the parish so there wasn't the impact there would otherwise have been.

Ecumenical developments 1972-80
Towards the end of 1972 I received a letter from a young Roman Catholic whom I had met on the Coventry course four years earlier. He was now in his final year of preparation for the priesthood at the Divine Word Missionaries House at Maynooth. Michael Cleary had been given permission from the College President to invite me to speak at a Bible Service in the forthcoming Week of Prayer for Christian Unity. This turned out to be a very inspiring experience and I received wonderful hospitality. It was an opportunity to speak bluntly about the problems of ecumenism in Belfast in the early seventies, as I said that probably more than half my congregation would not approve my being in Maynooth at all. The Divine Word Missionaries were one of the victims of the vocation shrinkage in the Roman Catholic Church in Ireland and they disappeared from Maynooth a few years later. I often wonder what became of that young priest.

About this time I was invited by Principal Jimmy Haire of the Presbyterian College to meet from time to time in his house with a number of priests and ministers of what were to become known as the four mainline churches. Here I met a number of Presbyterian and Methodist ministers as well as Padraig Murphy, then Parish Priest of Ballymurphy, Brendan Murray and one or two younger Roman Catholic clergy, all of whom were concerned about the way in which the Troubles were affecting their people. I found these gatherings to be very encouraging and very much missed the opportunity when illness meant Dr Haire had to call a halt.

Towards Christmas 1974 an invitation to a carol service for young people was received by the three ministers at school assembly, with a request that we should publicise it. The service was to take place in the new St Bernadette's Church. The Baptist pastor said he would not publicise it on principle, the Presbyterian minister said that he had no personal objection but that his elders would not approve and I agreed to announce the service. This was a very good example of attitudes to ecumenism.

A growing relationship with Methodists had marked 1972-73 during which I had preached at Ballynafeigh Methodist Church in Unity Week and we had a joint service in Church of The Transfiguration when Cyril Haire preached. In the planning of the Belvoir Park estate, the Housing Trust had given the Methodist Church the opportunity to acquire a site for a church, as had the Presbyterians and ourselves. They did not immediately proceed with building. Late in 1971 the Methodists were seeking to use the Primary School for a Sunday School and there were rumours that the Methodists were about to activate the plan for a building and, with the approval of the Select Vestry, I approached Cyril Haire to see if there were any way in which we could help. I had a horror of another church building being erected for one hour's use per week. Was there no way in which we could perhaps share our facilities at least to help gather a Methodist congregation? Cyril Haire responded very positively and, although some Belvoir Methodists wanted a church of their own from the outset, they accepted the hospitality of Church of The Transfiguration for a 5.00pm service in the first place, and during the summer months there were Anglican and Methodist evening services on alternate Sundays. After long negotiations, it was agreed that the Methodists should acquire a site adjoining ours where a hall would be built; that we should facilitate the Methodists for regular Sunday services at 11.45am (the time of our principal service moving to 10.30am from April 1975), and that we should share facilities in the Methodist hall for Sunday School classes displaced from the church and for organisations like the Ranger Guides. We had half-yearly joint meetings where we thrashed out any problems. By ensuring that on very special occasions, like Confirmation with Holy Communion, our Methodist friends were consulted well in advance to be able to alter their time of worship, and by exercising discipline to make certain that the 10.30 service finished by 11.30, until I ceased to be rector in 1980 we had minimal problems.

The Methodist centre was opened after a service in Church of The Transfiguration by the President of the Methodist Conference, with Bishop George Quin also present. There remained an element in the Methodist congregation that felt unhappy with only having a hall and wanted a Methodist church. These people were to find their voice under my successor when the time-interval between the two morning services proved too short. By 1981 Cyril Haire and Derek Ritchie, the Methodist ministers involved with me, had also moved on and our successors hadn't the same ecumenical vision. Sadly, a new Methodist church was erected and the symbolic connecting path was closed off. There is a plaque in the Methodist Hall 'in recognition of the practical help and encouragement of the Church of Ireland Parish of Belvoir and a spirit of true Christian friendship which helped to make the opening of this centre possible'.

A new minister came to Belvoir Park Presbyterian Church in the person of Kenneth Weir, rather more senior than his predecessors, but we continued a good relationship as he became acquainted with the area. We got to know one another through school and in shared services built round a summer community festival that was organised for several summers. Kenneth Weir was a very serious person, of total integrity. He encountered a degree of difficulty within the congregation as some of the elders disagreed with his exegesis of the scriptures. I tried to give him as much moral support as possible, but after I left the situation deteriorated. This was in fact symptomatic of something that was happening in the Presbyterian Church as people who took a very conservative fundamentalist attitude to the bible were rising at every level. When elected as elders, they could make ministry difficult for the minister. I am always thankful that Select Vestries have no jurisdiction over the rector or curate as far as their preaching or pastoral ministry is concerned and that only the approval of churchwardens is required for the introduction of trial forms of service. A wise rector consults the Vestry but makes it clear that forms of service and choice of bible versions are outside their constitutional function. One of our young people, who occasionally visited the Christian Endeavour Group in Belvoir Presbyterian Church, reported to me that on the prayer wall was a request that members should pray for the Christians who were members of the Church of Ireland and that they should be defended from the false teaching given from the pulpit!

In 1975 I became, in addition to my other responsibilities, Church of Ireland Chaplain at Forster Green Hospital. This involved an afternoon service one month in three with the Presbyterian and Methodist chaplains. I also came into contact with the Roman Catholic Chaplain and we used to lunch together most Mondays after completing our mutual rounds. The first was also Parish Priest of Drumbo whose parish included Belvoir. Later the task was added to that of the chaplain at Musgrave Park Hospital. We organised a joint carol service for the walking patients for Christmas 1979. Here again, we were making progress!

CHAPTER NINE

Involvement with the Ministry of Readers
1969-96

In the autumn of 1969 W. J. Whittaker resigned from his responsibilities as Episcopal Convener of the Lay Readers in the diocese and suggested to Bishop Mitchell that I might be a suitable
replacement. When I was offered the appointment I was very
happy to accept as I had already some experience in
Knocknagoney and Belvoir of the value of this ministry and of
its potential in the years ahead. I did ask that the title should be
changed to Warden of Readers as in other dioceses in Ireland
and in the Church of England. At the beginning of December, I
invited the diocesan readers to meet me over tea in Belvoir Hall
and thus began a relationship in which I sought to look after
their well-being and encourage them in their ministry.

Readers are authorised unpaid lay ministers who, after training, are licensed to read Morning Prayer and Evening Prayer
and to preach. It is thought that the office derives from the medieval order of lectors and was revived in the Church of England
in 1866. The first lay readers were admitted in Ireland in 1911,
hence the all-Ireland service of thanksgiving in St Patrick's
Cathedral in 1991 at which Robin Eames, a one-time reader who
had helped me in Knock in 1960-61, by then Archbishop of
Armagh and Primate of All-Ireland, was the preacher. In the
1940s readers were few and far between. Often in country areas
a competent educated layman was invited by the bishop to become a reader, often with a minimum of training. This led to
what can most generously be termed congregational reluctance
to accept their ministry. In some places they were thought to be
what in the Presbyterian Church were called 'stickit ministers',
trainee ministers who for one reason or another failed to get
ordained but could be called upon in emergency situations to
officiate.

Training until the 1960s was very variable. Some had been

appointed on the grounds that they were schoolmasters who were used to teaching religion and conducting school assemblies. In the dioceses of Connor and of Down and Dromore, from about 1960 the General Readers' Examination of the Church of England had been used, a great advance. I had several times invigilated these exams for W. J. Whittaker and had shown interest in the syllabus. There were some incredible episcopal regulations; for example, a reader when receiving the collection was instructed not to place the collection plate on the Holy Table but to take it at once to a credence or side table, being careful not to offer any prayer concerning what was being received. As a sign of their office, readers wore a medallion on a ribbon round the neck like an olympic medal. At my first meeting with them, the Down readers asked that they might be allowed to wear the blue scarf which was the almost universal badge of office in the Church of England and in Connor diocese. The incoming bishop, George Quin, readily agreed to this request.

Soon after my appointment I was invited to London at the end of April 1970 for two day conferences about a major revision to the General Readers' Examination. This gave me the opportunity to meet the Honorary Secretary of the Central Readers' Board, Canon George King, who was rector of a small parish in the diocoese of Winchester, and gave himself to the promotion of the office of reader and who had played no small part in the total acceptance of reader ministry in England. There were more readers than priests in the Church of England and Sunday by Sunday they were involved in the worship life of their parishes, not just when no priest could be found. Over the next twenty five years, I maintained a close relationship with the CRB, with George King and with those who followed him as Honorary Secretary, as well as with the bishops who chaired the Board, among whom were Hugh Montifiore and Michael Baughen. I even persuaded the Board not to hold its AGM one year on 17 March as I pointed out that was a major festival which would mean that the Irish fraternal delegate could not be present!

As soon as I became warden for Down and Dromore it was clear that structures needed to be set up and a Diocesan Readers' Board to advise the bishop was the first step. The DRB's first task was to form selection meetings at which those who applied for consideration as possible candidate readers would be interviewed and recommended for training or not. The bishop could, of course, overrule the recommendation as Canon Law gave him total control over those who would be appointed. In my experience, he never did. It was useful to have him as a last resort for occasionally someone recommended for training proved totally unable to grasp what was required in a reader. I used to say to them that a priest might not be a good preacher or might conduct worship in a strange way, but because he was a holy man of God going about the parish might be an effective minister, but that a reader stood or fell by his ministry at the reading desk and pulpit. Next, the DRB adopted the revised GRE, which differed from the previous syllabus in that candidates were required to 'earth' their answers to ministry situations. No one could pass this exam just by mugging up a lot of facts. Several of our candidates had trouble with this and complained strongly to me, even suggesting that there was a bias against 'bible-believing evangelicals'. One graduate, a teacher, was mortified by being given a fail mark for his paper on the use of the bible. It was the first exam he had ever failed, but it was the first time he had been asked to apply his knowledge of the scriptures to life situations. He did a re-sit and passed. I was personally sorry when, after five years, the GRE was replaced by an essay system with continuing assessment. This led to the House of Bishops of the Church of Ireland setting up its own programme of training and assessment system.

Having said to the diocesan synod that I believed that we needed a reader in every parish, I encouraged people to offer for this ministry. However, one of my main tasks as warden proved to be dissuading the more obviously impossible candidates from proceeding. Sometimes an inquirer of whom I had high hopes went away. One who came to see me in 1972 didn't begin training until 1986, and had only two months of active ministry before succumbing to a terminal illness. In the early years of the 1970s we had a steady stream of candidates of excellent quality whom I was delighted to assist by advice and teaching. As part of the training before admission and licensing, new readers had to serve for six months with an experienced rector, hand-picked by the DRB. Many of them after licensing continued to minister in these parishes: Paul Hooper, who trained in Belvoir, became as well accepted a preacher as the rector himself. These well-qualified readers transformed the acceptability of the office throughout the diocese. This led to more and more people realising that this ministry might be one to which God was calling them.

As the office had been opened to women some time in the 1960s, for the first time we began to see women officiating and preaching. I knew that the first women candidates would have to be exceptional and indeed had to wait almost to the end of the decade before the admission of a woman reader, but in 1979 Eva Hales, who also did practical training with me in Belvoir, was admitted at a service in the Church of The Transfiguration. I had first met Eva when we were introducing junior badminton to Knocknagoney and she was part of the St Clement's Parish junior team. In some ways she was 'fast-tracked', being a specialist religious education teacher and was about to become one of the Church Missionary Society team. I have never forgotten her first trial sermon – only a woman could have thought it through – absolutely fascinating. Nor the fact that I had to comfort her in the vestry afterwards. She was so convinced that her sermon had been so awful that she burst into tears.

There were rumblings about the changes when the General Readers' Examination became the General Readers' Certificate and the House of Bishops, through Arthur Butler, bishop of Connor, asked me to convene a meeting of the wardens of all the dioceses. As a result, a sub-committee began preparing a purely Church of Ireland programme of study, and an arrangement that wardens would send candidates' essays to tutors in other dioceses to ensure that a national standard was achieved. I don't know that this was ever totally successful although I regularly moderated essays from Armagh diocese and reciprocated by sending to that diocese. By the time I moved to Waterford, the system was in its infancy.

When I arrived in Waterford Bishop Willoughby asked me to continue my involvement with Reader Ministry and to maintain the cross-channel link. I worked with Adrian Empey and Bill Parker but we found the distances involved in the South East made tutorial work much more difficult and only achieved a couple of Saturday gatherings of readers and trainees. As I describe elsewhere, I found myself the tutor of a group of six candidates in Waterford and came to see the potential for self-teaching and group work. The day in 1983, when five readers were admitted and licensed, was the high point in my involvement with Reader Ministry.

On return to Down in 1984 the warden, John Dinnen, persuaded me act as tutor in two departments, Worship and Doctrine. I insisted on working with tutorial groups and over the next fifteen years had over forty students. They travelled from all over the diocese to meet with me in Down Cathedral. Most of these actually became readers – some indeed have proceeded to ordained ministry, both auxiliary and full-time. There were two or three who found that they couldn't keep up with the work and I had to advise them that if they couldn't find time at this stage, what would it be like if they were actually out in parishes. The training regime is part of the testing of vocation.

In the Lecale Group, I relied heavily on the support of readers. Jim Sims had been allocated to the Group on its formation by Bishop Eames, travelling three Sundays per month from Holywood. Over the next fifteen years I invited readers to join the ministry team, usually seeking commitment for one Sunday a month on which they conducted worship in two churches. Goff Mason, Brian Parker and Richard Dadswell, like Jim Sims, discovered vocations to ordained ministry partly as a result of their readership. Others who became regular members of the 'team' were Marsden FitzSimons, Sam Magowan and Derek Capper. One or two others came as 'emergency' cover. The parishioners accepted their ministry as on a par with that of non-stipendiary clergy and the full-time priests and deacons – a far cry from the day when knowing that the officiant was 'only a reader' meant a fall-off in attendance.

The House of Bishops was concerned that there was no church-wide co-ordination of Reader Ministry and I was asked in 1986 if I would become Central Co-ordinator. Having been assured of a modest budget, I was happy to do so and, with Bishop Willoughby as link to the House of Bishops, an annual or semi-annual meeting of wardens was held. I visited some diocesan readers' gatherings in Derry, Armagh, Cork and Waterford. The

approved programme of training was revised and I revived the
link with the Central Readers' Conference, under whose new
constitution, representatives of the Church of Ireland, the
Scottish Episcopal Church and the dioceses of the Church in
Wales were given voices but not votes. This allowed me to share
in the annual summer conferences where I used time to educate
readers about the Church of Ireland and the realities of living in
a divided community. Those visits to Lancaster, York, Lincoln
and Bournemouth were perhaps the 'perks' of being CCO but
were also unique opportunities for personal ministry and building up relationships within the Anglican Communion in these
islands. As CCO, I organised the all-Ireland eighty years celebration in 1991 and a very useful all-Ireland residential conference, based on the pattern of the English conferences, in County
Meath in 1994.

In 1995 I came to the conclusion that twenty-five years at the
front of organising reader ministry was enough. As a young
warden I had brought vision and enthusiasm and, on reflection,
had achieved much. Reader ministry was much more widely accepted than in 1970 and appeared to have a continuing place,
even with the emergence of non-stipendiary ordained ministry.
In 1995 I had little sympathy with the concept of 'parish readers'
– either as mere service takers – or who would be given sermons
written by the diocesan warden or others to read. I am firmly of
the opinion that, given proper training, such people can become
readers who can take material from commentaries and books,
make it their own and so communicate the faith as lay people to
lay people. I advised the House of Bishops in that year that I intended to step down on completion of ten years.

The diocese of Down and Dromore has continued to ask me
to tutor in Worship and Doctrine. When I retired in 2001 I indicated that I was still prepared to cover the first of these parts of
the Readers' Training Course but have bequeathed the adventure of tutoring in Christian Doctrine to a younger man!

CHAPTER TEN

Belvoir II

Diocesan Renewal 1969-80

During almost all my ministry in Belvoir the diocese of Down and Dromore was engaged in a Campaign of Renewal. Although elements from the almost contemporary charismatic renewal became involved, that did not play any part in its conception or central direction. Some day someone may research the history of this attempt to allow God to renew his church in the diocese; that is not my purpose here. Involvement in the Campaign of Renewal changed my outlook on ministry and re-shaped it for the future. My experience was also the experience of many other priests and lay people in the diocese and, in so far as there were parallel developments in other dioceses, brought changes to the whole Church of Ireland.

It is often said that the concept of the Campaign of Renewal was that of George Quin on his election to Down and Dromore, never by George Quin himself. The concept was a development of an idea floated at a meeting of the clergy of Hillsborough Rural Deanery by one of its members early in 1969. In reaction to what he felt was a spiritually lack lustre plan to mark in 1970 the centenary of the disestablishment of the Church of Ireland, William Neely proposed a national mission, involving study, prayer and evangelism. The clergy were persuaded by the careful thinking that had gone into Neely's proposal and he was charged to take the ideas to Bishop Mitchell and to the Centenary Committee. The latter decided plans for 1970 were complete and that they were satisfied with them. Bishop Mitchell commended Neely's suggestion to the archdeacons, George Quin and Samuel Crooks, and told the diocesan clergy at his farewell gathering how encouraged he had been with this vision for the future.

Thus it was that, after his consecration, Bishop Quin decided to make Diocesan Renewal the mainstream of his episcopate and appointed William Neely as Diocesan Missioner. From then on a flow of ideas, proposals and plans flowed from Mount Merrion rectory. An advisory committee was called into being of which three future bishops were members, Robin Eames, Gordon McMullan and James Mehaffey. I was also a member and became one of the leaders of clergy study groups which were set up throughout the diocese. Neely wrote a book, *Into the Future*, for study at monthly meetings and on which feedback was co-ordinated by Colin Capper, then a rector in Lurgan. These groups, because they didn't coincide with rural deanery chapters, had a life independent of the diocesan structures and became important in breaking down barriers which had existed between clergy of the diocese, either on the basis of churchmanship or seniority. The use of Christian names as a matter of course, rather than 'Archdeacon' or 'Dean', made a tremendous difference. Several of the groups also met regularly for shared prayer early in the morning. A series of two-day mid-week visits to the diocese of Coventry in England, a diocese in mission, further facilitated this coming together of clergy. What were sometimes referred to as 'Neely's Package Tours' involved three carloads of clergy travelling overnight on the Belfast-Heysham route, a drive down the M4, staying together in the diocesan retreat house, meetings with key leaders, clerical and lay, visits to Coventry Cathedral and taking in Choral Evensong at Lichfield, followed by dinner together.

It was April 1972 before I got my turn to go to Coventry. My critical faculties were working overtime as I detected rather more Christian Union type of thinking in the Coventry team than I was completely happy with, until I met the rector of Holy Trinity, Coventry, Lawrence Jackson, one of the bishop's right hand men. He met us in his rectory, dressed in grey cassock, greeted us as 'fathers' and spoke from a full Anglo-Catholic perspective of how mission and renewal worked in his parish. I saw that one could affirm the best in the evangelical and catholic traditions.

That evening, having met the laity, I decided that I would have to learn how to pray informally with others, for this was not something that had been in my SCM tradition upbringing

and I had never used anything other than collects known by
heart in one to one ministry. I spoke to another new area rector
about this who agreed that it hadn't been part of his tradition either. We decided to meet for a few weeks and try to learn by
doing. That rector was Robin Eames and from May 1972 until his
consecration as bishop in 1975 we used to meet for half and hour
on Friday mornings in one another's churches. Experiencing
informal prayer was probably the most significant change in my
way of ministering. It was the kind of change that meant that
when clergy from Down and Dromore spent a night at the
Theological College a few year's later, the principal was taken by
surprise with the natural way clergy of different traditions engaged in a time of open prayer during the late evening service.

From time to time people with a particular contribution were
brought to Ireland. I remember meeting Terry Waite, then working on lay training for the Church Army, one of the few people
who topped me in height, and Geoffrey Paul, later bishop of
Bradford. Each year a major diocesan service was held. To these,
leading English bishops accepted invitation – Cuthbert
Bardsley, bishop of Coventry, and Stuart Blanch when bishop of
Liverpool among them.

Renewal wasn't only for clergy. By 1972 we had set up inter-
parish lay-clerical study groups to which each rector was asked
to nominate three or four representatives according to parish
size. Study guides, on the lines of the SCM study guides of my
university days, were written by William Neely. The success or
failure of these was in proportion to the enthusiasm of the leaders. In Holywood and Bangor they went very well. In rural
areas, these lay-clergy study groups did not work well, partly
due to people being unwilling to travel on winter evenings because of possible IRA violence. The groups attended by parishioners of Belvoir – I wasn't involved as the advisory committee
members stayed out of these – were a mixture. One of my main
hopes for future leadership dropped out because of acute theological disagreement with a conservative evangelical curate
about the meaning of salvation! Members of these groups were
also offered weekends at Holy Trinity, Coventry, Stratford and
Rugby. I was able to send two or three parishioners for these and
it certainly opened eyes as to possibilities.

Members of the basic groups were offered the opportunity for further lay-training. William Neely and Bishop Quin conceived the idea of having authorised lay workers who would assist clergy in passing on the ideas and principles of renewal. I cannot remember that the advisory committee were given any opportunity to discuss this in any detail, or any idea of how the 'bishop's workers' might be deployed. We were simply asked to be responsible for area-training and I worked with Jack Mercer in the Bangor area training group. This was most rewarding even if it meant journeying to Bangor once a month (and as time went by, a very late return for fellowship tended to continue into supper in the homes of one or other members).

In 1974 and 1975 the advisory group was taken to Oxford after Easter with the opportunity, with clergy from Coventry, to meet with and listen to really top theologians like Professor John Macquarrie. This was important because it emphasised that renewal had to be fully intellectual, with those in leadership keeping their minds renewed. The members wrote two series of essays which were circulated for discussion in the diocese. My contribution to the first had been a honest appraisal of the ecumenical situation in Northern Ireland, where I saw a lot of lip service being given to ecumenism and prophesied that the Presbyterian Church would draw back from any deeper commitment. For the second, I contributed an essay on worship and, at the last moment, one on something that I had begun to research – charismatic renewal.

York 1975

Until April 1975 this had been almost entirely academic: I read the increasingly large amount of literature and was aware that Cecil Kerr, whom I had known at Trinity, had given up his position as chaplain at Queen's University to found a Christian Renewal Centre at Rostrevor. Another lay weekend had been planned: this time to a very thriving church in York, St Michael-le-Belfry. William Neely had sensed that there was probably little left for clergy or laity to learn from the Coventry experience and had gone to visit various people in the North East of England whom he thought might help with future clergy in-service training. This had brought him to the 'tweedy' archdeacon of York who suggested that it might be worth his while seeing David Watson, who was doing some 'interesting' things. David Watson was able to see Neely and they instantly 'clicked' as they talked about what the former was discovering about shared ministry in his church. Watson declined just to come and share his ideas, but invited people from Down to 'come and see', offering hospitality for a weekend. Four parishioners from Belvoir were to be among the party. There had been a certain amount of publicity about David Watson's parish and Bishop Quin asked me to go with the party to 'keep an eye on things'!

On arrival I was immediately captivated by the personality of David Watson and the introductory talk that he gave us was everything I could have wished in its biblical content, application and awareness of the reality of life in 1975. I had my doubts about the programme, with Holy Communion 'tacked on' to the Evening Service. I reacted rather strongly to what I considered bad exegesis by David Smith, one of the ministry team, on the first evening and had to be restrained. Sunday morning's family service introduced me to the use of an overhead projector and cartoons to illustrate a fairly bland biblical story for children. The music was of a completely new kind – light, bouncy and memorable – a singing group and a children's orchestra. Different. I sat in the balcony and parishioners sat in pews near the front which gave them a view of the congregation. They simply couldn't get over the looks of sheer joy and enthusiasm in the faces of the congregation. In the afternoon, in response to a request, a member of the congregation talked very simply about the place speaking and praying in tongues had in her devotional life.

Evening service came and a superb sermon on the life of the early church and how that could be experienced today, from David Watson. After an hour and a quarter, those who wanted to leave were given the opportunity. To my surprise of a total congregation of over five hundred not more than one fifth left and we went on to the communion according to the English *Series* 3 experimental form, north side celebration, surplices, scarves and hoods being worn. Yet, there was something different. It was a very prayerful congregation and, once administration of communion began, the singing group began singing gentle worshipful hymns. I had a tremendous sense of the presence of God in which I was as it were caught up, with angels and archangels and all the company of heaven. It was as if my father, who had died a few months earlier, was with me in the pew. I was overwhelmed with a sense of peace and tears poured from my eyes. Only once before had I experienced anything like it as I walked up to receive the sacrament and returned to my place. That was on that St Patrick's Day where the sense of the presence had confirmed my path to ordination. After the service, William Neely wanted a time for 'assessment' of what we had learned that day. I protested and was backed by the vast majority: 'Not tonight. Tomorrow.' It had been an experience of personal renewal, some would call it being filled with the Spirit. It hadn't been sought or prayed for. It just happened.

Next day I found that others had had a similar experience, one that would change their lives, at least one was set on a road that led to ordination and others found their prayers coming alive. They were set to play decisive parts in the future of parish and diocese. There were some whose experiences were rather less positive; this was to be expected. Partly that was due to insensitive hosts and hostesses whose extreme evangelicalism was found to be off-putting. Partly it was the newness of the forms of worship – no chanted canticles, the use of electric guitars and so on. Unfortunately they didn't recognise the hand of a real musician in the arrangements performed. On return to Ireland, some of these were not slow to acquaint those in leadership with their negative reactions and the fact that Brian Mayne, the one sent to ensure stability, was enthusiastic and believed there were lessons to be learned.

Follow-up
The five of us from Belvoir decided to meet the following week to consider what we could take on board from the weekend. We recognised that the people in York claimed that the growth of their congregation and the way lives were renewed stemmed, not from Sunday worship, but from their weekly evening of prayer and bible study, and we concluded that that was one thing we could commit ourselves to – one evening a week we would meet to study the bible and to pray together. For six

weeks we did this in our homes and invited one or two others to
join us. After that we 'went public' and for the next five years the
Thursday evening prayer and bible study became part of our
parish programme.

I visited York in December 1975 and shared in a Thursday
night bible study. There were elements in it with which I was
less than happy; next morning I spent time in an almost deserted
Minster where I encountered a Swedish nun who recognised me
from the previous evening and, during our talk, she spoke of her
concern about the evening. When she found I had shared her
unease she said that I had lifted a burden as she thought the
fault had to be in her. I suggested that she went and talked to
David Watson himself. There were always problems in a gathered congregation as there were people with their own agendas
who were not prepared to wait on God for guidance.

A further weekend lay visit took place in 1976 by which time
David Watson had accepted an invitation to lead a diocese-wide
mission in 1977 with a team from his church. Once again I was
accompanied by some parishioners, already partners in our
Thursday evenings. There had been developments in the worship life of the York congregation in the twelve months –
Sunday evening service was now a complete Holy Communion
and on Saturday evening we shared a typical Praise and Bible
Study evening during which we looked forward to Mission in
1977. Elements of 'prophecy' were now accepted in the Sunday
service; with this I had considerable difficulty. On this occasion
the strong point of my worship experience came during traditional Choral Evensong in York Minster when the second lesson
spoke directly to me, and I knew that I had to be obedient and
seek reconciliation with someone who had offended me.

Mission 77
By the time Mission 77 began, William Neely had left the diocese
for a parish in Cashel and Jim Mehaffey was the diocesan missioner. I worked very closely with him and was present at almost all the events. One that gave me special pleasure was the
Sunday afternoon youth rally which was held at the Church of
The Annunciation, Knocknagoney, which was packed solid
with young people, sitting on hassocks from the Chapel of The

Magnificat when they ran out of clinging space on the pews. The 'theatre' at the front was ideal for the singing group and the drama. David Watson held those young people spellbound and I know at least one for whom it was a defining moment in her faith-journey.

Five nights in Belfast Cathedral were the core of the York team's week. And it wasn't only people from the diocese of Down and Dromore who came. On Ash Wednesday evening a rather sceptical Presbyterian assistant minister from a conservative fundamentalist background decided to see what this Anglican minister had to offer. What he heard changed David Armstrong's life, led him into ecumenical encounters of which he could never have dreamed and ultimately to what can only be called persecution from the closed mind. I don't know what were the words that changed David Armstrong's life but I remember two or three sentences which were spoken with special power: 'There are no Roman Catholics in heaven,' said David Watson. 'There are no Anglicans in heaven; there are no Presbyterians, Methodists or Baptists. There are only sinners redeemed by the blood of Jesus Christ.' It was a particularly powerful address. Over the five nights dozens of people found that God was challenging them to change their lives. It is estimated that more than half of the candidates for ordination in the next few years, as well as a number who went on to become readers, looked back to Mission 77 as being decisive in their lives.

For some the challenge both in clarity of David Watson's teaching and his own sacrifical lifestyle which had enabled the creation of a unique team ministry was almost too much. Yet others failed to see that this was no simplistic evangelical message but one that, while rooted in the sacramental life of the Church of England, was larger than any one denomination. David Watson felt that the tragedy of the Northern Ireland conflict could only be solved through deep repentance and a search for healing after centuries of behaviour that had stained all denominations of Christians. In the summer of 1977 he gave the address at the National Assembly of Evangelicals in England in which he described the Reformation as a tragedy: a headline catching phrase not immediately appreciated by those who celebrate it as the time when the errors of the western church in the

Middle Ages were confronted, and instead of reform happening within, the visible church became fractured. Since then Christians in different parts of the church have spent all too much of their time, digging in and fighting with one another. In Ireland the post-Reformation divisions have been linked in a political power struggle. Ian Paisley's Free Presbyterian Church fastened on reports of that summer address and their supporters picketed a Mission David Watson led in Carrickfergus Presbyterian Church in October 1977 and a Praise Service arranged for Belfast Cathedral at the end of it. Members of the congregation ran the gauntlet of the Paisleyite pickets who sang hymns outside as we began the worship within the cathedral.

After the York team went home in March, Mission 77 continued with parish study groups meeting. For this Canon Mehaffey had asked me to prepare some guidelines which were published in a booklet, *A Fleet of Ships – worship, fellowship, discipleship, stewardship*. Then we prepared for three further nights in Belfast Cathedral towards the end of June with Stuart Blanch, by then archbishop of York, as speaker. It was decided that some kind of home-grown singing group was needed. Jim Mehaffey encouraged Jim Sims of Holywood to gather such a group and I was asked to work alongside the group in preparing for the services. Because of Jim Sims' musical skills and the talents of the young people concerned, this was a very successful undertaking and although the archbishop did not draw anything like the numbers we had had for the gatherings led by David Watson, there were positive indications of ways forward for the church, particularly in affirming the new kind of music in worship. I was to have a continuing relationship with the Diocesan Singers until I went to Waterford, particularly with their participation in three special weekends for Belvoir and its neighbouring parish, Drumbo.

Bishop Quin invited Archbishop Blanch to conduct a Quiet Day for clergy in Church of The Transfiguration during his June visit and our parish provided lunch and refreshments. Stuart Blanch didn't know beforehand where he was going to be speaking. He had chosen to reflect on the transfiguration of Christ and there behind him in the stained glass window was the perfect visual aid.

The climax of Mission 77 was an open-air celebration of Holy Communion in the playing fields of Cherryvale, off Ravenhill Road. This was at the suggestion of Archbishop Blanch who had seen something similar in Liverpool diocese but I do not think had ever been attempted in Belfast before. We got a superb Saturday as far as the weather was concerned and, although the organisers were to some extent disappointed at the number attending, realising that as yet sacramental worship was not as central to the life of the Church of Ireland as in the Church of England, left us well satisfied.

Between September 1977 and May 1978 Bishop Quin attempted to carry on the momentum of Mission 77 with area services at which he became the missioner and for which he sought the backing and support of what became known as the Diocesan Singers. These services brought out the very best in George Quin and I have particularly strong memories of the service for the Lecale area, held in the lovely St Anne's Church, Killough, right on the edge of the Irish Sea and that for the Ards peninsular in Ballyhalbert. At the latter, when the bishop spoke of the weakness of our prayers there was such silence: everyone knew the bishop was speaking with an awareness of real need.

1977-80

I sought to anchor the Diocesan Renewal Programme in the parish of Belvoir as we moved on from Mission 77. Although I didn't expect Belvoir to become another St Michael-le-Belfry, I had a conviction that there was to be some spiritual development. It came in an unexpected way. For almost ten years I had attempted every kind of programme for involving young people in the life of the parish in a more positive way. Youth Guilds and Youth Clubs were started and collapsed. Some people in the congregation had taken offence when we allowed table tennis and darts on a Sunday evening. One in particular transferred her allegiance to the Presbyterian Church although her husband, a member of General Synod, stayed. The 1977 confirmation class was a most unpromising group, but I began praying for each one individually every morning and, when the time came for them to be confirmed, they asked if they couldn't have some kind of Youth Fellowship. There were two girls in their

very late teens who offered to help with leadership and so a
Sunday night Youth Fellowship was launched. Young people in
St Finnian's, Cregagh, helped to guide the leaders and they encountered other young people in larger youth gatherings once a
month at Dundonald Methodist Church, where the curate of
Dundonald Parish, Kenneth Clarke, now bishop of Kilmore, impressed me with his very clear biblical teaching about the nature
of the church. We were also supported by the new curate of
Willowfield Parish. Kenneth Good, now bishop of Derry, was
trying to allow the Holy Spirit to breathe new life in that area as
well. It was, as I have said already, one of the features of the
Renewal Campaign that people of varying shades of opinion
worked closely together. My two study outlines were used in
parishes of a strongly evangelical tradition; and I was able to
find in the two Kenneths evangelicals who encouraged my more
sacramental expression of faith. Even in the early days of their
ministry, I perceived in them teachers and encouragers of others; no wonder they were destined to become bishops in the
church.

Experience in the Youth Fellowship led a student at Newtownbreda High School to conclude that God was calling him to ordination. After over twenty years in Holy Orders here was the first
parishioner to come to tell me what I had told Canon Fred
L'Estrange, twenty five years before, that he believed he had a vocation. Francis Rutledge was still at school and he would have a
rocky path before he was ordained in 1986 for the curacy of
Holywood. At the time of writing he is rector of Carrigrohane on
the north west side of Cork city.

Hands across the border
At the end of 1977 in partnership with John Bell, rector of neighbouring Drumbo parish, we held a parish 'renewal weekend'.
We both agreed that this would anchor diocesan renewal in the
parish. I had also been very concerned since becoming a member of General Synod in 1976 of the danger of the Church of
Ireland dividing into two 'churches' – the Church of Northern
Ireland and the Church of Southern Ireland. Two 'locum' holidays in Gorey, Co Wexford in 1974 and 1975 had convinced me
that in both 'jurisdictions' members of the Church of Ireland

need to understand each other and seek God's guidance together. For that reason I invited a friend from college days to come and speak to both congregations. Stanley Baird was at the time Warden of the Church's Ministry of Healing. Both John Bell and I agreed that it was an appropriate time to introduce a public opportunity of receiving the ministry of laying on of hands with prayer for healing. This took place at the final evening service of Holy Communion when both congregations came together.

I have written above of my experience in my first curacy of ministering the laying on of hands in a pastoral ministry situation. I had continued to exercise this aspect of ministry to the sick but had refrained from doing so in church services. There had been unfortunate examples of 'healers' in the Belfast area who gathered large congregations and promised wonderful healings in the Lord's name but had proved to be tricksters and charlatans. The Church's Ministry of Healing worked quietly and sympathetically in three centres, the Mount in East Belfast, in Londonderry and at St Andrew's, Dublin, where Stanley Baird had been for several years Warden and director. I felt that I could trust Stanley in what he would say in the pulpit and in what he would do. I had also experienced for myself the ministry of laying on of hands at a service in York presided over by Bishop Morris Maddocks, author of the most sane and sensible book on the subject. The service was everything that I had hoped for – at the suggestion of Stanley the laying on of hands took place after the administration of communion as those who wished to be prayed for returned to the communion rails and two of the clergy laid hands while one recited the prayer. Very simple, very restrained: there were no dramatic occurrences.

At the beginning of Advent in 1978 we had a second such weekend. This time Donegal-born Billy Gibbons, rector of one of the liveliest Dublin suburban parishes, came to be with us and preached in the two parish churches separately in the morning and at a joint service of Holy Communion and healing in the evening. I had been to Kill o' the Grange earlier in the year to lead bible study at their parish weekend. So this was another case of hands across the Border.

A non-stipendiary curate

On St Andrew's Day in 1978 the first ordination service took place in Church of The Transfiguration when Andrew Stewart and Desmond Logan were ordained as the first non-stipendiary deacons in the diocese of Down and Dromore. Several years before, the General Synod had legislated permitting men to be ordained who would continue to earn their living in secular occupations. The House of Bishops had drawn up regulations for their training locally in the diocese, with standards being monitored by the staff of the Theological College in Dublin. James Mehaffey and I were appointed by Bishop Quin to co-ordinate and oversee the training of Down and Dromore candidates. Then Jim Mehaffey became Canon Missioner and responsibility was left with Alwyn Maconachie and myself. Two men had been accepted as candidates, Andrew Stewart, reader and parishioner of Dundonald, who had completed the Church of England General Ordination Examination as an extern candidate. He required little training to complete the bishops' requirements. Desmond Logan had to undertake the whole course and with the help of Richard Clarke, then curate of Holywood, who covered history and part of the doctrine, I tutored Desmond over a period of two years during which he used to come to the rectory for an hour once a week from 9.00am to 10.00am. This was possible because he was a civil servant, working nearby with flexi-hours. Both had satisfied the authorities; and the bishop and his advisors invited me to a meeting to agree placements after ordination. To my total surprise, after Andrew Stewart, who was taking early retirement from the Post Office, was placed at Ballymacarett, the bishop turned to me and asked me if I would be prepared to have Desmond Logan as a part-time curate. It gave us both pleasure, the more so when the ordination took place in Belvoir. So for the first time I had a partner in leadership, in leading worship, preaching and to a limited extent in pastoral ministry. Desmond Logan fitted in so well into the parish and we developed a strong partnership over the final fifteen months of my Belvoir ministry.

Because we had the same views on the ministry of healing we were able to offer the ministry of laying on of hands with prayer on a regular basis on the Sunday in the month when we had Holy Communion in the evening. We never saw startling cures take place before our eyes but we both believed that God was at work in this ministry. One parishioner who came forward regularly said to me after about a year, 'You know I suffered from vertigo. That is why I sought the ministry. All I can say is that I used to have attacks every few weeks but I haven't had any for almost a year. Yes. I believe God has answered our prayers.'

A pastoral council
Several times in 1979 I was approached by parochial nominators and I knew that my name must be on the list as someone to be given a different charge. I had met two sets of nominators and knew before they left that I wasn't what they were looking for. I had too many radical ideas in worship and ministry for two rather settled parishes. I was in no hurry to move as innovations like a parish council had just been introduced. This was totally unofficial, made up of members of Select Vestry and others whom I felt could advise me in planning developments in pastoral ministry for the new decade. Unlike the Select Vestry, this was advisory and those invited were people who were prepared to pray together. They were shy about it and so was I: it was very much a group with L-plates on.

In Advent 1979, just after Desmond Logan was priested, we had the third cross-border visitor to conduct a joint weekend. This time it was Horace McKinley, with whom I had developed a good relationship following a visit with the Diocesan Singers to his parish in South Dublin. His hospitality offered and accepted had made Whitechurch Vicarage my base for General Synod from 1977. It was another memorable occasion. Chatting after supper on Sunday evening, Horace suddenly said to me, 'Brian, would you ever think of taking an appointment in the South?' How I kept my composure I don't know, because the Bishop of Cashel had phoned earlier in the week to ask me if I would allow my name to be considered for the vacancy in Waterford, and as we had sat at lunch I had taken a call from Austin Earl, arranging for Valerie and myself to travel down there the following week.

CHAPTER ELEVEN

Waterford

New parish, diocese and province

The biggest change of my ministry came when I was nominated rector of Holy Trinity with St Olaf's, St Patrick's and St Thomas, Rathculliheen and Kilmacow in the diocese of Waterford and, on acceptance of the nomination, appointed dean of the Cathedral of the Blessed Trinity. That was 14 December 1979. How did it come about that a rector of a Belfast new area parish could move over 200 miles? In fact it was symptomatic of the realisation that diocesan boundaries were becoming more flexible with the continuing shrinkage of the ordained ministry.

The bishop of Cashel and Ossory, John Armstrong, had been the preacher at the fifth anniversary of the consecration of the Church of the Transfiguration in 1970. He had seen me in action at General Synod in 1978-9 when I had put through a private member's bill to allow designated lay persons approved by the bishop to administer the chalice, thus freeing many readers from a monthly commitment. A late night phonecall asked if I would be interested in being considered for the vacancy in Waterford. 'What vacancy?' was my reaction. I wasn't aware that Fergus Day had retired. Anyway, I allowed my name to go to the Board of Nomination and in due course was invited by Austin Earl, brother of the dean of Ferns, to travel to Waterford with Valerie 'to see and be seen' by the parochial nominators.

It happened that the evening of the interview was our fifteenth wedding anniversary, so we let people know that we were going away to celebrate it. I'll never forget my first sight of Waterford City. Driving in on the road from New Ross on a wet December afternoon with the smoke drifting over the River Suir, it looked what I imagined one of the worst Welsh mining valleys would be like. Austin Earl was waiting as we arrived at the Tower Hotel and immediately took us to see the Deanery – apologising that we would see it at its worst – plans were in hand for double-glazing, re-decoration etc. It was a good modern house in the suburbs – by no means off-putting. Then it was on to the cathedral – already dark but well-lighted. A liturgical nonsense – classical 1777 building, re-ordered in the late 19th century with Gothic choir stalls but with a spacious sanctuary, free-standing altar laid out for westward celebration. The moment I walked into that building I knew that I could say my prayers there. It had that numinous atmosphere, and although I could see that there was evidence of years of neglect and decay, there was also hope of renewal. We learned that, since Bishop de Pauley's time, a programme of restoration had been slowly in hand, financed by Waterford millionaire Ambrose Congreve.

The nominators, Austin Earl, Bob Morrison, David Bate and Robert McBride, entertained us to dinner. When Valerie and I toasted one another with pre-meal sherries they discovered the significance of the evening and made the meal a real celebration. Afterwards we drove out to Grantstown – the Earl family home on the Dunmore Road. There, with Valerie present, I was interviewed – the best and fullest interview I ever had by nominators. My method of answering was to refuse to say what I'd do in the future but to relate the questions to my past experience. When asked how I'd tackle the responsibilities and problems it may have sounded a bit pious – with reliance on the guidance and strength of the Holy Spirit, using the gifts I had been given for ministry.

However, there were many practical problems to face – financial, transferring from one jurisdiction to another, and, most significantly, education for our two daughters. We had a good look round Waterford – and in 1979 it wasn't a very prepossessing city. Of course we had to have the required tour of the Waterford Crystal factory. Little did we think it would be the first of dozens of such tours. As we left the city late on Friday morning and talked together in the car on the long drive home, the practical problems seemed so great that we felt sure that even if appointed it was unlikely that we would ever return to Waterford. I would have to let the bishop know very soon if I wished to leave my name on the table.

When we got back to Belfast on the Saturday I told my sister, who was just about to announce her engagement to Bishop Arthur Butler of Connor diocese, what we had been up to, and gave her permission to tell Bishop Butler to see what he had to say. This was especially valuable as a former dean of Waterford, Noble Hamilton, was his uncle. They both encouraged me, and I recalled a promise I had made years before: that I would never seek a parish but if it seemed good to a Board of Nomination and the Holy Spirit, I would go where I was called. If God was in all this I had to be available, so I phoned Austin Earl to confirm that I was still interested. The following Tuesday, by coincidence, the bishop of Cashel and Ossory was giving the addresses at the diocesan quiet day in Down Cathedral. On his way in he saw me, raised an eyebrow in a characteristic way, and said, 'Well?' I replied, 'I am available.' He said, 'It's up to the Board. I'll phone you on Friday night.'

Friday night came. I sat in my study all evening. The phone never rang. Then at 10.30am Bishop Armstrong phoned, apologising for being so late but he expected I'd been out in the parish. At 7 o'clock the Board had nominated me for the vacant parish. Would I accept the nomination? On my answering in the affirmative, he appointed me dean of Waterford. Would I please get in touch with Alan Johnston, the Church of Ireland Press Officer in Belfast? (Alan would later be one of my Lecale parishioners.) That was one of the first indications that the way the diocese of Cashel and Ossory operated was very different to the efficiently organised Diocesan Office in Belfast. And Cashel (at least) needed to change very quickly. I was to find myself the catalyst for the change, so much so that after I left the diocese someone described me as a 'six foot four inch steamroller'. That would lie in the future. Family members were pleased. With my sister's engagement announcement earlier in the week – now this – the Mayne family couldn't keep out of the papers. Bishop George Quin professed to be shocked when I phoned him. Of course he knew that I was being considered, but he never thought I would accept.

It was from then on in a very strange Christmas – my last in Belvoir. Three further flying visits to Waterford – one with daughters to arrange schooling – one thanks to gracious overnight half-way house hospitality both ways from Bishop

Donald Caird of Meath and his wife in Leixlip – the adventure was on. I scarcely remember the months of January and February going past. There were all kinds of farewells including those from the Diocesan Singers, the Bangor Bishop's Worker Group and the parish of Belvoir at which the star attraction of the evening was the Youth Fellowship's 'Cultural Delegation from Waterford' complete with mufflers, shillelaghs and many begorrahs! Whether they really thought we were going to the bogs, they certainly knew that we were to experience many kinds of change. On our penultimate Sunday in Belvoir Bishop Quin came for confirmation and among those confirmed was daughter Barbara, about to be up-rooted from a school into which she had happily settled. Tuesday 26 February came. The furniture van was loaded. We set off for life in the Republic of Ireland.

Institution and installation
It was indeed a very different Deanery, vastly transformed from what we had seen in early December. Through the windows we could see brightly burning fires in both grates. Terry Hilliard, the wonderful cathedral Treasurer, had been in to prepare for us. A parcel containing a cooked chicken was in the hall, a present from Miss B. Finnegan, just a sample of fantastic kindness that parishioners showered on us for the next four and a half years. Overnight we stayed with the cathedral Secretary and his wife, Edward and Mildred James, round the corner from the Deanery. Next day the furniture van arrived. That evening the 'mafia' rallied round to help unload and set us up in the house. We can still hear David Coulter directing the men of the church and see David Bate on his back helping to manoeuvre a bed into the fourth bedroom. We had Friday to adjust, and then came Saturday 1 March – institution and installation. Family and friends came from the North; W. J. Whittaker, who was to 'preach me in' on Sunday morning, came from Dublin. We arrived at the Cathedral to be met by Alex Bell the verger: 'Welcome, Mr Dean.' The service sheet had had to be revised at the last possible moment, for earlier in the week Bishop John Armstrong had been elected archbishop of Armagh and had instantly taken office. There would be prayers for John, archbishop

of Armagh and Brian, our dean. All this had been capably taken care of by Canon Leslie Enright, retired from Limerick, who had cared diligently for the parish in the months of the interregnum. Leslie had smoothed the way for a young dean – in eight months of pastoral ministry re-built the people's expectation after years in which a dean with declining health had been just about able to keep the machinery of the parish ticking over. However, Brian Mayne's document of institution to the cure of souls in all those parishes mentioned earlier, had been written in the name of John, bishop of Cashel and Ossory, and the see of Cashel and Ossory had been vacant for five days! Was I ever legally incumbent or dean? Strictly speaking a new deed should have been drawn by which Henry, archbishop of Dublin as guardian of the spiritualities of the vacant see, would have conferred on me the cure etc. But Cashel didn't worry too much about the niceties. I couldn't imagine Dr Breene or Rossy Good, registrars with whom I'd had to do at institutions in Connor and Down, allowing it to pass.

What struck me first was that there were two bishops in the sanctuary, Archbishop John Armstrong and Bishop Michael Russell, the Roman Catholic bishop who was accompanied by John Shine, President of St John's College. The Minister of the combined Presbyterian and Methodist Congregation was there but I would have expected that. The Mayor in full regalia and the Waterford Branch of the Knights of Malta in their robes were part of the procession. One couldn't help noticing the evident age of the rest of the clergy in procession: only one of the diocesan clergy was less than twenty years older than me. The canons of the Cathedral were in their seventies. Clearly change was going to take place. How would they accept a dean at the age of forty-five?

Archbishop John was a favourite in Waterford city where he had lived until the merger of Cashel and Ossory in 1977. The community regarded him as their friend. This gave me a clue to the ecumenical dimension. The Church of Ireland was a welcome partner in the gospel, and John Armstrong and Michael Russell had forged that relationship. The archbishop's sermon dwelt on the fact that he was going North and I was coming South, emphasising the thing that I most wanted to stress, the unity of the church in this island and how we must strive to work together seeking peace and reconciliation throughout this island. RTÉ news cameras filmed parts of the service for the evening news. I wasn't so big-headed to think that it was because of me. The first public outing of the newly-elected Primate of All-Ireland just happened to be the installation of the Very Reverend Brian Mayne as dean of Waterford.

Ruthless change had already taken place over the past twenty years in the Church of Ireland in Waterford City. The Anglican population of Waterford parishes had fallen to a mere one per cent of the population of the city. There were hardly any 'working-class' members but an inordinate number of elderly spinsters in their seventies and eighties, the sweethearts of the huge number of Protestant men from the city who had lost their lives in World War I, whose framed sepia photographs I was to see on their mantlepieces. A good number of the cathedral congregation were 'blow-ins', who had come to Waterford through banking, insurance and other businesses. Some had come from Great Britain and some from continental Europe. These were the folk most ready for change, seeking more than just going through the motions when it came to Sunday worship.

Only the cathedral was now open for worship. St Patrick's Church had been handed over to the Presbyterian Church years before. An attempt had been made to use St Thomas's Ballynakill, about six miles out, for youth work: from its weathervane the church was locally known as the Brasscock Church and the Youth Club had incorporated that name in its title, but when I arrived they had decided it was too far out. Only the parish church of Rathculliheen (on the Ferrybank side of the river) was still usable. One request that the out-going bishop made was that I should investigate how to re-employ it as a place of worship. The total number of parishes which would be under the Waterford Group umbrella by January 1984 was actually twenty-nine – twenty nine parishes which in 1870 when the Church of Ireland was disestablished each had their own minister. Just thirty years earlier there had been six fulltime priests, including a curate, serving the ancient diocese of Waterford. In 1980 there were three and by 1984 just one. Ministry in the South-East was in a process of change. Little did I realise that

John Armstrong had already foreseen that Dunmore East and Tramore were no longer viable. It would fall to me to bring them into the Waterford Cathedral Group. He had kept this under his hat, probably realising that it would have dissuaded me from being interested. Leslie Enright however soon revealed what he knew to be the plan.

Further responsibilities
Amalgamation of parishes in the South and West had been on-going for decades. The Church of Ireland population had been shrinking at least since the establishment of the Irish Free State, after which a number of Protestants had moved out either to Great Britain or to the North. My wife's parents had been a case in point, her father having transferred to the Northern Ireland Civil Service. On top of this, the effect of the *Ne Temere* regulations in regard to marriages between members of the Church of Ireland and members of the Roman Catholic Church, requiring the children of such marriages to be baptised in the Roman Catholic Church and brought up as Roman Catholics, had been devastating. I could see this in Waterford City. There were family businesses that had been 'Protestant' a generation earlier. In the 1980s all the family members were Roman Catholics. Again, the changes in farming practice which also affected rural parishes in the East and North of Ireland meant there was no longer the same employment prospects: this had led in the Republic to a drift of young people to Dublin and emigration to England or further afield.

A decline in vocations to fulltime ministry had begun at the end of the fifties. There were the priests and there wasn't the money to maintain ministry and rectories everywhere. Ivan Biggs, priest-in-charge of Dunmore East, was anxious for a move to a more demanding ministry than the small number of families that made up that parish. Canon Jack Porter, rector of Tramore and Annestown, was not physically very strong, and wanted to retire as soon as he reached the age at which he could receive his state pension – although at that time the clergy retirement age was two years after that. The new dean was expected to take over responsibility.

Once I had been in office for about nine months the bishop

and the diocesan council reviewed the situation and I acknowledged that, though technically I could have declined to operate the scheme, there was no alternative. As there was no prospect of a fulltime curate, I said that I was prepared to go along with it provided the parishes would produce six readers. They rose to the challenge and by the time Jack Porter retired at the end of 1983 we had five readers, trained and equipped. It was one of the most exciting, demanding and satisfying tasks of my ministry, preparing that group of readers. It was possible because we didn't have Sunday evening services and every second week for two years the group met and I took them through the agreed programme of training for readers. In September 1983 Bishop Noel Willoughby admitted and licensed David Bate, Maureen Coulter, John Galloway, Edward James, Sheila and Stanley Johnson – later Stanley went forward for fulltime ministry and Sheila became an auxiliary priest.

While this was going on in March 1982, pastoral care of Dunmore East became part of my responsibility. Every Sunday after the Cathedral main service I drove the 13 miles to St Andrew's. What began on their part, and probably on mine, as a somewhat reluctant relationship blossomed into that of part of the family of God. I was very touched by the kindness shown to me by the congregation. Leaving them was not the least of the wrenches I felt when I moved to Downpatrick in 1984. They had had to come to terms with the fact that they no longer had a resident presence of an Anglican minister. They had had to sell their rectory, making the residence of the incumbent in Waterford better equipped for someone who had to 'manage' an extensive pastoral area.

With Dunmore East came a special ministerial relationship. Life centres round the sea and every summer there is a ceremony of 'blessing the boats'. Originally this was for the fishing fleet but by the eighties the recreational boats were included and it took place in connection with regatta week. In 1982 the parish priest deputed his curate to share the service with me and we drew up a form of service which was much appreciated. There was almost an ecumenical disaster when at the end the curate invited us to dedicate the whole proceedings to Mary, Star of the Sea, by saying together a decade of the Rosary! My parishioners were very embarrassed for me. I was learning that there was still a lack of ecumenical awareness around. The next year the elderly parish priest, Father Aylward, came himself and left the whole ordering of the service to me, professing himself happy to do whatever I thought fitting. No one can tell me that someone hadn't passed on their awareness of the previous year.

In 1983 Father Aylward invited me to speak at the annual district service for the South East for the Boy Scouts of Ireland which was to be held in Killea Church. I prepared to give a Scout Yarn and arrived in the sacristy to find the local TDs, the Minister of State for energy and most of the local civic dignitaries. What I took to be a Distrct Commissioner arrived; it was the Chief Scout of Ireland. A little local service turned out to be almost a national occasion. What struck me most forcibly looking down at the congregation was how many cub scouts had caps on and many scouts were wearing their berets in church. The Scout Association of Ireland was wholly integrated. That was why Killea Parish had chosen SAI rather than the Catholic Boy Scouts of Ireland although that had much closer ties to the church. Unexpected change. I don't know what the VIPs thought of my talk but it did hold the kids' attention – I was trying to relate my scouting experiences to following Jesus.

Being Dean
Bishop Noel Willoughby succeeded John Armstrong and it fell to me to welcome him to his cathedral of Waterford and enthrone him on 28 May 1980. Bishop Noel was enthroned in six cathedrals, presiding over a bishopric of six ancient sees. He immediately set about a programme of rationalisation, effectively constructing a single chapter for the cathedrals of Cashel, Waterford and Lismore by making each dean a canon of the other two cathedrals. His plan included appointing one of the deans as archdeacon after George Hogg retired, and for a short time I acted as archdeacon. On my departure David Woodworth, dean of Cashel, took over.

There was clearly something awry with the financial administration of Cashel and Waterford: the accounts at the Diocesan Synod in 1980 revealed a heavy deficit in the Waterford/Lismore account and a healthy surplus in the Cashel account.

Cashel wasn't prepared to agree to an amalgamation of the accounts. At my frist diocesan synod, the new boy asked a couple of awkward questions and received contradictory replies. Then he was elected to the diocesan council (the executive which used to meet each quarter). Armed with advice from a former professional accountant later ordained, Canon Leslie Enright, I kept up the pressure and searched for explanations. Finally, it was discovered that contributions to the Clergy Pension Fund by mistake had not been assessed to parishes where rectors were over the age of sixty-six, but the diocese had been paying these each month to the Representative Church Body in Dublin. It had only taken a couple of years to run up a deficit. Once that was sorted, in a very few years the deficit was turned into surplus and a process of amalgamating accounts could go forward. Bishop Noel persuaded Waterford's representative Edward James, bursar at Newtown School, to take over and a new era of efficiency in diocesan administration began.

Cathedral worship
The Cathedral of the Blessed Trinity, commonly called Christ Church, had a variety of Sunday worship. At 8.00am there was Holy Communion, 1972 rite, with a congregation of twenty or so, sometimes augmented by Newtown boarders for whom attendance at 8.00am covered their obligation to attend church on Sunday.

The principal morning service had a different pattern each week. On the first Sunday it was Choral Communion using the Merbecke setting of the *Book of Common Prayer* service. On the second Sunday there was a Family Service which was basically Morning Prayer according to the 1969 booklet but somewhat simplified, at which the children of the Sunday School were involved. Third Sunday was Family Communion, using the 1972 service, children going to Sunday School after the gospel. Fourth and fifth Sundays there was Choral Matins. I made one change almost immediately: the children had been accustomed to leaving Matins before the Venite, now they remained until after the second lesson. I gave a very short child-orientated 'word' based on the kind of thing I had done in Belvoir Primary School, we sang a children's hymn, and Matins resumed with the canticle. It added hardly anything to the length of the service. Although technically unlawful, and for a liturgical purist unsatisfactory, I deemed it necessary to meet the pastoral need of a quarter of the congregation. I also insisted on choosing the hymns with the cathedral organist, Eric de Courcy, and this ensured that a wide repertoire of hymns were sung, familiar to all, but not hitherto in the lists of Waterford cathedral. Eric, having had sole responsibility for chosing of hymns, welcomed my input positively.

After I had been dean for twelve months we invited the Select Vestry to the Deanery for supper and an informal meeting at which I asked for and got their reactions to my first year. There was general approval although one man said that for him my preaching was too personal. Exactly what he meant I never discovered. I hope it meant that my exegesis and exposition of the scripture was being understood. As a result of that informal meeting, the canticle after the children's hymn was dropped and we varied the canticle sung between the readings.

We experimented a bit with the time of the principal service until I became responsible for Dunmore East when we settled on 10.00am. To my surprise there had been no midnight Holy Communion at Christmas but this innovation was enthusiastically welcomed in 1980 but without music – a step too far for the Cathedral Choir. My successor, John Neill, would have a fully choral midnight eucharist and a fully choral Easter Vigil. For the latter I carried on the practice I had in Belvoir and each year the small congregation was growing.

Public role of the dean
The dean of Waterford is accorded special recognition in the city. The holder of the office in a very real way 'represents' the Church of Ireland community. In the eighties there was a warm welcome accorded to the dean from the overwhelmingly Roman Catholic population. I discovered this very quickly for St Patrick's Day was only a few weeks away and I was invited to sit on the reviewing platform outside the City Hall for the celebration parade and to recite with Bishop Michael Russell prayers for peace. On that first St Patrick's Day it was bitterly cold and the showers of sleet that had been threatening descended at the end of the parade: so the prayers were said into the gale with

definitely declining earthly audience! The bishop and I had envied the Lord Mayor and members of the Corporation who wore
their ceremonial robes over their overcoats, giving them an extra
layer against the elements.

The dean is also invited by Waterford Corporation to be a
member of the City Vocational Education Committee which is
responsible for all public education beyond primary level. This
meant a monthly meeting with elected members of the
Corporation and others who held public office in the City. The
chairman was Monsignor John Shine. To my surprise the office
of vice-chairman had been held vacant since the retirement of
Dean Fergus Day and at my first meeting I was asked if I would
accept nomination to the post. In fact, I only took the chair at one
meeting in four years but I did chair the Adult Education sub-
committee.

It is a testimony to the relationships of the late twentieth century that nothing of moment can take place without an ecumenical
dimension. The Church of Ireland bishop, like his Roman
Catholic opposite number, receives an invitation to every major
social event. Because of his wide responsibility for the rest of the
bishopric, frequently the dean is required to deputise. Bishop
Willoughby had one rule during my time: he did not accept invitations to social events taking place on a Sunday, and neither did
he ask me to do so. I believe that there is still a value in making
the Lord's Day different and the erosion of that element in the
Protestant tradition is one change that I have been unable to welcome. South and North I have been able to resist pressures to ac-
commodate myself to fetes, football matches and public dinners
on Sunday.

Among the ecumenical events, ecumenical blessings at the
openings of factories, schools etc were of major importance.
Normally, Bishop Russell would discover if Bishop Willoughy
was coming, in which case he would officiate. If the bishop
could not be present the local parish priest would normally pre-
side with the dean. I shall never forget my first ecumenical blessing – of a new toilet roll factory! My former colleagues in the
North wouldn't believe me. I have very happy memories of
these occasions, perhaps especially the new Bausch and Lomb
lense factory on the western outskirts. This state of the art factory

was a forerunner of the many 'high tech' developments which were to transform the Republic in the next decade. I can always say I was in at the birth of a 'tiger cub' and I have a superb magnifying glass as a reminder. I also got a laugh or two from these blessings. Once, in the week before Christmas, the administrator of the Roman Catholic Cathedral and I officiated at the opening of the new shopping-mall. My colleague offered thanks to Dean Martin for so kindly sharing in the ceremony!

The dean is also hospital chaplain and, apart from the normal rounds and provision of Holy Communion for patients, each year I was invited to talk to the student nurses about differences in the way in which Church of Ireland patients approached their faith compared with Roman Catholics who made up ninety-five per cent of patients. I was also involved each year in the Graduation Day Mass of Dedication, either reading the gospel or the Prayers of the Faithful. I found the ceremony of anointing the hands of each graduating nurse very moving.

This was also the period during which almost every town and city in the republic had a pirate radio station. Changes in technology meant low power FM radio was feasible and many of the stations were very popular. Clearly in a few years these would be legalised and it was in anticipation of it happening that the churches became involved. I was asked to record a Christmas message to the people of the City and it was played half a dozen times a day in the week before Christmas. A message from Bishop Russell or one of his senior priests was also broadcast on Waterford Local Radio. One of the priests from St John's College – the local seminary – Father Michael Mullins had a chat and music show on Saturday mornings. One week he invited me to 'explain' the Church of Ireland and I had a very enjoyable experience. On another occasion he invited me to 'report' on the General Synod the week after its meeting.

Ecumenical dimensions

In common with the rest of the church, the Week of Prayer for Christian Unity in January was still an exciting event. It was different to my experience in the North. All the denominations except the Baptists and the Pentecostals were involved, including the Society of Friends. In 1981 I was the preacher in the Church of Our Lady and Saint Benildus, one of the modern churches, on Dunmore Road, opposite Newtown School. In my sermon I traced the developments that had taken place over the previous fifty years – noted that the Scottish churches had that month publicly recognised each other's baptisms. When, I asked, would this happen in Ireland? Immediately after the service Bishop Russell protested that the Roman Catholic Church in Ireland had done this five years before: he knew because he had written the section in the ecumenical directory. I apologised and expressed delight that it had happened. Next day I wrote to the chairman of our Church Unity Committee, Bishop Samuel Poyntz of Cork. It was news to him. He had it checked and, of course, Bishop Russell was correct, but, he commented, it is something that had been kept rather quiet. On the same Sunday in 1982 the said chairman highlighted the fact that all the churches in Ireland now recognise each other's baptism in a sermon which got major publicity. What the good sisters called my 'very honest' address had wider repercussions and on the ecumenical baptism certificate the 'Catholic Church in Ireland' (sic) is now listed with all the other denominations.

Relationships with the Presbyterian/Methodist congregation which shared a minister with the Kilkenny Presbyterian congregation were friendly enough but I didn't find the minister an easy person with whom to relate. A minister of the Church of Scotland, hailing from the Isle of Skye, he had come to Waterford from a ministry in Buenos Aires and was about as opposed to everything Northern unionists stand for as it was possible to be. In many ways we just weren't on the same wavelength, although he wasn't an enthusiastic evangelical. I feel that the fact that the city community gave public recognition to the Church of Ireland may have rankled. But as I had discovered in Knocknagoney and Belvoir, there are difficulties in working alongside Presbyterian ministers. They don't wholly trust 'Episcopalians' as they liked to call us. After he moved to a congregation in the Midlands, it was the Methodists' turn to appoint a minister and the Rev David Neilands and his wife Lynda arrived in 1983. David and I 'clicked', as they say, and we found we were able to co-operate in many different ways. It wasn't always to my advantage! Having invited him to preach at Harvest

Thanksgiving at St Andrew's Dunmore East, his preaching was so attractive that one of the Dunmore 'backbone' families decided that they had always been Methodists and transferred allegiance.

For Holy Week 1984 David proposed a joint 'mission', offered a preacher, the Rev E. Todd, and proposed two nights in each church beginning at St Patrick's. This turned out to be the high point of my four and a half years. Church of Ireland folk were supportive at the first two services. Mr Todd was a quite exceptional preacher. We had an amazing congregation at the Maundy Thursday communion. Probably quite unlawfully, David and I 'concelebrated' at the cathedral altar and a congregation, including Baptists and Brethren (yes!), Anglicans, Presbyterians, Methodists and Roman Catholics, came to the altar rails. It was indeed a foretaste of the heavenly banquet. Good Friday produced an even larger attendance. David and I were full of plans for future co-operation. Then I was called away to Downpatrick.

Working with the Society of Friends – the Quakers – centred on Newtown School. The Friends had been probably the second largest non Roman Catholic community in the county. In 1798 they had founded the School and it had continued as a Quaker secondary school with a preparatory department. When Bishop Foy's, the Church of Ireland boarding school in Waterford, had had to close because of falling numbers and financial problems in the 1960s, Newtown School had accepted the Church of Ireland scholars and the Bishop Foy's Governors (of which the dean of Waterford was chairman) awarded scholarships to assist Church of Ireland entrants. Three of the governors were welcomed as members of the Newtown School management committee. This was conducted as a friends' meeting. It begins with silence and no decision can be taken if even one person expresses their unhappiness with the proposal. This could have been a recipe for chaos but in fact once you accept the principle it ensures that very careful consideration is given to each matter. A minute is written, read and agreed before proceeding to next business. Since the Newtown experience I have applied the principles to meetings of Select Vestries – to the frustration of those who like to proceed by divisions and votes! It wouldn't be honest not to record that some Quakers have grave suspicions of the Church of Ireland. Some chose to send their primary age children to our national school and one parent wrote to ensure that I did not require his son to learn the Creed by rote. My reply was to remind him that his children could withdraw from religious education classes and that learning 'by rote' was not part of my approach to Christian education. The children stayed and I reckon they were perhaps among those with the clearest understanding of what the creeds mean.

My elder daughter was a day pupil at Newtown for the whole of her time in Waterford and the younger had one year. Both found things that irked but on the whole the liberal education and the respect shown to each pupil as an individual was streets ahead of anything experienced North of the Border. It fell to me to prepare Anglican pupils who so wished for confirmation. I thoroughly enjoyed the task although it wasn't easy, since the only time that could be allocated was after prep – 8.30 to 9.30. I have seen members of the class fall asleep. I don't think my teaching was all that boring! As I have said there was a very liberal disciplinary regime – frequently abused, I fear, with smoking and consumption of alcohol by some seniors. In a way this was either an anticipation of what was going to become a larger issue for teenagers in Ireland or there was less cover-up than in other mainstream schools. Co-education, of course, meant boy-girl relationships. At Newtown these were so open that they did not become unhealthy.

'Early Christians'

During my second year in Waterford I concluded that the formation of a group who would form an advisory pastoral council would strengthen ministry in the parish. I felt we needed a smaller group than the Select Vestry which could think about and give me their advice on pastoral issues. Above all it needed to be a praying group. By Easter 1982, I had discerned those I wanted to invite and everyone of them agreed. How to find time each week for a group of busy people to meet for prayer was a serious question. One of the group came up with the solution: they had all been able to attend the early Holy Communion services in Holy Week, surely 7.30-8.00 once a week was possible.

We decided to try this, building our prayer into an informal communion service which we held in one of the Sunday School rooms in the Cathedral, and towards the end using photocopies of proof pages of *Alternative Prayer Book*. I found that this gathering became a power house for my ministry. As time went on most of those preparing to become readers came along in addition to the original group. They called themselves the 'early' Christians. So vital did those times of worship become for them that they persuaded Canon Leslie Enright to keep the service going until my successor as Dean arrived.

Called away

It was the last thing in the world that I expected when I went to General Synod in May 1984. As a result of a chance meeting with Robin Eames, now bishop of Down and Dromore, I received a challenge to consider returning to Northern Ireland, and pioneering a Group Ministry, similar to that which I now had in Waterford. This would involve care for the most significant Patrician sites of Saul and Down Cathedral. Should we think about this? There were practical considerations. Barbara was about to embark on training as a speech therapist in Edinburgh. There were family considerations – my remaining aunts were not in the best of health and perhaps being in Downpatrick would take some of the care responsibility from my sister. All Valerie's friends were in the North. She had not, as the wife of the dean, found it particularly easy to make friends in Waterford. I knew that I would always be a 'stranger in a strange land' but I had been prepared to accept that. What I hadn't expected was the feeling of helplessness in the face of reports of continuing violence in the North. Could I, as a priest, have done anything by word or deed to prevent any one violent act? When I reflected I reckoned that I had accomplished many positive things in the four previous years. In particular I felt that although Dunmore East was now firmly wedded to Waterford, Tramore and Annestown would always feel I belonged more to the other parts of the Group. A new leader could be on the same footing with everyone. When I consulted Bishop Noel Willoughby he said he was not surprised that I felt drawn back to the North for which he knew I had an ongoing concern. With his understanding, I allowed my name to be considered and on 8 June 1984 the appointment was confirmed. Waterford parishioners were very understanding, all imagining that I would be going to care for much larger numbers. In fact there were fewer households in Lecale Group than in Waterford Group. When the time came at the end of August, our family was given a wonderful farewell. I was especially moved by the kindness of the congregation of St Andrew's Dunmore East, who had received me so reluctantly in 1982 but with whom I had built up a great rapport. So it was that we went from Waterford to Downpatrick in one of the hottest Augusts on record.

CHAPTER TWELVE

Lecale 1984-2001

It was so unexpected to be going back to the North. Within a month it was settled and 7 September was fixed for my institution as rector of the Lecale Group of Parishes. Lecale means Cathal's Quarter and was applied to the area between the Quoile and Blackwater rivers to the east of Downpatrick. In many ways it would have been easier for the grouping to have been called the Down Cathedral Group but that decision, along with a whole lot of others, had not been mine to make. As Bishop Eames had said there was a plethora of small parishes in east Down, none of which had been viable in their groupings, so he had taken the opportunity of several retirements to create a group of five parishes. There were two rectories, one for the rector and the second would be for a curate. The bishop had pointed me towards Alan Abernethy, who had completed three years in orders, and whom he was finding difficult to place for a second curacy. I already knew Alan from his student days and I wrote to him suggesting we meet to discuss his joining me in the new venture. Early in July we met in the grounds of Trinity College in Dublin and it was immediately apparent to both of us that a partnership in ministry would have possibilities for both of us. He would give three months notice and join me in October.

In addition to Alan I would have a reader in the team, Jim Sims, and there was a retired English priest, Charles Simpson. As Robin Eames said, 'There's your team.'

Re-wiring and some structural alterations were being made to the rectory. By putting on pressure and announcing we were making our first move in mid-August, the house was ready for us. I sent in a list of those I wanted invited to the Institution, expecting the Rural Dean and the parish to add to it with official and ecumenical guests. No other invitations other than my list were ever issued. It was clear that I wasn't altogether welcome.

However, I found that the cathedral wardens, Joy Wilkinson and Mary Love, were deeply embarrassed over the matter and put it down to experience. Raymond Press of Saul Parish organised overnight hospitality for a small group who travelled from Waterford and who shared with me the first Holy Communion of my incumbency in St Patrick's Memorial Church Saul, on the festival of the Birth of the Blessed Virgin Mary. That service meant a great deal to them and also to me.

On the first three Sundays I celebrated Holy Communion in turn at the five churches, St Nicholas, Ardglass, St Mary's Dunsford, St Patrick's Saul, Loughinisland Parish Church (which was actually outside the Lecale district but had become part of the group as it was unable any longer to be a separate parish and had declined amalgamation with Magherahamlet to the west), and Down Cathedral. At the Cathedral there was a mid-afternoon service of Evening Prayer, choral once a month. Evening Prayer was in Ardglass at 6.30pm. For services at which I couldn't be present, Jim Sims officiated three Sundays a month and I had to find help for the other service as Mr Simpson had gone on holiday. I drew up a schedule of services and circulated it on the back of a letter introducing myself to my new parishioners. This letter was immediately welcomed and I was asked to make it a regular communication. Thus *Lecale Letter* was born – typed on an electric typewriter, with many typographical errors and printed on a small hand-fed photocopier.

Within a few weeks I had to tackle the question of where responsibility lay in respect of the cathedral. Although it was part of the Lecale Group and the bishop had held my institution there, because it was not a parish, I wasn't technically 'rector' of the cathedral parish. The dean of Down was Rosmond Good, rector of Carryduff, my former neighbour when in Belvoir. When I discovered that he was making pastoral calls on cathedral parishioners it became clear that we had to establish demarcation areas and I arranged to go and interview him. I said that whatever he may have felt about my appointment and the arrangements for the Lecale Group, it was now a fact and we needed to work out how we could work together. I rejected his suggestion that I become a minor canon of the cathedral; having been a dean a month earlier such a suggestion was rather insensitive. But we came to an amicable agreement: pastoral care of the congregation and the arrangements for Sunday services would be my responsibility, while diocesan services and chairmanship of the Cathedral Board would be his. He would step down from the *ad hoc* body which the Diocesan Council had set up to over-see the Lecale Group and leave that to me as rector. I have to say that from that moment until his untimely death in 1987 we never had the slightest disagreement.

In general, the conviction in Connor and in Down and Dromore, that the cathedral dean is a senior diocesan figure who is more often than not a rector of a parish other than that in which the cathedral is situated, is really problematic. The Church of Ireland should recognise that being a 'senior diocesan figure' has nothing to do with the office and work of a dean. A dean should be on the spot, leading the cathedral's worship and life. I was able to work with three deans of Down because I was con-vinced that concern for the life and witness of the cathedral church was my priority. It was a little easier when I was made a canon and appointed to the chapter in 1987, although General Synod provided in 1985 that the rector of the Lecale Group should be *ex officio* a member of the Cathedral Board if not a member of the chapter. I am delighted in 2002 to see a hint in the appointment of the rector of the cathedral parish of Dromore as dean of Dromore, a sign that one bishop has recognised the anomaly, and I look forward in due time to a successor as rector of Lecale Group being dean of Down.

Liturgical life in Lecale parishes
When I arrived, Down Cathedral was using modern language services for everything except Choral Evensong once a month. Ardglass and Dunsford used the 'red' book for Morning Prayer and Evening Prayer, and Holy Communion 1972 in alternate months with *Book of Common Prayer* Holy Communion. Saul used the 'grey' book except for one Book of Common Prayer Holy Communion service a month, and at Loughinisland all the services were *Book of Common Prayer. The Alternative Prayer Book* was about to be launched and I preached about the new book at a Group Service in Ardglass at the end of September. Where trial services had been used, there was no problem with *Alternative*

Prayer Book and it was soon in regular use except in Loughinisland. I decided that the priority for that congregation was to make it a worshipping and witnessing community, who would know and trust my leadership, before we changed forms of worship. In Dunsford parish Mervyn Kingston, as group curate had overcome a lot of hostility in getting the congregation to accept the 'new' form of Holy Communion but after my first Sunday one of those who had been most opposed confessed that hitherto she hadn't liked the service but had done so on this occasion. There is obviously something in the way the priest presides which helps.

Ecumenical life in Lecale

At the time of my institution, the parish of Down and Hollymount, whose congregation accounts for the vast majority of members of the Church of Ireland in Downpatrick, was vacant following the death of Ralph Peters. I was delighted when Mervyn Dickson was appointed and looked forward to a good relationship. At his institution I was introduced to Canon Joseph Maguire, the parish priest, and to Roy Packer, minister of the Non-subscribing Presbyterian Church. David Knox, the Presbyterian minister of Downpatrick, had already called at the rectory to make himself known to me.

Within a few weeks there was a meeting of the Downpatrick and Area Inter-church Caring Project, the brainchild of Canon Maguire, a committee with representatives of all the churches, clergy and laity. This sought to organise practical help for the elderly and to make the best possible use of the government scheme, Action for Community Enterprise (ACE). At this meeting Dean Good, who had been at the inaugural meeting, stood down and I was elected as vice-chairman in his place. The ACE scheme was for over ten years one of the chief weapons in combating the high level of unemployment and deprivation in the province. Our particular scheme proved to be one of the best organised ACE undertakings and directly employed hundreds of young men and women in the town, more than a third of whom learned skills and gained the self-confidence that enabled them to obtain and hold down successful jobs in a variety of industries and professions. We in the cathedral benefited from having full-time workers present at the cathedral, the majority of whom we were able to encourage into good jobs. As a good number of these were young members of the Roman Catholic community, it enabled them to learn how the Church of Ireland regarded St Patrick and how the Church of Ireland worshipped. At least one came back to faith as he shared in the life of the cathedral, learning to pray and read the bible, without any question of his transferring denominational allegiance.

The Downpatrick churches observe the Week of Prayer for Christian Unity with a united service in each of seven churches in turn. In 1985 it was the turn of the Non-Subscribing Presbyterian Church in Stream Street to be the host. It is the second oldest church building in Downpatrick and is little changed from the 18th century. My colleagues asked me to be the preacher. It was an amazing experience for the preacher goes out from the church through a lobby, up stairs and emerges into a pulpit halfway up the wall, looking out on a nave and transepts stretching out on either side. I preached a revised version of the address I had given in Waterford a few years before and had a very good reception. However, in subsequent years the host congregation also took the responsibility of finding a preacher from its tradition. I know that this was to save one or two of the congregations having the embarrassment of inviting a Roman Catholic preacher who would not be acceptable. Down Cathedral had taken the lead earlier in the decade when Canon Maguire had preached there. It was, however, something that detracted from the vitality of the Week of Prayer Service and which has now been re-addressed. Towards end of the 1990s a Unity Week service became established in Strangford and, from the outset, the parish priest and I made sure that the preacher came from another denomination to the host church.

I shall refer later to the very special relationship that developed between the Roman Catholic and Church of Ireland congregations of Loughinisland.

Cathedral Restoration
I arrived to find scaffolding in place within the cathedral and work in progress on the outside. A massive task of restoration had been undertaken and all kinds of fund-raising initiatives

were in hand. Thankfully my remit did not involve me too closely in this but I did find my input in meetings of the Cathedral Board, after Waterford experience, was positive. On one issue I clashed with the cathedral architect as I was deeply worried about the lack of ventilation in the cathedral and the potential damage that condensation could do to the wonderful work of restoration. My ideas were not taken into consideration but in the beginning of the new century investigations are showing that I may not have been wrong in sounding warning bells. We managed to continue services in the building until Epiphany 1986, after which we closed for twenty two months. The parishioners of Saul hosted the cathedral congregation and choir during those months of waiting. We looked forward to returning to the cathedral in 1987.

Bishop Robin Eames had become archbishop of Armagh and Gordon McMullan had been translated from Clogher diocese in his place but had not yet been enthroned in Down. Rosmond Good had sadly died and Hamilton Leckey had been appointed as dean. The holder of every office in the chapter had changed, either by promotions to fill vacancies or new appointments like those of John Bell and myself. Alan Abernethy was now rector of Helen's Bay and I had James Carson as my curate assistant.

Re-hallowing was fixed for Thursday 27 October, 1987 which would include the bishop's enthronement. An all-ticket service was organised at which 550 people were present. Sunday 30 October was to be marked by a service of Holy Communion for all the Lecale Group, a service at which the dean and canons were installed, and an open ecumenical praise service for the people of Downpatrick in the evening. Quite a weekend! It was complicated for us in that elder daughter Barbara was to graduate in Edinburgh on the Saturday morning and the family had to be there. We managed to be at all these events and to host a special preacher for Sunday, Bishop Kenneth Pillar, bishop of Hertford, whom I had invited the previous autumn. Everything went extremely well. Down Cathedral was back in business!

CHAPTER THIRTEEN

Lecale II

Accident

In the spring of 1985 I had an adventure which could have meant that these reminiscences never saw the light of day. On a Friday afternoon I parked my car and was walking through the shopping centre to the library. I pushed what I took to be the door beside the supermarket and to my horror my hand went through the glass and I tumbled after it, large splinters of glass entering my neck below my chin. I knew enough of anatomy to know that it could be dangerous. As I stood up I seemed to hear a voice, 'Do not be afraid, I am with you all the way.' I cannot account for it, nor did I understand what it meant. If it meant through the way of death I had a sense of peace. The nearest shop was a hairdresser and I went in asking for towels which I pressed on my neck from which blood was pouring and asked that an ambulance be called. In a few moment an off-duty district nurse was on the scene and took control. In no time the ambulance arrived and she came with me to the Downe Hospital. It just happened that the senior surgeon, Alan Archbold, was in the hospital, and I was in theatre, where the anaesthetist was someone whose children were in the Cathedral Choir. The next thing I knew was waking up in intensive care with my wife beside me and Bishop Robin Eames, who had been down the road at Ballykinler, when word of my accident came.

I received wonderful care in the Downe and often wonder whether, if it hadn't been there and I had required transport to a Belfast hospital, I would have survived. The large glass slivers had cut into the lower tongue muscles and saliva glands but had missed the major artery by millimetres: truly, the Lord was with me all the way.

Alan Abernethy was superb in his priestly care of his 'boss', bringing me communion and otherwise ministering. Bishop Robin simply took over my responsibilities for St Patrick's Day at Saul in addition to his own at the cathedral. I determined to get back to work as soon as possible – and used the Holy Week communion services in the cathedral to get back my confidence in reading, not easy when your tongue had been cut into. I conducted Holy Communion on Easter Day, finding the *Book of Common Prayer* service the most difficult because of the long sentences. Probably it was too soon and I had to take time off later. When I went for a final check-up with Alan Archbold he was delighted with the results of his surgery. He looked at me with a quizzical look. 'Brian,' he said, 'as a result of your accident your left side saliva glands should not be working. They are. I don't know why but I think you do.' A Presbyterian elder recognised that the healing power of God was involved as well as his skills.

We took Lecale Youth to a post-Easter praise service in the Hall of the Assembly's Buildings in Belfast at which the speaker was Ken Clarke, returned from Chile, then a rector in Dublin. When he saw me, his greeting was: 'Hello, Lazarus!' In June I attended a Church of Ireland Renewal Conference in Dublin, during which I received laying-on-of-hands with prayer for healing from Archbishop John Armstrong that the slight difficulties I still had in speaking would be healed. And they were. From that day to this I thank God I have had no problems with speech as a result of that accident.

Adult education
It seemed to be a priority that within Lecale parishes there should be some opportunities for enabling adults to understand their faith at a deeper level. To this end Alan Abernethy and I launched in 1984 a programme based on John Finney and Felicity Lawson's *Saints Alive*. After an initial gathering in Ardglass about ten people decided to take part and we met mostly in private houses from January on. The skills that Alan and I had intertwined and I think we got as much from the experience as the participants. It proved to be the way to instruct one who had come for confirmation as an adult. Indeed I presented him for confirmation at the very beginning of his joining the group. Two couples who were to be married in 1985 were part of

the group as well as a member of the cathedral choir and a cathedral warden. The unstable nature of society meant that within a few years all but three of the group had moved away from Lecale but the lives of all were enriched. Sixteen years on the adult confirmed began training for full-time ordained ministry in the Church of Ireland. Richard Hare, bishop of Pontefract in the 1980s, used to say that he considered that often when he laid hands in confirmation he was not just implanting a seed but sometimes laying a time-bomb!

Subsequent attempts to suggest courses in Christian education either produced no response or were 'hi-jacked' by people with their own agenda which soon put off the genuine inquirers. We had most success with a joint Roman Catholic and Church of Ireland Lent Group in Strangford but finding even a night in five successive weeks proved beyond the impossible for people busy with all kind of cultural and community activities. Often, I was to be thankful for the Waterford Sunday evenings which had worked for study groups, and the Reader Training Group.

Team Ministry
Charles Simpson had hardly resumed ministry in October 1984 when he suffered a stroke and was never able to officiate again. It was a blow to the Loughinisland part of the Group but in a way it proved a blessing in disguise as each parish learned to look to me as their rector and to Alan Abernethy as their curate. Jim Sims continued to be our reader although I had to seek extra assistance on some Sundays. My work with reader training enabled me to invite the 'best of the bunch' to join the team as gaps occurred, such as when Jim Sims was accepted for ordination and began full-time work with CMS. This brought Goff Mason, Richard Dadswell and Brian Parker to the team. All three eventually found their vocation to ordained ministry. The Group also benefitted from the reader ministry of two school-teacher readers, Derek Capper and Sam Magowan, not forgetting one of my former teachers at Inst., Marsden FitzSimons, who qualified as a reader in his late sixties. When Goff Mason and John Gowen completed their training for auxiliary ministry, Bishop McMullan assigned them to Lecale Group on a two Sunday per month basis. Once they were priested they provided cover for

eucharistic ministry and enabled Bishop McMullan, as priests seeking second curacies became almost non-existent, to assign deacons to the Lecale Group. So I became responsible for the nurture in turn of newly ordained Brian Cadden, Charles Mullen and Gordon Freeman. Each of these contributed their gifts as did Lecale's one local contribution to the ordained ministry of the diocese, Dr Graham Savidge, an Englishman residing in Ardglass whose secular occupation is as a reader in marine biology at Queen's University. Pat Mollan and Gordon Graham were two other non-stipendiary priests who, initially doubting whether they could contribute to such a variety of parish situations, came to find the worshipping community of the Lecale parishes warm and enriching their discipleship. At the very end Nigel Kirkpatrick, already a priest, joined me, to gain experience of rural ministry and to be cover for my retirement which at that time I expected to be autumn 2000. Nigel's particular gifts were just what were required at the time and parishioners were delighted when he was appointed to the parish of Killinchy Union in the diocese. In 2000 my first curate, Alan Abernethy, rector of Ballyholme, was appointed as a canon of the cathedral, someone who shares with me a very real sense that Down Cathedral is one of those special places which seem to draw people close to God.

Members of the Group, contrasting their experience with the average parishioner in a parish with just one minister, said that they had come to value the variety of presentations of the Gospel received from members of the team. I believe that it is a positive indication that the worship life of the Lecale churches has encouraged so many to move on from reader ministry to ordained ministry.

I often said that each Sunday when I was officiating in a particular church I felt that I badly wanted to be there again next week meant that I was in a good relationship with God's people in that place. It was the longest time I served in any one appointment but it was a time of personal enrichment and, I hope, faithful service.

It was hard to persuade people that they were part of a group and not of a parish. One method we tried was always when there were five Sundays in the month to have one central morning service only. Unfortunately there were those who refused to travel, taking that Sunday off. And there were a few who, rather than worship in another church of the group, went to the local Presbyterian Church or a non-group parish church. However, the quarterly Group Services were times of huge encouragement, both as regards numbers, with nearly full buildings, but they also gave opportunity to introduce new hymns, to use new worship forms like Service of The Word, to offer the ministry of laying on of hands for healing and to get to know one another better.

Loughinisland

Perhaps Loughinisland found it more difficult to be part of the Group than any other unit. As a parish it had a 'chip on its shoulder', having had a full-time priest of its own for longer than any of the others, latterly a 'light-duty' charge of elderly priests with some kind of physical disability, housed and continuing to minister until reaching pensionable age, which until the 1980s was 70. This had an effect on the congregation, as the younger members voted with their feet and didn't go to church. Attempts had been made to amalgamate Loughinisland with other places, which they had fiercely opposed, until finally accepting the Lecale Group, where they hadn't the expense of rectory upkeep and with pastoral care from a lively retired priest, Charles Simpson, who was immensely popular with many parishioners.

There were more 'singles' in Loughinisland in proportion, bachelors, spinsters and widows, than in any of the other units. Many of them walked to church on Sundays and for some reason were embarrassed to ask other parishioners to take them to Group Services.

Alan Abernethy and I found the spiritual atmosphere in Seaforde Church cold and hostile at first. And there were a number of bad relationships between families. It took a lot of praying before this began to change but it did happen. One catalyst was the infusion of new life as new people moved in and showed a willingness to contribute positively to the life of the parish. I became more accepted when it was realised that I was as close as a telephone call, and on one occasion of a sudden death was present before the undertaker summoned at the same time. It was pastoral care by rector and curates that won the people round. And it required extraordinary sensitivity, as well as a thick skin, particularly when a delegation from the parish visited the bishop to suggest that a retired priest living in the parish be put in charge as that would cost the parish less than two clergy in Lecale Group! When I drew up a list of the giving level of each parish per week, based on dividing direct giving income by the number of families, and presented it to the Group Committee Loughinisland's representative pleaded with me not to publish it in *Lecale Letter* (our bi-monthly Group leaflet) for their parish average was about a quarter of that of the best. By the mid 1990s this had changed as parishioners faced up to the cost of maintaining their church and sharing in the increasing cost of maintaining ministry. By then the chronic deficits of previous years had been turned around, the church secured from the ingress of damp, the heating replaced and the church re-decorated. Although primarily traditional language rites were used, worship had been re-invigorated: Service of The Word was enthusiastically appreciated and the proposed baptismal rite was being used.

Loughinisland became a nationally known name in 1994 when a murderous atrocity took place on 18 June in the Heights Bar when a UVF terror group burst in and killed a number of men who had been watching World Cup Football on television. All the victims were Roman Catholics. On the Monday evening before the funerals, knowing that I couldn't be present, I called on the parish priest Canon Bernard Magee to express my sympathy and that of the Church of Ireland parish of Loughinisland. This message was read out before the first of the funerals, which some of our parishioners attended. A week later I was invited by the BBC to broadcast a morning service in August from one of the Lecale churches. I decided it should be Loughinisland and hit upon the idea of an inter-church service of prayer for peace. I went again to the parochial house, put the idea to Bernard Magee and he agreed to think about it. A day or so later we were in touch and he agreed to share in the service and invite his people to come to Seaforde for the occasion. The organists and choirs were to combine and each church would provide readers and people to lead the intercessions – I would preach and we would give a joint blessing at the end. We agreed that we would not talk to the news organisations beforehand to forestall any protests by Paisleyites or other extremists. However, by the Thursday before the broadcast the press had got hold of the story and we had to fend them off, saying they were welcome to be present but that we would give no interviews. Sunday morning came and I was early at the church wondering whether people would come. As I stood at the door people streamed up most of whom were strangers – the Roman Catholics were seizing the opportunity – and then our own people were arriving. Press photographers were everywhere. A correspondent for *Chicago Herald Tribune* asked, 'How was it we could do this while people in Northern Ireland were at each other's throats over religion?' My reply was that these were literally neighbours, who farmed together and were accustomed to practical sharing. I didn't tell her that it was the first time they would have worshipped together on a Sunday. Her next remark was a request, 'Can my cameraman shoot the congregation?' I smiled and said, 'Hardly an appropriate way of putting it in the circumstances!' The service went well and was well-received by the radio congregation. It led to an annual worship gathering round Christmas, alternatively in St Macartin's Church and in Seaforde Church – gatherings which have survived the retirements of Canon Magee and myself. One devout Roman Catholic from the Seaforde area meets me from time to time and avers that the Lord answered our prayers that day: coincidence that within a month the IRA announced its cessation.

Loughinisland ceased to be part of Lecale Group on my retirement becoming part of a new re-organisation in the area, and is now part of the Down Group where ministry is shared on a similar team basis.

The political scene
Valerie, Hilary and I returned to a no-less divided Northern Ireland than that we had left in 1980. In the meantime there had been the hunger strikes at the Maze, the ramifications of which had touched Waterford, where Sinn Féin intimidation had forced shops to close on funeral days. People there began to re-

alise just how a very small grouping could exert control through
violence or the threat of it. The Lecale area and Downpatrick
town are predominantly nationalist areas within which
Provisional IRA and the Irish National Liberation Army had areas
under their control. But the majority was constitutional nationalist
represented by the SDLP. On the local council, although that
party had a built-in majority, each year the chair of the council al-
ternated between Unionist and SDLP members. When we arrived
Cecil Maxwell, a member of the cathedral congregation, a
Unionist, was the Chairman. Each year the chairman in office was
invited to read a lesson at the Cathedral Carol Service. Canon
Joseph, later Monsignor, Maguire made an immense contribution
to good relations within the town and district of Down. Building
on a long tradition of the Presbyterian, Non-subscribing Presbyterian and Methodist churches also helped to make Downpatrick a
sign of hope in dark times. We regularly welcomed cardinals and
other distinguished visitors to the cathedral as well as each of the
Secretaries of State between 1984 and 1997. Both Peter Brooke and
Sir Patrick Mayhew arranged privately to attend morning service.
They were dedicated to a search for a peaceful solution to the
years of inter community disorder.

The local battalion of the Ulster Defence Regiment was accustomed to attend Remembrance Day service at Down
Cathedral and presented chairs at the time of the restoration to
commemorate each of its members who had lost their lives due
to terrorist action. One of the few local major terrorist acts occurred in 1991 when the IRA blew up the vehicle in which members of a UDR patrol were travelling on the Tuesday morning of
Holy Week. The Holy Week murders were roundly condemned
and the community response was a walk of peace from the town
centre to the site of the murder. This procession was led by all
the clergy of the town. We led prayers for peace in the community
and for those who suffered as a result. One of the last IRA bombs
before the 1994 cessation was aimed at Downpatrick Police
Station and caused considerable damage. In this incident one of
my honorary treasurers received minor injuries when the windows of his workshop were blown in by the blast. On another
occasion a young policeman, also a parishioner, was injured
when the IRA ambushed his car in South Armagh: although he

recovered physically he was so emotionally damaged as a result of his colleague being killed beside him that he was unable to resume duty and is only one of thousands in Northern Ireland on both sides who are scarred for life.

Not surprisingly, the Anglo-Irish Agreement entered into by Margaret Thatcher and Garret FitzGerald, was not welcomed with total approval by the Protestant community in our area. Many viewed with scepticism my experience of living safely and with respect in the Republic, but there were others who recognised that ultimately some kind of power-sharing would have to be accepted. In the spring of 1988 I was entertained to lunch by Canon John Collins at Holy Trinity Church, Brompton, London and was introduced to his churchwarden Michael Allison, who had been a junior minister at the Northern Ireland Office, and continued to be one of Margaret Thatcher's advisors on Northern Ireland affairs. He wanted to know from a grass-roots minister (!) just how people were by then reacting to the Anglo-Irish Agreement. I had to tell him honestly that, pressed, most of my people would still reject it but that as it wasn't having any disastrous consequences they were now prepared to accept minimum involvement of Dublin in the affairs of Northern Ireland. I remember him saying, 'Margaret really wants to bring peace to Ulster.'

In the autumn of 1997 I received an invitation from the local SDLP Member of Parliament to lunch at a Newcastle hotel to meet the Foreign Minister of the Republic – a Presbyterian minister and Monsignor Maguire were there as well with several influential non-political members of the community. At that reception and lunch it was clear that two objectives were involved: one, to impress us with the wholesomeness of the Republic's involvement in the negotiations which would lead to the Good Friday agreement and, two, to discover from people like me just how some of the plans that were being shaped might be acceptable. David Andrews gave an address and shook hands with everyone. His officials were subtly seated beside people like myself and away from SDLP party officials! My official came from near Waterford and as a result he probably got less politically than he was looking for. At least he discovered someone who did not consider that the road across the border was the road to

outer darkness! I was broadcasting the mid-day Protestant service on RTÉ from Down Cathedral on Good Friday in 1998.
Apart from the fact that it was a very meaningful service involving people from all the parishes in the Lecale Group, it was a
time of prayer at a critical time in our history. Was a historic
agreement between unionists and republicans imminent? Could
the wreckers destroy it at the last moment? History relates that
before the cock crew next morning an agreement had been
signed. In the next few weeks we worked for the referendum
that would 'ratify' the agreement. I was happy that so many of
our people were positively in favour, including men who had
organised 'No' rallies over the Anglo-Irish Agreement. I was
also shocked to visit on the day of the vote an intelligent elderly
parishioner who was now displaying a portrait of Dr Ian Paisley
on her mantlepiece. 'He's the only one speaking for us', was her
declaration and I knew she had voted 'No' in the referendum. It
was the traditional anti-nationalist attitude that is deeply en-
trenched in the Ulster countryside, like that of another who said
to me, 'Rector, dear, the border begins the other side of Clough
(a militantly Protestant hamlet in Loughinisland parish).'

The Church of Ireland leadership was so anxious not to be
'party political' that it failed, in my view, to give clear guidance
about the Agreement. I would except from this assessment the
contribution of Bishop Harold Miller, an article by whom I
reprinted in our Group newsletter. We were so anxious not to
drive from our churches those who were unconvinced that the
Good Friday Agreement represents the only viable way forward, that we temporised and suggested that it was equally
valid to be pro or anti. Dare I suggest that failure to endorse the
Agreement may have led to a smaller Protestant 'Yes' vote than
was expected? I have also seen pro-agreement Unionists change
horses after Sinn Féin seized the key ministries of education and
health in the Executive. At the time of writing, it is unclear just
how much longer the Executive which came into office in 1998
can survive. The changing island has not yet become stable.

Relations with the Orange Order

The parish clergy in Northern Ireland, for better or worse, come
into contact with the Orange Order. It gave colour and ceremo-

nial with a religious tinge to men who otherwise in church life opposed both because these were seen to dominate Roman Catholic worship. It also helped many to come to know their bible and to become better churchmen and Christian disciples. But it fostered, in spite of its foundation documents, suspicion of Roman Catholics. Politicians played on Orange fears to bolster the Unionist state. Paradoxically, it was unrest within the Orange Order that started the undermining of the state. In 1965 the local papers headlined 'Hecklers' Twelfth' as fringe members attacked Prime Minister Terence O'Neill for seeking better relations with the Republic by meeting Sean Lemass, the then Taoiseach.

I have described my minimum interaction with the Orange Order in Belvoir. I could not expect to be isolated from it in Lecale. Saul Select Vestry had resolved some years earlier to discontinue an annual service held by the Lodge of St Patrick in the church as it was regarded locally as sectarian and out of keeping with the reconciling role of the memorial church in the community. This was a very brave resolution but possible since not one of the Saul congregation was a member of the said lodge. In my first year, the Seaforde Orange Lodge requested a service in Seaforde on a July Sunday afternoon and a very orderly quiet service took place to which the lodge members paraded with a number of friends, accompanied by a pipe band. It was straight Evening Prayer at which I preached on the role of men in church and society – in no way political. The only addition to a normal service was the singing of the National Anthem at the end. The next year Ballyculter was in my charge and I was informed that the local lodge paraded to church for Evening Prayer on the first Sunday of June each year and would I be the preacher. Once again it was a straight-forward service and I used basically the same sermon. I found within the congregation a man who had been in our Bishop's Worker training class in Bangor a decade earlier, whom I knew to be totally dedicated to the service of his church, and I asked him to read the lesson. I wrote before of the need of deans to be devious. If I had been thinking of being devious I couldn't have chosen a better way to become accepted by the congregation, as this elderly saint was beloved by them all and my request, I understand, led to his singing my praises!

Over the remainder of my time in Lecale I was able each year to bring as preacher someone who could speak to men, sometimes as fellow orangemen, sometimes as those outside the order who brought a message of primary duty to God and love to neighbour. On two subsequent years I exercised my right to preach and gave strong messages of the need to heed the lessons of history and no longer to live in the past but face a changing future. On both occasions I was thanked for thought provoking addresses. What was noticeable between 1986 and 2000 was the decline in the numbers attending. Some parishioners told me that they had left the Order after the Drumcree altercations: others just ceased attending.

I had different experiences at Loughinisland. There were no problems until after 1990. There were services at which members of the Orange Order and the Royal Black Preceptory attended but these were not every year. However, in 1995 the Worshipful Master arrived at the Rectory to request the service as before but he also came with his choice of preacher, a minister of the Church of The Nazarene. Invoking the bishop's ruling that the preacher at such services must be a Church of Ireland minister, I refused to accept this. A stand-off occurred and, thankfully, Bishop McMullan backed me to the extent that he would permit a Methodist or Presbyterian minister as preacher. The Lodge met and came back; reluctantly they would accept the bishop's ruling, but they would not have me because I had stood beside a Roman Catholic priest in Seaforde Church. They hoped I would allow my curate, Charles Mullen, to be the preacher. Highly amused I conceded the point for little did they know that their chosen preacher was a staunch Irish republican which his English Midlands accent concealed from them! Charles Mullen duly preached but I conducted the service. Charles Mullen was also their choice for an open-air dedication of a new banner later that summer. Two years later, the Black Preceptory arranged their service for a Sunday in August and at their request I invited the new Presbyterian minister in the area to be the preacher. To my surprise, three weeks before the service I saw it advertised in a local newspaper for a different Sunday to that which had been booked. I contacted the Secretary and pointed out the error. A day or so later he phoned back to say that they wanted to cancel

the service and thanked me for being ready to receive the preceptory. I left a message for the minister and am still awaiting
his return call. After Sunday I heard that the service had taken
place in the Presbyterian Church. It was reported in the district
that I had refused to have the service in the Church of Ireland.
That was untrue. Someone had made a mistake about the book-
ing: but I got the blame. And until my retirement there were no
more requests for Orange or Black services at Loughinisland.

Inter-church marriages
Probably in no other aspect of ministry have I seen more change
than that of marriages between members of the Church of
Ireland and the Roman Catholic Church. When I was ordained
these were always spoken of as 'mixed marriages'. The Roman
Catholics still describe them as marriages with those of another
religion – as if Church of Ireland is not Christian. Nowadays we
speak of 'inter-church marriages'. Soon after I went to Knocknagoney in 1963, the brother of one of our Boys' Brigade NCOs
was to be married. I was told in hushed tones that his fiancée
was a Roman Catholic, that the wedding was taking place in her
church and that he was 'turning' and being re-baptized. This
was devastating to the family and meant that he was no longer
accepted in the local community.

   In Belvoir there were two weddings involving a member of
the Roman Catholic Church. When notice of the intended marriage was sent to the parish priest by the diocesan licenser, a
reply was received that there was an impediment to the wedding of incompatible religion. This was not a recognised impediment but it meant that within the Roman Catholic Church the
marriage was not recognised. I had to obtain a signed statement
that the man involved accepted fully that he was freely entering
into marriage and accepted it a fully binding undertaking. It was
interesting that this couple were able to live in the neighbourhood – to my knowledge they were still there when I went to
Waterford. Their first child attended Sunday School but she was
not baptized nor did her parents attend church. By the time of
the other wedding the licenser had given up sending copy notice of intended weddings to the church of the non Church of
Ireland partner. The couple wanted to share the heritage of both

traditions and decided to leave Ireland and live in Canada to do so. This was a very happy celebration, tinged with sadness that they felt they had to go abroad. The bridegroom was to die suddenly a few years later in Canada, leaving a young widow.

Waterford weddings were few and several were 'inter-church'. On occasion I was invited to share in the ceremonies and accorded a warm welcome, except that the groom, his family and I were excluded from the nuptial eucharist. On another, the groom refused to sign the documents presented to him under the new Directory of 1976, saying he had too much respect for his future wife and her church to promise to do all in his power to bring up their children as (sic) Catholics. They were married in the cathedral, attended together regularly and their first child was publicly baptized there. But there were already a number of inter-church marriages within the congregation – some with inter-church families, boys being Church of Ireland with their fathers, girls being Roman Catholics with their mothers. From time to time they wanted to worship together and they were made welcome. When the issue of receiving Holy Communion arose, and I was asked, I gave an assurance that the Church of Ireland welcomed as communicants any who were communicants in their own church. I know just how much it meant to one parent in such a situation when on Mothering Sunday in 1984 his wife and daughters walked with him to kneel at the Lord's Table in his church. They had earlier found a sympathetic priest who had been willing to give him communion with his wife in a Roman Catholic church, knowing that he was a member of the Church of Ireland. Increasingly this has been happening *de facto* despite the efforts of the Roman Catholic authorities to prevent it.

Around Downpatrick there were more inter-church marriages and the number was to increase in the 1990s. It was my experience that as the clergy of the two churches got to know one another better the problems of obtaining dispensations disappeared. Indeed in one instance the fact that it was clear that attending a wedding in the church of the bride would have caused great difficulties in the family of the groom led the parish priest concerned to send the couple to me, suggesting that the marriage ceremony should be in the groom's church. I supplied him

with a copy of the marriage certificate for validation in his registers. So different from 1963! One marriage between members of
the two churches stands out: it was the BBC Clothes' Show Bride
of the Year wedding. It took place in St Patrick's Memorial
Church Saul. The fact that it was inter-church had clinched their
winning the competition. It had already been planned. The bride
to be, Heather, told the producers that for her it was the ceremony
and not the clothes that mattered. She received the promise,
which was honoured totally, that the cameras would not be in-
trusive. The BBC gave me a video of the complete service which
I have used in many subsequent wedding preparation classes. It
was a very straight service using the 1987 modern language rite.
There were members of the congregation, friends of the groom,
who were not aware that the church was not a Roman Catholic
church and that it wasn't a Roman Catholic ceremony!

On another occasion I was able to welcome my former fellow
history student of the 1950s, Monsignor Ambrose Macauley, to
share in another inter-church wedding at Saul. How little did we
imagine sharing such a service when we were both looking forward to ordination in our respective churches.

I was happy to be invited to share in a working group from
the four main churches in Ireland who drew up guidelines for
the clergy of the four churches on inter-church marriages and
the kind of sensitivity that is required. I saw this wonderfully
demonstrated in a service in which I shared in 2000: the curate
did not bat an eyelid when the parents of the bridegroom came
up to receive communion. The groom and I were the only non-
communicants and I don't think that the Roman Catholic building was defiled!

With inter-church weddings goes inevitably inter-church baptisms. In only two instances have these occurred in a Church of
Ireland context and on each occasion I invited the visiting Roman
Catholic priest to hold the baptismal shell and repeat the words of
baptism with me. I felt that this recognised any problems the
Roman Catholic members of the wider family might have. With
the best will in the world, no Roman Catholic priest has felt able to
take that step when I was invited to share in a baptism ceremony
in his church. At most I was permitted to join in the signing with
the cross, to read the gospel and give a homily and jointly to say

the blessing at the end. But at least there was a willingness to involve the clergy of the non Roman Catholic partner.

One of my friends who ministers in the South of Ireland and who is in an inter-church marriage, said to me not so long ago, 'We've sorted inter-church marriage and inter-church baptisms, but we'll pretty soon have to sort out inter-church funerals that will respect both church's doctrinal positions on death.' And that is a major problem.

Technological revolution
While in Waterford I had become interested in the new technology of computers. I had bought one of the first super calculators and had experimented with one of Clive Sinclair's ZX machines which linked to a cassette recorder. On arrival back in the North one was hearing of clergy like Jack Shearer, rector of Seagoe, finding computers useful in parish work. A new generation of super calculator arrived which was capable of a link to my electric typewriter and I began using it to compose the material for the Group newsletter and to draft service sheets which could be run off on my personal photocopier. But it was the week before Christmas 1986 that the breakthrough came. I came home from Belfast with my first personal computer, an Amstrad PCW, which had an attached printer. I promised myself that I would leave experimenting until after Christmas Day but the bug had bitten and I sat up to the very small hours trying to master Locoscript, the word processor built into this machine. I found it absolutely fascinating and I was able to get it to work. So from the next issue, the Lecale Letter was wholly produced on the computer – the strange dotty style of print declaring its provenance. I also discovered a database programme and was able to transfer my parish register to computer. And so it developed. As computers improved I moved up with them and by 1989 was regarded almost as a 'guru'.

To someone coming new to parish work in 2002 it would be almost inconceivable to be without a computer. It has made possible immense advances in communication and in liturgical churches has facilitated locally produced order of service of a really professional standard. When the service sheet for my institution in 1984 is compared to that which I prepared for my

final service in January 2001, the extent of this change is immediately apparent. Perhaps it is now too easy to run off newsletters,
service sheets, etc and perhaps more thought needs to be given
to the conservation of paper. It was said that computers would
herald the paperless office. Just look at the waste bins of 2002!
Having said that, I am really thankful for the word processor
and all the other bits and pieces that have made so many adventures in ministry possible during the last decade of my stipendiary ministry.

CHAPTER FOURTEEN

Liturgical Renewal

I have described in earlier chapters liturgical change as it affected the parishes in which I served. I want in this chapter to describe the changing liturgical scene and my involvement with it on a wider front.

This began when Diocesan Liturgical Advisors were appointed in 1972, as the modern language Holy Communion liturgy was being introduced. Bishop George Quin appointed me as the advisor for Down and Dromore, with Mervyn Wilson, rector of St Patrick's Newry, to assist. The advisors were briefed by the Honorary Secretary of the Liturgical Advisory Committee, Dean Gilbert Mayes and some of those who had prepared the rite, at a gathering in the Theological College in Dublin. We then returned to the diocese and arranged meetings of clergy (and laity, where possible) to explain and demonstrate *Holy Communion 1972*. I did this for Bangor in Bangor Abbey, for the Belfast area rural deaneries, and for Ards. By and large these were friendly occasions – the only difficult person was encountered when Hillsborough Rural Deanery met at Belvoir and I first encountered Canon John Barry's criticisms of modern liturgy. More significant was an evening gathering of the Lurgan area rural deaneries when lay people were present. Tom Rainsford, a leading evangelical layman, a member of the Liturgical Advisory Committee, who had been on the Holy Communion sub-committee, accompanied me. I was very glad of his presence for after my introduction, the then rector of Knocknamuckley, A. J. Finch, rose and attacked the service for being a change in the doctrine of the Church of Ireland in direction which he felt led straight to Roman Catholicism. Tom Rainsford replied in no uncertain terms, speaking from his unimpeachable evangelical standing, completely debunking the

charge, as if anyone from his perspective could possibly have
countenanced any such thing. Otherwise introducing *Holy
Communion 1972* was always a pleasant experience. Indeed, I
was even invited to Hillsborough Parish for a joint meeting of
Select Vestry and Men's Society to discuss *Holy Communion 1972*
being used in Hillsborough. Canon Jack Barry knew that I
would be under attack from a well-known artist, Patrick
Stevenson, son of a former Dean of Waterford, for whom nothing short of the language of Elizabethan England would suffice.
I believe I gave as good as I got and *Holy Communion 1972* was
occasionally used while 'Cromlyn' was rector. The DLAs were
called again when the 'Grey Book' was issued in 1973 with modern language versions of Morning Prayer and Evening Prayer
but there was no great demand in Down and Dromore to promote these and in only a few parishes, including Saul and Inch,
were they much used.

When I was appointed Dean of Waterford, Bishop
Armstrong told me I was being nominated for election by
General Synod 1980 to the Liturgical Advisory Committee. I can
scarcely describe how pleased I was for I felt that I might have
something to offer through the LAC to the whole church. I
wasn't aware until much later that, because of my 'perceived
churchmanship', evangelicals had barred my election or co-op-
tion on previous occasions. They were obsessed with the idea of
'balance' and feared a preponderance of those who were perceived as 'high church'. That at that time those who had expertise in liturgical scholarship were more likely to be found on the
on the more catholic wing of the church was simply a fact of life.
Thankfully, by the end of the century there were a good number
of evangelicals who had embraced liturgical scholarship. Much
of that is due to the influence of Colin Buchanan, principal of St
John's College, Nottingham, and member of the English
Liturgical Commission which produced the *Alternative Service
Book* in 1980. That two members of the present English
Commission can cheerfully describe one another as 'High
Jeremy' and 'Low Jeremy' and respect each other's scholarship
and integrity shows the progress that has been made. As we shall
see there are still times when the two schools of thought clash in
Ireland.

My first meeting of LAC was rather a post-mortem occasion, for the laity of General Synod, under the influence of the Evangelical Fellowship of the Irish Church, had failed to give *Holy Communion 1972* the two thirds majority needed for it to be part of the proposed alternative service book. Synod had been led to believe that there was something sinister is saying, 'Accept through him our sacrifice of praise and thanksgiving' before receiving the sacrament. Several options were open to LAC, to alter the wording or to find a compromise that the Committee could unanimously propose to Synod in 1981. Archbishop Henry McAdoo would not hear of making a change in something that was part of the classic Anglican eucharistic prayer. It was John Neill who suggested two alternative prayers of thanksgiving, and the evangelicals indicated that they would support this if the second prayer came from a province with a sound evangelical pedigree. As a result the eucharistic prayer from the 1978 Australian Prayer Book was included. Having a little more inside knowledge than the evangelical protagonists, I was sure that Father George Every SSM, who had drafted the Australian prayer, would have been amazed to discover that it was especially evangelical. Whatever, it is a fine prayer and after many years of using it in Down Cathedral at Sung Eucharists I believe that within it is the heart of what we want to say to God as we give thanks over bread and wine.

Archbishop John Armstrong remained Chairman of LAC even when he became primate, but his attendance was erratic. The Church of Ireland tradition is that on Synod Committees in the absence of the Chairman the senior bishop takes the chair, and, if there is no bishop present, any dean usually in order of seniority. Archbishop Henry McAdoo was a 'Cheshire cat' like figure at meetings of LAC, slipping in and out of meetings, and declined to take the chair. Thus it was that at only my third meeting as the only dean present except for the Honorary Secretary I found myself in the chair for a long meeting that went on to 10.00pm. I must have done a reasonable job for at the next meeting, although the deans of Christ Church and Ardfert were present, I was again asked to chair the meeting. And so it went on. In the absence of the Primate, the dean of Waterford chaired the meetings, meetings which determined the shape of the occasional offices, like marriage and confirmation, as well as finalising Holy Communion services for Synod 1982. One of the tributes I received was from the doyen of the evangelicals remarking on my complete fairness to all viewpoints. We rarely took a vote, proceeding largely by consensus. I even got the committee to agree to my proposing as an addition to the eucharistic prayer, the alternative salutation, 'The Lord is here...' seconded by an evangelical layman, David Williams, even though the majority opposed including in the resolution anything other than, 'The Lord be with you...' It is a matter of history that Synod accepted the amendment and that in the 2004 book it stands in pole position with 'The Lord be with you' as the alternative.

The solution of two alternative prayers commended itself to General Synod in 1982. There was a disastrous amendment to the Nicene Creed by Archdeacon William McCappin, removing a comma, and leading some users of the *Alternative Prayer Book* to declare that God made 'all things seen and unseen'. We tried to indicate the proper breathing in the lining out when it came to printing, but that was second best. Another amendment proposed during the debates in Synod left an extra 'let us pray' in the prayers after communion. As a result standing orders were amended and now liturgical amendments have to be submitted well in advance of their appearing on the order paper.

The year 1982-83 saw the LAC finalising work on the baptismal service and anything else that was outstanding that would be included in what was now being called *Alternative Prayer Book* and 1984 was to see its publication. At General Synod the carefully crafted service of Holy Baptism suffered the same fate as Holy Communion in 1980, failing by a small majority to command a two-thirds majority among the laity. We had the unusual spectacle of a layman at the rostrum trying to teach Saint Paul's theology to Archbishop Henry McAdoo. This gave the very real prospect of a Prayer Book without a baptismal rite. However, the bishop of Kilmore, Gilbert Wilson, put down a last-minute resolution to include the highly successful *Service for the Baptism of Children* from the 'red book' of 1969. And this, although not the preference of LAC, was duly included at Synod 1984.

Some time before General Synod in 1984, LAC had to decide what version or versions should be used for the readings to be printed in *Alternative Prayer Book*. England's *Alternative Service Book* used several versions including *Jerusalem Bible* and the *New English Bible*. Consensus was that we wanted one version, but which should it be? *New English Bible* did not read well. In areas of the Church of Ireland the Roman Catholic *Jerusalem Bible* would be unacceptable and *Revised Standard Version*, the preference of most members, dated from 1951 and used 'thee' and 'thou' language, hardly what we wanted for a prayer book in contemporary language. The *New International Version* was another option. It was the most recent major translation and some members felt that it might meet the case. This was suggested at one meeting and members unfamiliar with it undertook to look at it before the next meeting. At it I was in the chair. Archbishop McAdoo had been with us for an hour before having to leave for another meeting. He was rising to his feet so I asked the meeting to bring the item forward and as he went to the door I asked for his opinion. 'Since the last meeting,' he said. 'I have used the *New International Version* for my daily office and in my study. I think it is excellent.' That decided the matter. Our publishers negotiated with the 'owner' of the translation to expand numbers and expressions like 'He'll' – he will. To this they readily agreed, stipulating that so doing did not imply any intention to change the published text. There are some renderings that the majority of LAC did not like, but it proved fairly acceptable through the life of the *Alternative Prayer Book* lectionary.

At some stage it was suggested that instead of continuing with the lectionary, which had been in trial use since 1973 and was in the *Alternative Service Book*, we might think of using the same lectionary as the Episcopal Church of the USA which was virtually the same as that in use in the majority of churches in Ireland. It was an idea before its time. It would not be until 1996 that permission would be given to use the ecumenical *Revised Common Lectionary*.

In the spring of 1984 I was asked to be one of the team which read and corrected the proofs of *Alternative Prayer Book*. This was a time-demanding task but I had the thrill of knowing that I was contributing to the desire that the new worship book would be as accurate as possible. We worked on our own, then in groups and finally in a two-days session for which I had to travel to Belfast. In spite of this, errors did pass unnoticed. Partly this was due to the need for frequent re-typing of pages – it was before the days of the word processor. Before the new book came into use Dean Mayes and I wrote small pamphlets to explain the services in it. My little commentary proved more useful than I could have expected, seeing that it was originally prepared with confirmation candidates in mind.

The coming into use of *Alternative Prayer Book* coincided with my coming to Lecale. The new book was immediately welcomed in the parishes where the trial books had been used in the seventies and early eighties. Where trial had not occurred there was a rush of opposition, mostly on the ground of language. I never heard any complaint about doctrine.

LAC continued its work in preparing the remaining pastoral rites. I used to sit beside Dean Mayes at LAC and assist in preparing texts and, as with the *Alternative Prayer Book* itself, with the proof-reading of the 1987 booklets for Confirmation, Marriage and Funerals. These were still published by Collins Liturgical under the guidance of Mrs Sue Chapman. After his retirement, Gilbert Mayes remained as Honorary Secretary for another year and then Bishop Edward Darling approached me and asked me if I would be willing to take over because I had a word-processor! Thus in 1989 I became Honorary Secretary of the Committee and served in that role for the next ten years. Only his successor knows just how much dedicated work Gilbert Mayes put in as Honorary Secretary and how much the worshipping church of the past twenty years owes to him.

It fell to me to bring the remaining modern language rites before General Synod and to pilot them through the complex stages that are required of liturgical business. I found that, provided everything was made clear to the president and to the secretariat, the tangles that had beset the process of the *Alternative Prayer Book* through General Synod could be avoided. The remaining rites were not controversial and gave the Church of Ireland a modern language service for the Institution of an Incumbent, resources for use in Ministry to the Sick and a set of services in modern language for use at ordinations. For a number of years the House of Bishops had stalled the preparation of this last section. In 1989 permission to go ahead was given, and by 1991 the modern language ordinal had also passed through General Synod.

It was suggested in 1992 that now that all the pastoral services had been passed, they should be collected in a second volume of *Alternative Prayer Book*. I was advised by the then General Manager of APCK, the Church of Ireland bookshops, that a print run of 20,000 in a paperback edition, with 1,000 in hardback, would be required. The publisher of *Alternative Prayer Book*, now Harper-Collins, part of the News International conglomerate, offered to print them and deliver in one lot to APCK, the cost being met out of the royalties which had been earned by *Alternative Prayer Book*. This turned out to be a disastrous over calculation. Between the decision to publish and the arrival of the books in 1993, desktop publication of service sheets had become a real possibility and there just wasn't any bulk sale for the cheap paperback edition. These were eventually sold off at 25p a copy, less than half their cost price.

LAC had turned its attention to the demand for authorised forms of Family Service. After looking at what was available elsewhere, a sub-committee representing Cork, Dublin and Belfast met, with a remit to bring proposals to LAC. It considered a draft based on the Ministry of the Word part of the Holy Communion rite and suggested a structure into which variable elements could be inserted. At this time I was invited to attend a meeting in London at which the English Liturgical Commission was sharing its thinking about what was to replace *Alternative Service Book* when its authorisation ran out in 2000. I arrived an hour early and met Archdeacon Trevor Lloyd who was having a short meeting of a group preparing a similar rite. We swapped details and as a result we included a couple of ideas that the Church of England has arrived at and they took on board one of ours. This led to the production of *A Service of the Word* – a structure with some worked out examples and resources. The House of Bishops gave its approval and it went out for trial. Although it began life in the search for a family service, what emerged is a very flexible format which can be used on many different kinds of occasions, from Mothers' Union festival services to the instal-

lation of canons in a cathedral. Provided the structure is followed, it is possible to insert material from all sorts of sources. It
is tailored to the use of desktop publishing and in its final form
in the 2004 edition of the *Book of Common Prayer* structures and
guidelines are given, resources being available separately. In one
diocese the bishop conservatively restricted use of *Service of the
Word* to one Sunday in each month, but signs are that in the future it will have a much wider use.

In 1994 Harper-Collins informed the Standing Committee of
General Synod that a third printing of *Alternative Prayer Book*
would be needed and that the selling price would have to be
stg£14.95, an increase of £9.00. I was asked to go to London and
talk to the publisher. As a result of these negotiations, an offer
was made that the publishers would arrange for a bulk printing
to be delivered to Church of Ireland House in Dublin, after
which it would be the church's responsibility to distribute
copies to shops. This enabled the book to be sold at £9.95 per
copy with discounts to parishes through APCK – five pounds
sterling less than the publishers had wanted. The bookshops got
their normal discount and the church as wholesaler more than
recouped the advance from the royalties fund which Standing
Committee had made. The only people who had more work
were officials in Church of Ireland House who had to make
available parcels for the shops from the store in the nearby
College of Education.

After ten years, *Alternative Prayer Book* was widely used in
the church but a division had arisen, and appeared to be growing, between parishes which 'only used the Prayer Book' and
'APB parishes'. LAC recognised that this was a problem and
made a suggestion that the way to overcome this was to produce
a 'Sunday Service Book' containing services from both *Book of
Common Prayer* as it was commonly used and *Alternative Prayer
Book*. A resolution was introduced in General Synod 1996 with a
version of *Book of Common Prayer* services with modified rubrics.
This failed by one vote to pass in a very thin house at the end of
the day.

At this meeting of General Synod, I was not an elected representative, having lost my seat at the 1993 elections. It was suspected that this was the result of a nasty piece of electioneering

in our diocese. A number of clergy were targeted because we were perceived to favour the admission of children to communion before confirmation. I had made a speech supporting the setting up of a commission of Synod to investigate this practice, which in the previous decade was being tried in various provinces of the Anglican Communion. I had seen it in practice in the Scottish Episcopal Church in two places; one experience had been dreadful, the other had seemed totally fitting. I had also given communion to American visitors in Saul Church when the children had come to rails with their parents, blessed themselves and held out their hands for the consecrated bread. I could not withhold the sacrament, I had told the Synod. And I was not elected for that three-year period.

APCK asked for a meeting in June 1996 with members of LAC at which the market demand for the so-called Sunday Service Book was queried. Perhaps we hadn't done our homework but we were very anxious to reconcile two integrities. APCK informed us that the Oxford University Press wanted to re-set the *Book of Common Prayer* for any reprint and as joint publishers it was asking what, in the light of Synod's decision, was the view of LAC. One member present queried the legal standing of the Sunday Service Book if its rubrics were deemed to conflict with those in the standard prayer book. Was the answer not a comprehensive and thorough revision of *Book of Common Prayer* itself? I don't think that up to that moment this had been considered by any member of LAC. We only knew we had a problem. The stock of the *Alternative Prayer Book* reprint would last three or four more years; *Book of Common Prayer* needed to be re-set and, if it was, what would be the cost and sale prospects?

LAC gave careful consideration throughout 1996-7 and went to General Synod in 1997 with a proposal for a thorough revision of the Prayer Book, one that would include services in traditional language and in contemporary language, omitting those parts of the *Book of Common Prayer* which were no longer required or where there were anachronisms. A resolution was passed asking LAC to return to Synod in 1998 with detailed proposals and a timetable. This was also approved and work began towards a new edition of the Prayer Book to be ready in 2004.

International Liturgy

I had been developing relationships with other parts of the Anglican Communion in the field of liturgy. In 1988 I went to Sarum College in Salisbury to a gathering of liturgists who wanted to consider the future of daily prayer in the Church of England. My interest in this went right back to those summer days in which as a teenager I had discovered daily Matins in St John's Malone. This was one element where liturgical change as represented by *Alternative Service Book* and *Alternative Prayer Book* had been minimal. All kinds of ideas which I found exciting were being suggested and I met, among others, George Guiver of the Community of the Resurrection, author of *Company of Voices*, a book about the history of the Daily Office, and Brian Hardy, of the Liturgy Commission of the Scottish Episcopal Church, which was at that time working on a new simpler form of Daily Morning and Evening Prayer. Brother Tristram of the Anglican Franciscans was working on a revision of the his Society's office book, *The Daily Office SFF*, which I saw for the first time. I talked for hours to him and to one of the Anglican Sisters of the Church, who kindly made available to me a copy of the service book used by them. Using my word-processor I began experimenting with forms of prayer to use when I said my daily prayers in Down Cathedral or at home.

After becoming Honorary Secretary of LAC in 1989, while visiting Church House in Westminster on Reader business, I made myself known to David Hebblethwaite, Secretary of the Church of England Liturgical Commission, and arranged an exchange of minutes between our two committees. This led to my being invited to meetings when members of English Diocesan Liturgy Committees were briefed by the Liturgy Commission, and to a gathering in April 1991 at St Michael's College, Llandaff, the Theological College of the Church in Wales. This latter was an opportunity to think about baptism and baptismal practice as the third millennium approached. For the future there were three significant encounters. I was in a discussion group led by Michael Perham, then a rector in the diocese of Salisbury, who was to become a major player in the English Liturgical Commission and Synod. One of the main speakers was David Stancliffe, then provost of Portsmouth; he was to be chairman of the Commission and someone I would be meeting frequently in the next decade. The third encounter was with my opposite number on the Liturgical Committee of the Church in Wales, Robert Paterson, who kindly supplied me with copies of all the recent worship books of the Church in Wales. We promised to stay in touch.

The Church of Ireland sent Harold Miller, by now a member of LAC, to represent the Church of Ireland at the International Anglican Liturgical Consultation in Toronto in 1991. It was at that meeting that a statement was issued about Holy Baptism and its relation to confirmation. The Toronto Statement from accredited liturgists from all over the Anglican world would have a strong influence on any revision to baptismal services, and those prepared for the 2004 edition of the *Book of Common Prayer* reflect the thinking of Toronto 1991. In 1993 an 'interim' Consultation was held in Austria at which Harold Miller and John Paterson, dean of Christ Church, were the Church of Ireland representatives. The 1995 Consultation was to be held in Dublin and it would be up to us to provide the local organisation.

The autumn meeting to which the Church of England issued its invitation in 1993 gave Robert Paterson and me the opportunity to suggest to Michael Perham that the four independent Anglican churches in these islands should in some way liaise closely together so that, as far as possible, we would remain in step in regard to calendar and lectionaries at least. From this what we formally called the Interprovincial Liturgical Consultation came into being. Michael Perham and Jane Sinclair represented England, Robert Paterson and Keith Denison represented Wales, and Brian Hardy and I represented Scotland and Ireland respectively. The IPLC soon became known from the rugby union analogy as the 'Four Nations'. Our meetings led to the calendar changes, including the Epiphany Season, which are found in *Common Worship* (2000), the *Welsh Alternative Calendar* (1996) and were approved by our House of Bishops in 1995. It was also decided to adopt the three-year cycle of readings in the *Revised Common Lectionary* in all four churches as well as a set of revised collects. Each one of these was considered by the group; but the wording of a handful could not be agreed as I wasn't able to recommend them to LAC. For these Ireland was sticking

by the equivalent prayers we had in *Alternative Prayer Book*. The
Four Nations meetings also have given valuable opportunities
to exchange information and ideas between the four commissions or committees. It was a great delight after the English pre-
Common Worship conference in York in September 2000 to see
that all four committees wanted the 'Four Nations' to continue,
with Robert Paterson as convener, deciding to meet in each
country by rotation. The Church of Ireland was delighted to host
the 2001 meeting in Dublin and in 2002 the meeting was held at
the office of the Scottish Episcopal Church's General Synod in
Edinburgh.

'In 1995 the place of liturgical excellence was Dublin': that
statement was made to the Church of England's National
Liturgical Conference in Cambridge. A superb week of summer
weather greeted the International Anglican Liturgical Consultation when its members convened at the Church of Ireland
College of Education in Dublin. Representatives from all over
the Anglican Communion met for five days' hard work, drafting
a Statement on the Eucharist which it was hoped would assist
provinces in any future prayer book revisions. The final
Statement on the Eucharist was approved on the last morning
by consensus. It was an immense achievement, realising the
varieties of 'churchmanship' present, from the ultra-conservatives
from Sydney, Australia, to the ultra-catholics of Southern Africa
and the ultra-liberal positions held by some of the North
Americans. I found myself in a section dominated by some of
those ultra-liberals and, with Ian Paton from Scotland, constantly
pressed to try and find words that would be understood in a
British Isles context. In our group we had also a professor from
Brazil, whose first language was Portuguese, and a bishop from
Africa who appeared to sleep through most of the meetings.
Group findings were printed and debated in plenary sessions
with the result that visitors to such sessions found the proceedings baffling. The worship was 'out of this world' as we shared
Holy Communion according to the rites of Australia, Cuba and
a very extravagant interpretation of the American Prayer Book.
Receptions by the Government of the Republic of Ireland and
the diocese of Dublin provided a social dimension to an amazing week, and the hospitality of the Church of Ireland College of

Education set a standard that has not been approached at any of the three other Consultations I have had the privilege of attending in Finland (1997), Kottayam (1999) and Berkeley, California (2001).

A new prayer book

For the General Synod of 1998 we prepared a list of proposed contents for the new edition of the prayer book and set 2004 as the hoped-for publication date. I seconded the adoption of the Report which was proposed in a brilliant speech by Bishop Richard Clarke, the Bishop of Meath and Kildare. The proposal was carried by a huge majority. The Synod also passed at resolution stage an adaptation of the ecumenical *Revised Common Lectionary*, with provisions for occasions not included in it, like St Patrick's Day. A very tiny group objected to a small number of passages from the Apocrypha being included. Most Protestant denominations reject the Apocrypha, books in the Greek version of the Old Testament, which were not originally written in Hebrew. In the Thirty Nine Articles the Church of England reformers distinguished between the canonical books and those of the Apocrypha but stated that we should continue to read the same for 'example of life and instruction in manners'. I was able to inform General Synod that the highest legal authority of the Church of Ireland had ruled forty years or so before that it was quite proper for lessons from the Apocrypha to be included in tables of readings. My successor was to have to make a similar statement in 2002.

The hard work was now on. Most of the services like Morning Prayer required very little adaptation for the new edition and LAC worked on these throughout 1998-9 presenting them as resolutions in that year. I had given notice that I intended to stand down as Honorary Secretary after General Synod in 1999 and Canon Ricky Rountree had agreed to take over the reins. We worked very closely together and exchanged texts on our computers. I was planning to retire from full-time ministry in the autumn of 2000 and, when the need for someone to edit the new edition of the *Book of Common Prayer* was perceived, I agreed to take on that role as a fitting occupation for active retirement. The Standing Committee of General Synod agreed to the appointment and gave me a small supporting advisory committee. General Synod in 2000 met in Belfast and in that year Ricky Rountree proposed all the bills and resolutions and I formally seconded them, reversing our roles of the previous year. I spoke briefly of how I saw my role as editor of the prayer book and pledged my determination that the book, as well as being functional, would be a beautiful book. I am working to achieve that.

Whatever changes in forms of worship that are to be incorporated in the new edition of the *Book of Common Prayer* in 2004 will reflect the changing scenes in worship that have developed through the Liturgical Movement of which I first became aware in that SCM study group in Queen's in 1952. It will give worship leaders opportunities to bring those gathered in Christ's name closer to him, that they may receive the proclaimed word, celebrate together at the Lord's Table and go out as God's people to effect the changes he wants in his world.

Epilogue

I planned to retire from stipendiary ministry in the autumn of 2000. The problem was not having a house in which to live when that happened. Valerie and I had always supposed that when that time came we would return to Belfast. But by the mid 1990s there was no attraction to return to the city. Our elder daughter, Barbara, married, was a speech therapist, living in Leeds. Our younger daughter, Hilary, having had a succession of illnesses brought on by a back injury in her schooldays would probably follow her sister to England. My sister, Elizabeth, was still likely to be living in County Down. And we liked the area and were used to living in the country. So we searched for a house in the neighbourhood throughout the latter part of 1999, found one we liked near Ardglass but every bid we made was covered by a higher one. An attractive building site with a wonderful view over Dundrum Bay to the Mourne Mountains might have been ideal but there was no knowing when it would be available. Every month the agents told us: 'Call in again in a fortnight, and we'll have news for you.'

In January 2000 we gave up and started looking again. And although it was beyond our original budget we found what we wanted and it was capable of extension. So on 1 April 2000, Valerie and I became first-time house owners! With all the delays in getting permission, extension work couldn't start until the end of July – and I postponed retirement until the end of the year, finally deciding on 31 January 2001, so that I could benefit from new church pension rates by staying in stipendiary ministry for a further thirty-one days. We moved into our home between Downpatrick and Clough on the road to Newcastle. From the new lounge I look out each morning at the Mourne Mountains – an ever-changing scene.

Forty-five years of ordained ministry has also been a changing scene. The Church has been changing in its understanding of ministry, in its worship and in ways in which its ministers seek to fulfil their calling. But one thing never changes: the rock on which it is all built – the good news of God's love for us in Christ, experienced in the Power of the Holy Spirit. I echo the words of Nahum Tate and Nicholas Brady, perhaps not the greatest of the eighteenth century poets, but men who taught the Anglican church to sing:

Through all the changing scenes of life
In trouble and in joy,
The praises of my God shall still
My heart and tongue employ.